THE COLLECTED WORKS
OF HERMAN DOOYEWEERD

Series A, Volume 8/I

GENERAL EDITOR: D.F.M. Strauss

Encyclopedia of the Science of Law

Introduction

Series A, Volume 8/I

Herman Dooyeweerd

PAIDEIA PRESS

Library of Congress Cataloging-in-Publication Data

Dooyeweerd, H. (Herman), 1884-1977.
   Encyclopedia of the Science of Law
   Herman Dooyeweerd; translated by Robert D. Knudsen, edited by Alan M. Cameron.
     p. cm.

   Includes bibliographical references and index
   ISBN 978-0-88815-222-0 (soft)
   Encyclopedia of the Science of Law; Volume 8/I: Introduction

   This is Series A, Volume 8/I in the continuing series
   The Collected Works of Herman Dooyeweerd
   (Initially published by Mellen Press)

   ISBN 978-0-88815-302-9

   The Collected Works comprise a Series A, a Series B, and a Series C
   (*Series A* contains multi-volume works by Dooyeweerd,
   Series B contains smaller works and collections of essays,
   Series C contains reflections on Dooyeweerd's philosophy
   designated as: *Dooyeweerd's Living Legacy*, and
   Series D contains thematic selections from Series A and B)

A CIP catalog record for this book is available from the British Library.

The Dooyeweerd Centre for Christian Philosophy
Redeemer College Ancaster, Ontario
CANADA L9K 1J4

All rights reserved. For information contact

©PAIDEIA PRESS 2012
Grand Rapids, MI 49507

Printed in the United States of America

Series A, Volume 8/1

Encyclopedia of the Science of Law
Introduction

Herman Dooyeweerd

Translated by

Robert D. Knudsen

Edited by

Alan M. Cameron

This is the second print-run (containing a few minor text corrections) of volume one of a five volume series. The manuscript used in the translation of this volume is entitled, *Encyclopaedie van de Rechtswetenschap: Inleiding* and dated 1967.

The other four volumes of this work are:

Volume 2 – A History of the Concept of Encyclopedia and the Concept of Law
Volume 3 – The Elementary and Complex Basic Concepts of Law
Volume 4 – The Typical Basic Concepts of Law and the Theory of the Sources of Law
Volume 5 – Revised Introduction (Unfinished)

The Dooyeweerd Centre for Christian Philosophy wishes to thank the Stichting Zonneweelde for the generous donation that contributed to the translation and publication of this work.

Table of Contents

Foreword xi
Editor's Introduction. 1

PART 1

The Philosophic Idea of Encyclopedia in the Light of the Cosmonomic Idea. The Theory of the Law-Spheres as the Primary Foundation of the Encyclopedia of the Science of Law

1.1 Introduction to the Science of Law and the
     Philosophic Idea of Encyclopedia 11
1.2 Science and Reality 21
1.3 Philosophy, the Special Sciences, and Naive
     Experience of Reality. Cosmic Time and the First
     Transcendental Basic Problem of Any Conceivable
     Philosophic System 26
1.4 The Second Transcendental Basic Problem of
     Philosophy: The Archimedean Point 34
1.5 The Christian Transcendence Standpoint and the
     Critical Immanence Standpoint in Philosophy.
     The Third Transcendental Basic Problem of
     Philosophy. 37
1.6 The Four Religious Ground Motives of Western
     Thought 48
     1.6.1 The Form-Matter Motive 50
     1.6.2 The Motive of Creation, Fall, and Redemption. . . 58
     1.6.3 The Nature-Grace Motive. 61
     1.6.4 The Motive of Nature and Freedom 63
1.7 The Cosmonomic Idea as the Transcendental
     Ground-idea of Philosophy: The Transcendental
     Critique of Theoretical Thought and "Metaphysics" 75
1.8 The Cosmonomic Idea and the Method of
     Concept-Formation in the Science of Law 85

1.9   The Law-Spheres and their Modal Structures.
       The Concepts of Law and Subject in the Science of
       Law 94
1.10 The Cosmic Order of the Law-Spheres and the
       Method of Analysis of the Modal Structures. 100
1.11 Antinomies and Illegitimate Fictions in Scientific
       Thinking: The Fictions of Legal Method. 112

PART 2

The Opening Process in the Normative Aspects of Reality:
Law and History

2.1   The Sphere Universality of All the Modal Aspects
       and the Opening Process in the Normative
       Anticipatory Law-Spheres. The Relationship of
       Causality, Attribution, Unlawfulness, and Fault 123
2.2   Law and History: The Relationship of the Science of
       Legal Dogmatics to the Science of Legal History 135
2.3   Law and History: The Modal Structure of the
       Historical Aspect 138
2.4   The Modal Meaning of History in its Opened
       Structure: The Relation of Historical Ethnology and
       the Science of History 155
2.5   The Relationship between Law and History
       Revisited: Is the Opposition between Historical and
       Systematic Thinking Correct? 165
2.6   The Modal Structure of Faith as the Temporal
       Boundary Function and its Place in the Opening
       Process 173

PART 3

The Subject-Object Relation within the Modal Structure of the Law-Spheres and its Significance for the Science of Law

3.1 The General Significance of the Subject-Object Relation in the Modal Structure of the Law-Spheres with particular reference to the Jural Aspect. 185
3.2 The Limits of the Subject-Object Relation. 188

PART 4

The Theory of the Individuality-Structures of Reality and their Forms of Interlacement as a Second Foundation for the Encyclopedia of the Science of Law

4.1 The Place of the Various Branches of Law in an Encyclopedia of the Science of Law 197
4.2 The Relationship of the Modal and the Individuality Structures of Reality. Law-Type and Law-Modality. 204
4.3 The Interlacement of the Individuality-Structures: Enkapsis and the Enkaptic Structural Whole. 216
4.4 The Enkaptic Structural Whole of the Human Body and Act-Life: The Relationship of Psychology and the Science of Law 222

Glossary. 233

Index 243

Foreword

The *Encyclopedia of the Science of Law* constitutes the first scholarly domain in which Dooyeweerd tested his radically new understanding of created reality, informed by the biblical basic motive of creation, fall, and redemption. The *Science of Law* represents the academic discipline in which Dooyeweerd was trained and in which he developed exceptional expertise. Therefore, it must be clear that the publication of this comprehensive and authoritative multivolume series will contribute significantly to the ever growing legacy of reformational philosophy.

Although many philosophical trends throughout the history of philosophy and even within the contemporary scene ventured to categorize our understanding of created reality, the dominance of reductionistic approaches frequently precluded an integral account of the diversity and unity of reality. What is particularly attractive about Dooyeweerd's program in the *Encyclopedia* is that he applies the method of *immanent criticism* so effectively in his analysis of alternative theoretical trends that it enhances the argumentative force of his own approach. Combined with his sincere aim to do justice to empirical reality in all its facets and dimensions – exemplified in what became known as the *transcendental-empirical* method – this resulted in a comprehensive account of the basic concepts operative in scientific endeavors.

The *Encyclopedia* opens up unexpected vistas within this domain, starting with an elucidation of what Dooyeweerd calls the *elementary* (or analogical) basic concepts of the science of law and proceeding with a scrutiny of the *complex* basic concepts as well as the *typical* concepts of law.

The first volume is not only an introduction to the *Encyclopedia of the Science of Law*, it is also a magnificent introduction to Dooyeweerd's entire philosophy. It will appeal to all scholars with a basic interest in philosophy, regardless of what discipline they are coming from. This introductory volume may turn out to become the cornerstone of the entire Collected Works of Herman Dooyeweerd.

D.F.M. Strauss
General Editor

Editor's Introduction

This is the first of the five volumes to be published which will comprise the complete *Encyclopedia of the Science of Law* by Herman Dooyeweerd. It is appropriate therefore in this introduction to provide a brief description of these volumes, some information about the Dutch texts on which the English translations are based, as well as more detailed information about this introductory volume and the editing of its translation. Some general observations will also be made about the Encyclopedia as a complete work and its significance within *The Collected Works of Herman Dooyeweerd*.

The Encyclopedia Volumes
The five volumes of the *Encyclopedia* comprise 1 *Introduction*, 2 *A History of the Concept of Encyclopedia and the Concept of Law*, 3 *The Elementary and Complex Basic Concepts of Law*, 4 *The Typical Basic Concepts of Law and the Theory of the Sources of Law*, and 5 *Revised Introduction (Unfinished)*. As a systematic theoretical account of law and legal phenomena volumes 1 and 3 are the key volumes. Volume 3 is the next in the set planned for publication.

The first volume outlines Dooyeweerd's general philosophical perspective specifically orientated to the academic field of law. The general philosophical systematics is known both within and without reformational Christian circles as the Philosophy of the Cosmonomic Idea. This orientation of the latter to the major theoretical problems of law in the first volume is intended to serve as an introduction to this field of study and to a new method of juridical analysis.

Volume 3 provides the systematic framework of basic concepts which are the foundation for the special science of law. This volume is the detailed and comprehensive application of the philosophical perspective and the juridical methodology introduced in the first volume.

The fourth volume comprises two monographs that expand upon complex basic concepts introduced in the preceding volume. The complex concepts build upon the application and expansion of the theory of individuality-structures which, along with the theory of the modal aspects, is one of the two fundamental pillars of the Philosophy of the Cosmonomic Idea. Not only legal, political, and social science theorists, but also learned legal practitioners who read this volume will discover the contemporary relevance of this volume's examination of the public/private distinction and the concept sources of law. The final volume is an unfinished revision of the *Encyclopedie van de Rechtswetenschap* consisting largely of an incomplete new introduction.

Some Background on the Dutch Texts

Whilst a detailed historical study of the development of Dooyeweerd's legal philosophy is yet to be undertaken there is ample evidence to suggest that Dooyeweerd was developing the idea of the *Encyclopedia* at the same time as he was developing the major elements of the Philosophy of the Cosmonomic Idea. It would be very surprising if this were not the case because the stimulus for the development of his general philosophy was his early wrestling with the problems of legal theory. That the development of the legal philosophy and the general systematics went hand in hand is further supported from evidence that a version of the *Encyclopaedie* in the form of lecture notes was already in existence in the 1930s, the same decade in which he produced the first definitive form of his original philosophy, the three volume *De Wijsbegeerte der Wetsidee*. According to his biographer the *Encyclopaedie* obtained a definitive written form during the period of the Second World War.

Although a contract was concluded in the early 1950s between the author and the publisher H. J. Paris for the publication of the entire *Encyclopaedie* this did not take place. In the meantime it continued to be printed as "notes" (dictaten) for Dooyeweerd's jurisprudence lectures in the Law Faculty at the Free University of Amsterdam where he was a professor for nearly 40 years. According to D.F.M. Strauss, prior to the 1960s, copies of the *Encyclopaedie* notes were made available by H. J. Paris.

The version of the notes which has been used as the basis for the English translation and publication of this first introductory volume was printed by the Students Council of the Free University and bears the date 1967, two years after Dooyeweerd formally retired from his university position. Although editors of the *Encyclopedia* are greatly indebted to the late Robert Knudsen for his translation of this first volume, considerable work was required in its editing which resulted from errors and omissions in the translation. Some of the main instances of the latter are mentioned below.

First, although Knudsen attended Dooyeweerd's lectures in jurisprudence at the Free University, his formal qualifications were not in law but theology, having held a professorship in apologetics at a North American theological institution, Westminster Theological Seminary, Philadelphia. An understandable lack of depth of legal learning is apparent in his translation. Secondly, there were some significant omissions of material from the 1967 notes which required translation. Longer omitted passages were translated by the General Editor, D.F.M. Strauss, other smaller passages by the Editor. Omitted quotations in German were translated by D.F.M. Strauss. Thirdly, there were also difficult shorter passages which sometimes required complete retranslation by the Editor.

Despite extensive checking against the Dutch *dictaat* this publication is not a complete retranslation which might well have brought to light additional errors of translation. A retranslation is a worthwhile project for the future. However, in view of a long and careful editing process the editors are confident that such errors have been kept to a minimum and are of a minor nature.

Further Background on the Dutch Texts: Limitations of the Encyclopedia as a Published Work

As an application of the general philosophy and its comprehensive systematics to the special discipline of law the importance of this *Encyclopedia* within the Dooyeweerd corpus can hardly be overemphasized. The significance of its publication for the development and advancement of the general reformational philosophy, and all of the special academic disciplines, not only (though especially) for the study of law, is therefore immense. Nevertheless, the reader needs to be aware of the limitations of the *Encyclopedia* as a published work of jurisprudence and the limitations of this introductory volume in particular.

One important limiting factor is that the *Encyclopedia* cannot be regarded as having reached the mature written state which the general philosophical systematics attained in *A New Critique of Theoretical Thought*. Dooyeweerd had intended to provide a completely revised version for publication. This never eventuated; only an incomplete revised *Introduction* was written. When all the volumes have been issued, the published *Encyclopedia* will still only be in the form of the lecture notes, albeit remarkably complete and polished, that Dooyeweerd provided for his students.

This failure of Dooyeweerd to get round to completing a revision for publication meant that an important development contained in the mature philosophical system was apparently not incorporated anywhere in the printed *dictaten* and certainly not in the key volumes 1 and 3. This remained the case although the *dictaten* had continued to be printed after Dooyeweerd's mature philosophical work had been completed and published.

The omitted development was the introduction of an additional modal aspect into the theory of the modal aspects, which allowed him to distinguish the aspect of movement from that of the physical aspect. This development took place some time between the publication of *De Wijsbegeerte de Wetsidee* in the mid-1930s and the appearance of the four volume *A New Critique of Theoretical Thought* from 1953 onward. Almost certainly it took place in the early 1950s. This is because first, his introduced distinguishing of the two modal aspects in question does not appear in the last printings of the *dictaten,* which seem not to have changed substantially from the early printings going back to the 1930s. But secondly, that development does not appear in the publication of an address by Dooyeweerd in 1950 to the Royal Dutch Academy on the modal structure of the concept of jural causality which Dooyeweerd used to illustrate the juridical application of the modal analysis and where one would certainly expect that development in the theory of the modal aspects to be reflected if it had already occurred.

Another important area of the general philosophy, which lacks its mature expression within the *Encyclopaedie,* is the treatment of the basic theoretical problems of philosophy contained in this first introductory volume. Whether or not his ideas in this area can be viewed as having undergone substantive development subsequent to their articulation in the *Inleiding (Introduction),* a much clearer and coherent statement of the basic problems are to be found in *A New Critique* than are to be found in this first volume of the *Encyclopaedie.*

A final observation relating to the provisional nature of the content of the *Encyclopedia* arises from reflecting on just a couple of the difficulties presented in the translation of the first volume.

It is not appropriate here to delve deeply into the complexities involving Dooyeweerd's use of *recht.* However, it may be helpful for a reader of the *Encyclopedia* to make the following point of explanation. A fundamental distinction within the *Encyclopedia* and Dooyeweerd's general philosophy is that between the modal structure of reality and the individuality-structure of concrete "social" and "physical" entities. Within Dooyeweerd's use of the term *recht* (in the sense of "law" not "right") there is some degree of unclarity as to whether he is intending this in the "modal" sense of the jural aspect (*juridisch aspect*) or in the sense of an individual law as a concrete totality which functions in all the modal aspects but which is qualified by the jural aspect as that which gives to the individual thing its jural character.

Although, in the latter part of the *Introduction,* Dooyeweerd explains and applies his theory of individuality-structures within the context of jural phenomena, nowhere does he address the issue of the individuality of laws as concrete totalities. Is this because he not only considered the idea of the jural aspect as essential for an adequate account of law but that law itself was nothing more than a modal aspect of individual, concrete social realities such as courts, legislatures, and nonstate jural institutions? In this respect there may be some force in the criticism of Arend Soeteman, the present holder of the professorship in jurisprudence at the Free University which Dooyeweerd himself held for many years, that Dooyeweerd goes too far in criticizing legal philosophy for regarding law as a thing rather than as the (modal) aspect of things etc. Certainly, the question as to the individuality of law is one which those who seek to take up and apply the reformational perspective articulated in the *Encyclopedia* will need to address.

This observation on a problem with *recht* leads to another closely related translation issue which goes to the very heart of this work and again called for the exercise of editorial discretion. It concerns the decision to frequently employ the term "jural" when *juridisch* is found in the text. The latter was used when referring to the universal aspect which for Dooyeweerd was not confined to explaining the nature of the conventional legal phenomena that is the typical subject-matter of legal practitioners – viz. state law and state legal institutions.

Although it is true that Dooyeweerd himself, throughout the entire *Encyclopedia,* uses examples taken from state law in explaining and applying his elementary concepts, it is vitally important to understand that these concepts and the cosmic aspect of reality that grounds them are *universal.* That is to say, this aspect for Dooyeweerd manifests itself not only in the state rules of the courts and legislatures but within every sphere of human life. Therefore the elementary concepts of "law" which are introduced in this volume, and systematically explained in the third, are not confined to explaining the rules and legal phenomena associated with the organs of the state. Hence the available but less common term "jural" is employed rather than "legal" or "juridical" whenever the author intends to convey this meaning of *juridisch.* Nevertheless, Dooyeweerd's less-than-always-consistent use of terms in this regard and the prevalence of state law examples to illustrate his philosophy requires one to constantly be alert to this "pluralist" feature of his philosophy of law.

Many of the above points that have emerged in the process of translating and editing the *Introduction* invite a word of caution for the reader in approaching this and other volumes yet to appear. Whilst the *Encyclopedia* should become an indispensable reference resource for students of reformational legal philosophy, on its own it cannot be treated as the mature statement of Dooyeweerd's legal philosophy let alone of contemporary reformational legal philosophy. It must be handled with care making proper allowance for the provisional and incomplete nature of the work and should be accompanied by an attitude of openness to its revision in the light of new insights that have emerged since the completion of the *Encyclopaedie,* not only within law and legal theory, but from across the whole range of scholarly disciplines. Not to do so would be contrary to the integrative multidisciplinary vision which the *Encyclopedia* embodies and the spirit of reformational scholarship. At the same time it would be unwise to underestimate the breadth of vision, comprehensiveness, and profound implications of this work, which even Dooyeweerd himself would have been unable to fully appreciate.

The Title of Dooyeweerd's Major Jurisprudential Work

There is another matter regarding the editing of this and the other volumes which deserves a mention and which also is relevant to the issue of how the work will be received amongst its prospective readers. It concerns a discussion amongst several of those involved in the editing about the main title to be given to this English translation of the five volume work. The outcome of that discussion was that the original decision to maintain a literal translation of the title given to the work by the author was confirmed. The alternative proposal was to adopt a title which, though adequately intimating the contents of the work, would have departed from the author's given title in favor of one that it was generally agreed would contain terms more readily understood amongst a readership beyond the jurisprudentially informed.

Although the English translation of the author's own title has in the end been maintained, the translation itself has slightly altered from that originally advertised by the Dooyeweerd Centre. The rendering of *Encyclopaedie van de Rechtswetenschap* that was adopted from the outset was "Encyclopedia of Legal Science." The title finally fixed upon is "Encyclopedia of the Science of Law." It is instructive for appreciating the nature and significance of this work to briefly consider both of the key terms *Encyclopaedie* and *rechtswetenschap* in the original Dutch title and the translation of the latter term.

Encyclopaedie presented no problems of translation. However, the meaning which Dooyeweerd attached to *Encyclopaedie* is not the meaning of that term or its English equivalent that is widely accepted either within or without the scholarly community as its primary or common meaning – the provision of a compendium of facts in a particular field of knowledge or on all branches of knowledge usually arranged alphabetically. In the *Encyclopedia,* as indicated in its title, Dooyeweerd was consciously endeavoring to reform this primary meaning or at least to re-establish another older meaning of the term denoting an integrating theoretical perspective.

That he both fully realized the difficulty of such a project and yet also was determined to contribute towards its accomplishment is manifest within the work. For not only does he carefully explain in this *Introduction* why he has adopted the term *Encyclopaedie* to describe the work and its method, Dooyeweerd went to the additional trouble of taking half of an entire volume (2) to examine the historical basis of this concept he uses to denote an overarching theoretical perspective for a particular field of study ("special science"). Whether or not he was wise in seeking to adopt this term to describe his theoretical perspective and its method, and whether or not he was being realistic in thinking this reformation in the meaning or meanings of encyclopedia could be accomplished, this reforming project must be accepted as being a central objective of the work as a whole.

So whilst the substitution of Dooyeweerd's own title for one with more contemporary resonance has obvious advantages, in addition to presenting problems of word economy in any substituted title, it loses the historical reference to which Dooyeweerd attached considerable weight. And what was the point of attaching so much importance to the historical connection? The answer I would suggest is that by elaborating that connection he would have expected his original jurisprudence and its method to earn greater respect from the community of modern jurisprudential scholarship that would be highly skeptical of its dependence on his assertion of a religious root for all theory and for legal philosophy in particular.

Although *rechtswetenschap* can be given different renderings in different contexts, within the context of the *Encyclopedia* it cannot be given as "jurisprudence." The reason is that if it is correct to apply the term jurisprudence to the complete work in the sense of that term which denotes an area of theoretical study of law, and clearly it is correctly so applied, then *rechtswetenschap* cannot mean "jurisprudence." Dooyeweerd uses *rechtswetenschap* in the *Encyclopedia* to refer to the special "science," that is, the discipline, of law. For Dooyeweerd, an encyclopedia of law is jurisprudence as the theory of law, or more precisely, the philosophy of law encompassing both the broadest philosophical questions and the basic concepts which provides an integrating theoretical perspective for the special science of law in a comprehensive and total fashion. As such it provides a truly critical, comprehensive, and scholarly introduction to the discipline of law (*rechtswetenschap*).

"Science" in the title involves some unavoidable ambiguity. Adding "social" to "science" to avoid misinterpretation of "science" as meaning the application of the natural sciences to legal phenomena (e.g. forensic science) would not have avoided ambiguity or misinterpretation. There is still a danger of "social science" being read in a positivistic or reductionistic manner along the lines of the "natural" sciences. "Science" is the only term that is sufficiently precise to convey the intended meaning of *rechtswetenschap*.

Why the substitution of "Science of Law" for "Legal Science?" The latter is common enough within jurisprudential scholarship not to be misinterpreted and is a perfectly acceptable equivalent for the former in most contexts. However, as part of the description of Dooyeweerd's jurisprudence "science of law" more clearly conveys the notion of the field of study itself as a special discipline and does not simply denote the type of knowledge associated with the discipline, which "legal science" simply conveys. The issues which his jurisprudence primarily addresses are not merely espistemological but also ontological. Furthermore, his ontology is not confined to explaining the structure of the jural dimension of "legal" and nonlegal things, but also examines the structure of the study of law itself as a special science alongside other special sciences and its necessary relationship to philosophy as an integrating theoretical perspective. The questions "What is legal knowledge?", "What is philosophy?" and "What is the relationship between philosophy and the academic study of law?" are for Dooyeweerd ontological as well as epistemological questions.

To conclude this discussion of the title translation, it is not insignificant that our "science of law" rendering of *rechtswetenschap* echoes the title of a jurisprudence text (*The Pure Science of Law*) by one of the outstanding legal theorists in the Western tradition, Hans Kelsen, for whose scholarly abilities Dooyeweerd had the greatest respect. Even more relevantly, Kelsen's theory is one of the main targets of the *Encyclopedia*'s critique; the encyclopedic method and conceptual framework was undoubtedly offered as a superior alternative to the influential Kelsenian legal positivism.

This brief introduction to both the introductory volume and the entire set of volumes comprising the *Encyclopedia* is concluded with a comment upon a central concept of the *Encyclopedia*. Dooyeweerd's identifying of retribution as the normative core or "meaning-kernel" (*zin-kern*) of the universal jural aspect of cosmic reality may be viewed as a major obstacle to the reception of this work as a significant contribution to the field of jurisprudence and legal scholarship.

At a time when there has been a move towards the idea of restorative justice in the criminal justice system and when Christian scholars and reformers are giving support to this move as reflecting a more biblical approach than a traditional one which emphasizes retributive ideas of justice, it might be considered singularly inappropriate to be publishing a work of legal philosophy in which retribution is located at the core of the normative meaning of justice, human law, and legal institutions. Especially is this the case, one would think, when the work professes to arise out of a Christian worldview which proclaims love and justice as central themes.

With respect to this particular matter, and in order to get to grips with this jurisprudential work in general, however, it is necessary to understand a distinction of especial importance to be found within it. For an adequate structural-theoretical account of the normative societal phenomena of law and legal institutions Dooyeweerd insists on making a distinction between societies in which the jural aspect remains in a "closed" or "unopened" state where law is bound to a strict or "undisclosed" concept of retribution and those where the jural aspect has been "opened up" or "deepened" by morality under the leading of (the Christian) faith. Only in the latter does law relax its strict retributive character (lex talionis) as it comes under the influence of a "regulative" idea of justice. Not every "positing" of a jural norm within a particular legal culture need evince this opened up character, guided by an idea of justice, in order to establish itself as law – to satisfy the "existence conditions" of (valid) law as some legal philosophers might say. In the encyclopedic perspective, all law and jural phenomena are "qualified" by their retributive character, but only in opened up legal cultures is this retributive core of law itself deepened into a recognisably "modern" or developed form where it is more appropriate to speak of the most fundamental principles of law requiring implementation being those of "justice" than of "retribution" (even where use of the latter concept is confined to principles of criminal law).

Legal theory that lacks such a structural distinction, on this view, would not be able to provide a clear insight into the relationship between justice and law and shed new light in the never-ending jurisprudential debate over the relationship of law and morality. Perhaps even more significantly, it was the view of the *Encyclopedia*'s author that the lack of a comprehensive structural account of the *constitutive and regulative* elements of law prevented the then prevailing legal theories from being able to provide an adequate explanation of a whole raft of important juridical phenomena within the legal concepts they utilized for that purpose. The genius of this work is to construct a theory of law which provides just such a structural account consisting of a system of "jural" concepts and an accompanying methodology. This is the theoretical foundation of a new approach to understanding law and a new method for the analysis of juridical phenomena.

But to return directly to the point concerning the appropriateness of designating retribution as the concept that correctly approximates the "meaning-core" of the jural aspect, it is within this account of the structure of jural phenomena that the concept of retribution plays a central role. Whether viewed from a Christian or any other perspective, to avoid complete misunderstanding and a hasty dismissal of the work as unsoundly based at its core on account of the central role assigned to retribution, it must be appreciated that Dooyeweerd employs retribution in a sense broader than, though not unrelated to, the commonly understood criminal and penal meaning of the term.

An argument may be put against retaining that particular term to describe the normative content, which Dooyeweerd intends it to convey in his theory, because of the predominance of narrower meanings in both popular and scholarly contexts. Or a more fundamental criticism could be mounted against Dooyeweerd's account itself. But it is what the author understood by retribution within the context of his entire framework of legal concepts that must be addressed by the reader before any judgement can be passed on the theoretical appropriateness of his characterizing of the normative core of law and legal phenomena as retribution.

Here a serious student of the *Encyclopedia* is brought to the heart of the work's overarching conceptual framework and to the basis of Dooyeweerd's account of the concept of law with its retributive core. This is the theory of the modal aspects, the most distinctive and original element of his philosophical systematics which includes his legal philosophy. Only by seeking to fully grasp this theory of the aspects and the theory of individuality-structures that builds upon it can the reader avoid mistaken and hasty judgements on specific elements of this reformational legal philosophy such as that concerning the concept of retribution.

No doubt there are many other aspects of the *Encyclopedia* that are open to misinterpretation. I have focused upon a central element of its theoretical systematics, the concept of retribution as an obvious target of criticism, in order to offer cautionary advice for the reader on how to avoid such interpretive mistakes.

This introduction cannot be concluded without a mention of those who have assisted in various ways in the editing of this first volume. Thanks are due first to the late Robert Knudsen for appreciating how important this work is for serious Christian legal scholarship that he made the considerable effort to produce the first translation; to Herman Dooyeweerd Jr., Johan van der Vyver, and John Witte for encouragement at an early stage; Keith Sewell and Marcel Verburg for advice on specific translation points; Gillian Cameron who retyped the Knudsen translation into electronic format; Jaap Zwart who provided copies of the *dictaten* and a copy of a Dooyeweerd bibliography; Danie Strauss who not only had oversight as General Editor but also provided notes to supplement those of the Editor, retranslated parts of the text, supplied translations of omitted sections, and provided advice on other issues of translation; Michelle Botting for her excellent work as style and format editor; and finally, thanks must go to the Herman Dooyeweerd Foundation and more latterly to Elaine Botha and the Advisory Council of the Dooyeweerd Centre for their support and patience over the years of waiting for this first volume of the *Encyclopedia* to be published.

Alan Cameron
Editor

PART 1

The Philosophic Idea of Encyclopedia in the Light of the Cosmonomic Idea. The Theory of the Law-Spheres as the Primary Foundation of the Encyclopedia of the Science of Law

1.1 Introduction to the Science of Law and the Philosophic Idea of Encyclopedia

The gradual eclipse of the title "encyclopedia of the science of law" by "introduction to the science of law" was sanctioned in the Netherlands by the *Academic Statute* established by Order in Council of June 15, 1921, p. 800, in which the former designation "encyclopaedia" was replaced by "introduction."

Although there is no basis for the conclusion that with the change of title the legislature also intended a material change of content,[1] nevertheless, it is symptomatic of a trend in which the original idea of encyclopedia has gradually been abandoned, even though the name itself still remains in use.

In the middle of the last century, Walter, the author of an encyclopedia of the science of law, which in the interim has achieved considerable recognition, registered his protest explicitly against the already growing custom of identifying encyclopedia with introduction to the science of law. His view, which was largely shared by the already numerous philosophically schooled jurists, was that encyclopedia is a philosophic science which indicates the place of the special sciences in the totality of human knowledge. It gives us insight into the internal coherence of the branches of a science which is founded on the concept of the field of investigation surveyed by the particular science in question.[2]

The thought that lies at the foundation of this conception therefore was that the various areas of scientific knowledge have an inner coherence and are not simply related to each other in an external fashion. In order to attain knowledge of the internal connection of the science of law with the other sciences it is necessary to undertake an investigation of the internal structure of the entire extent of human knowledge so that, in terms of its

---

[1] Willem Zevenbergen, *Formeele encyclopaedie der rechtswetenschap als inleiding tot de rechtswetenschap* ('s-Gravenhage: gebr. Belinfante, 1925), 2.
[2] Walter, *Juristische Encyclopädie* (n.p.,1865), 5.

place within this totality, we can deduce the inner structure of the science of law.

Considered in this fashion, encyclopedia is of necessity a "universal science" of a philosophic character. This universal science, however, is not so much oriented to the ever increasing fund of knowledge, which is being collected by the special sciences within this structure, as it is oriented to the structure itself, apart from which no special science would be possible.

This inner delimitation of the task of encyclopedia has been expressed in the term "formal encyclopedia." That is not a particularly satisfactory expression because the term is also used by those who have broken with the idea of a universal science and have reduced the encyclopedia of law to that of an introduction to the science of law.

An introduction, in contradistinction to an encyclopedia, cannot be viewed as an independent philosophic science. In an introduction to the science of law the pedagogical goal of giving such introductory knowledge as is required to obtain insight into the nature, the scope, and the various branches of this particular scientific discipline is predominant.

Now it can be asserted that it is only possible to obtain a thorough insight into this discipline by means of an encyclopedia in the sense described above. It then must be recognized, however, that this judgment rests upon two presuppositions: (i) an encyclopedia in the sense of a philosophic universal science is possible; and (ii) even from a pedagogical point of view such an encyclopedia is the best introduction to the science of law.

Since the second half of the last century, the idea of encyclopedia as a philosophic universal science has fallen into disfavor and has been virtually abandoned. The idea was identified with a speculative conception of it, discussed later, which was elaborated and defended by the great founders of German idealism, Fichte, Schelling, and Hegel. Frequently the philosophical basic conception that was shaped in the idea of universal science, was not even comprehended any more.

Without any justification this idea was branded as an a priori attempt to capture the whole range of the burgeoning knowledge of the special sciences in a subjective scheme of totality and thereby to lay down the law for the development of the special sciences in terms of an arbitrary philosophical conception. It goes without saying that, in the face of such a disparaging judgment concerning encyclopedia as the "science of the sciences," the question was no longer even raised whether, considered from the pedagogical point of view, encyclopedia could be regarded as the most appropriate introduction to the science of law.

The prejudice to which we refer rests upon a lack of real insight into the significance of the philosophical idea of encyclopedia. Nevertheless, we must not simply sidestep the issue of whether the idea in question does indeed only belong within the framework of a speculative system of thought, or whether it possesses a firm foundation in the structure of the life of law itself and in the structure of scientific thought which addresses itself to legal life.

In answering this question we do not wish to commence with substantial philosophical and epistemological considerations, but rather give a brief account of the multifacetedness of an ordinary activity in daily life.

I enter a store and purchase a box of cigars. A jurist, who considers this act in the role of a scientific observer, begins at once to abstract from the act its legal configuration. The transaction is taken into consideration by the jurist only as a jural transaction, as a legal agreement, out of which flow mutual rights and juridical obligations for the buyer and the seller.

Furthermore, it is clear that this legal configuration forms only one of many aspects of the transaction in question.

If an aesthetician were present among the scientific observers, that specialist would view the same transaction from the particular standpoint of its aesthetic aspect and would provide an answer to the question as to whether or not the attitude, speech, and the expressions of those who were involved in the transaction were harmonious.

An economist, however, would direct attention not to the jural, nor to the aesthetic, but to the economic side of the transaction. Another aspect is now brought into view out of the concreteness of the act of real life, namely, that of economic valuation and the economic measure which was applied in working out the price of the purchased goods.

A fourth scientific observer, who makes the social side of human society a subject of special study, focuses on what is taking place in the store between the buyer and the seller, and considers it specifically from the point of view of social forms. In the form and the tone of their greetings, and in their questions and answers, such an observer quickly discerns the degree of education, status, or importance of the buyer and the seller.

The aspect of language, which is unbreakably connected with the aspect of social intercourse, is interesting to the linguist, who pays particular attention to the lingual significance of the words, to the construction of the sentences, to the possible differences of dialect, and to flaws in pronunciation, etc.

A historian, who views the transaction from its historical aspect, fastens our attention on the fact that the cigars in their packaging, as well as the money with which payment is made, are typical historico-cultural objects which have come into use only in the course of the historical development of Western society. That specialist also directs our attention to the fact that in the transaction the typical forms of language and social convention, the fixing of a price, and the content of the positive law involved in the agreement rest entirely upon a historical foundation.

A logician directs attention to the logical side of the transaction. Does the answer conform to the question in a logical fashion, and are question and answer an expression of a logical train of thought?

A psychologist is interested more in the unique sensory aspect of the transaction. Which psychical strivings, emotional representations, and desires drive the buyer and the seller to an agreement of will? What mood manifests itself in their tone, their expressions, their entire attitude as they make the deal and carry it out? Is it possible to point out emotional aberrations and disorders?

A biologist is interested in the transaction only in respect of its organic aspect of life.

Finally, it would also be possible to invite a physicist and a mathematician to join the group of scientists. Even though, at first, they might well excuse themselves, observing that the event lies outside the field of their own scientific interests, they would admit, nevertheless, that this transaction manifests a physico-chemical, a spatial, and a numerical aspect, etc.,[1] that is to say, precisely those aspects of reality to which their scientific interest is directed.

The variety of aspects of the transaction is by no means exhausted by the foregoing. The theorist of ethics and the theologian also discover in it

---

1 *General Editor's note:* Initially Dooyeweerd distinguished only fourteen aspects. In his first designation of the physical modality he used the term "movement" (see *De Wijsbegeerte der Wetsidee*, vol. 2 [Amsterdam: H.J. Paris, 1935-36], 71: "den wetskring der beweging"). After 1950, he realized that the science of kinematics (phoronomy) can "define a uniform movement without any reference to a causing force" – an insight which inspired him to distinguish between the *kinematic* and the *physical* aspects (see *A New Critique of Theoretical Thought*, vol. 2, trans. David H. Freeman and William S. Young, The Collected Works of Herman Dooyeweerd, gen. ed. D.F.M. Strauss [Amsterdam: H.J. Paris, Philadelphia: Presbyterian and Reformed Publishing Company, 1953-58; reprint, Lewiston, NY: The Edwin Mellen Press, 1997], 99 [hereafter cited as *A New Critique*]). A noteworthy historical point in this connection is the fact that in 1930 the brother-in-law of Dooyeweerd, professor D.H.Th. Vollenhoven, introduced *fifteen* modalities in the first edition of his book, *Isagogè Philosophiae* – by distinguishing the *mechanical* from the *physical* aspect. However, in the editions of 1936 and later this distinction vanishes and Vollenhoven then only acknowledges the physical aspect (cf. K.A. Bril, "A Selected and Annotated Bibliography of D.H.Th. Vollenhoven," *Philosophia Reformata* [1973]: 216). Dooyeweerd, in this respect, rightly mentioned the law of inertia as formulated by Galileo (cf. *A New Critique*, vol. 2, 99). That this law was anticipated by thinkers from the fourteenth century was convincingly shown by A. Maier (*Die Vorläufer Galileisim 14. Jahrhundert,* Roma 1949, 132-215). In a different context P. Janich also emphasized a "strict distinction between phoronomic (subsequently called kinematic) and dynamic statements" ("Trageheitsgesetz und Inertialsystem," *Frege und die moderne Grundlagenforschung*, ed. Chr. Thiel [Meisenheim am Glan, 1975], 68). This explanation applies each time Dooyeweerd refers to the physical or the kinematic aspect.

aspects which comprise the field of investigation of their special sciences, respectively, the moral aspect and the aspect of faith.

Each aspect of the concrete transaction which took place in the cigar shop, having been described, of course, in general and provisional terms only, is abstracted from concrete temporal reality by the science pertaining to it.

Thus the thought might easily arise that every special science, as special science, would be able to close the gates of its own field of investigation such that the disciplines mutually separate themselves strictly from each other as each one studies its own, theoretically abstracted aspect. If we pay attention, however, to the differentiated aspects of reality themselves, we make the surprising discovery that, on the contrary, it is precisely the distinctive character of these aspects themselves that stands in the way of such isolation.

This is immediately clear from the following considerations. As already stated, the jurist abstracts the legal figure of a commercial agreement from the full concrete transaction between the buyer and the seller in the cigar shop. In this legal figure two divergent interests, which could enter into conflict with each other, are brought into a certain harmony.

It is quite evident that the harmony in question cannot be an aesthetic harmony in the proper sense of the word; here it is undoubtedly a matter of the jural harmonizing of interests. But does this jural harmony exist in isolation from the aesthetic?

According to an aesthetic view of social life, every unilateral invasion of the rights of others is instinctively sensed to be a disturbance of the aesthetic harmony of society, even though the aesthetician might remain quite aware of the fact that the harmony of law is something completely different from the beautiful harmony in the aesthetic aspect of reality.

In the above transaction, in which the jurist has discovered the jural figure of a commercial agreement, let us suppose for a moment that the buyer had specified a box of 25 authentic Havanas of good quality and, with the store owner's consent, had only paid one dollar for it. In such a case suspicion immediately arises in the jurist's mind as to whether the agreement was a genuine one. Is it a true commercial agreement, or do we have here a disguised gift, a sham transaction? Or if no gift is intended, is the entire matter suspect? Has the store owner obtained the cigars honestly? Does the agreement indeed have a "lawful cause?"[1]

Why does doubt arise here concerning the genuinely legal character of the transaction? It is because the sum of one dollar does not represent a

---

[1] *Editor's note:* "Lawful cause (*causa*)" is a Civil Law concept for which there is no exactly corresponding concept in Common Law jurisdictions. Contracts however, may be declared void or illegal for being contrary to "public policy" in some respect, e.g. a contract to commit an unlawful act (crime or tort). At the time when Dooyeweerd was writing, *causa* was a requirement of all contracts under the Dutch

real price for these expensive cigars according to their current market value, at least, if they have not been damaged. Without having to take on the thought-pattern of an economist, the jurist's task itself demands consideration of the economic aspect of the commercial agreement. The juridical character of the commercial agreement as such is unbreakably connected with this economic aspect.

In article 1375 of the Civil Code, the jurist finds a reference to "usage" which, in addition to the express stipulations of the transaction itself and the requirements of "fairness" and the "law," determines the extent of the responsibilities and rights of the contracting parties.

In having to consider "usage" (custom) the jurist is immediately brought up against the norms of social intercourse in that society. Yet the meaning of social intercourse may not be read into the concept "usage" as that is intended in the mentioned article. The social rules of courtesy, politeness, social appropriateness, and tact as such do not have any juridical meaning. But there exists such an intimate connection between legal custom and customs of social intercourse that it is impossible to consider the meaning of the former apart from that of the latter.

Consider, for example, under normal economic conditions, the commercial custom of not demanding payment from a sound trader immediately upon delivery of the goods. It is apparent that this custom is primarily a social one; it is initially a rule of courtesy. But it is not out of the question that in various lines of business this custom might have taken on such established forms that it would also have to be taken into account juridically in determining the extent of the mutual rights and responsibilities of the contracting parties.

The intimate connection between legal and social rules can also be irrefutably shown outside the context of an agreement. Think of the transgression involved in breaching a requirement of discipline in wearing a particular kind of clothing, or a requirement in the army to salute in a certain way. In a jural sense, these fall into the category of an unlawful act, but undoubtedly they primarily involve transgressing the rules of social intercourse.[1]

Civil Code. This requirement has now been abandoned. Common law jurisdictions such as the English still retain the requirement of "consideration" which is a more narrowly economic concept than the continental *causa*. See Samuel & Rinkes, *The English Law of Obligations in Comparative Context* (Nijmegen: Ars Aequi Libri, 1991), 72-73.

1 *Editor's note:* It is important to realize here that in Dooyeweerd's philosophy, as a universal modal aspect, the jural aspect not only manifests itself concretely as state law but in nonstate spheres of life as well. It is possible that when he refers to the breach of a disciplinary requirement of dress he has in mind an actual state law to that effect. However, it is also possible that he is thinking of what might be called a "dress code," i.e., rules of greater or lesser formality functioning within some sphere

The jurist, who has established that the earlier described transaction in the cigar shop, as a legal configuration, meets the requirements of the contract of sale, now discovers in articles 1378–1387 of the Civil Code an entire heading devoted to the "interpretation of contracts." The jurist, qua jurist, thereby comes into immediate contact with the lingual aspect of the transaction, and it is plain from the outset that the entire jural configuration of the commercial agreement can only exist on the basis of linguistic forms of expression in which contracting parties make a disposition of their jural agreement of will.

Having already established that we are dealing with a contract of sale, there is presupposed an explanation, an interpretation, of the lingual signs employed by means of which, as the jurist says, the parties express their intentions. Nevertheless, the legal interpretation, in its jural sense, is not merely linguistic.

For example, the interpretation of getting into a street car as a declaration of intention to enter into a transportation agreement with the street car company certainly cannot be understood as a linguistic interpretation. But law cannot exist without language, so unbreakable is the connection between the two.

That the jural aspect of the transaction unbreakably coheres with the historical aspect is immediately apparent when we account for the fact that the positive juridical content of the agreement, as well as usage, wherever recognized in the Civil Code, has a close connection with the modern stage of cultural development. The form of the contract itself has its own legal history and can only be understood scientifically in connection with it. In the most primitive phase of Roman and German law, the contract, as a source of legal relationships relating to property, was unknown. Here only a delict created juridical relations between members of the tribe.

Furthermore, it is already apparent from the first attempt at juridical interpretation of the sale contract under consideration, that the jural significance of the agreement is unbreakably connected with the logical aspect of the transaction. If there is no logical process of thought underlying the expressions of will of the contracting parties, it is impossible per se to ascribe to them a juridical meaning. As yet there cannot be any agreement of will, in the juridical sense of the word, if the declarations contradict each other logically.

As soon as the jurist, however, begins to consider the jural sense of the declaration of will, the unbreakable connection between the jural and psychical aspect of the act will also be encountered. Behind the declaration is concealed a psychical process of desires, imaginings, and

---

of societal life, but not originating in state law. In which case it would still be correct to speak of the transgression of those rules as constituting an "unlawful act" "in a jural sense" because, as a general jural concept, it can be taken to encompass both breaches of state law and nonstate law, even rules contained in a dress code.

strivings, which cannot be ignored by the jurist in questions relating to matters such as mistake, bad faith, and fraud.

A valid declaration of will, furthermore, can only be expressed in a jural fashion by responsible persons, and responsibility in a jural sense is unbreakably interconnected with a normally developed life of feelings and imagination. Young children, for example, cannot legally bind themselves.

No further demonstration is required to show that the psychical aspect in question is in turn itself completely bound up with the biotic aspect of the organic development of life. In this connection think of the juristic notion of majority, as a rule, a primary condition for complete legal capacity.

And finally, the configuration of a legal act such as a commercial agreement also unbreakably coheres with the following aspects of reality: movement, space, and number.

As the jurist says, a sale agreement is a legal ground for legal consequences. It introduces changes into the previous jural state of affairs. The purchased cigars, by being handed over, cease to be the property of the owner and become the property of the buyer. The money which is given in payment passes in the same fashion from the possession of the buyer to that of the seller. No demonstration is required to show that the jural aspect of the transaction is directly connected with the physical aspect of movement.[1] We here encounter the elementary legal configuration of jural causality, which cannot be understood apart from its connection with physical causality, but which nevertheless retains it own inviolable meaning.

Furthermore, a sale agreement is made in a particular place and thereby manifests its spatial character. Nevertheless, the location of the transaction in its jural sense is not at all a mathematical concept. This becomes clear if one considers the following case:

A German trader in Amsterdam orders by telephone a shipment of grain from Brussels. Immediately the jurist asks, Where did this agreement come into existence? It goes without saying that mathematics cannot provide us with an answer. But the place of agreement must be established for juridical purposes, because the question as to the applicable system of law depends on it. At the same time, this finally brings us to the expression of the unbreakable connection between the jural and the aspect of number. How does the difficulty arise here with respect to establishing the place of the agreement in a juridical sense? It is because the buyer and the seller are

---

1 *Editor's note:* In light of his later distinguishing of the aspects of movement and the physical aspect (see note on p. 14), Dooyeweerd would have been required to revise this analysis so as to distinguish two distinctly different "elementary legal configurations": (i) jural movement (e.g. *transfer* of legal title to goods); and (ii) jural causality."

two different persons who, since they are located in two different countries, express their intentions from different places.

The agreement of sale presupposes, however, that out of this dual expression of will there must come into being a jural unity within the voluntary agreement. If the agreement of sale in this sense is to be a jural unity, then juristically speaking it can only come into being at a single place. The question whether the location is to be that of the buyer or the seller is a legal question, which, however, could not arise apart from the numerical aspect of the act.

Now I have yet to say anything about the connection between the jural aspect and the moral and faith aspects. Nevertheless, the connection here is just as intimate, even taking into consideration the unique nature of the aspects in question. In article 1356 of the Civil Code, one discovers the provision that if agreement is to be reached there must be a "lawful cause." I cannot enter here into the various points of view concerning this concept. In the present context it will suffice to give an illustration of an unlawful cause which according to article 1371 of the Civil Code renders an agreement void.

Let us suppose that a person promises another a sum of money for spreading false rumors in the stock market by which means the first hopes to personally benefit. The other party agrees to this proposition. There is therefore mutual agreement. But such an agreement has an "immoral cause," and for this reason is legally void. The connection here between the jural and the moral aspects of the transaction is immediately apparent. Article 1374 of the Civil Code explicitly states that an agreement must be brought into existence "in good faith." Article 1357 provides *inter alia* that in an agreement assent is invalid if it is obtained by deceit. Article 1284 refers to the failure to perform an undertaking that is owing to the "guile" of the debtor.

The above mentioned sale agreement, which we have discussed earlier, is subject to all of the provisions of the Civil Code, and the unbreakable connection between its jural and moral aspects, at the same time, is thereby demonstrated.

An elementary legal figure in which the connection between the jural and the moral aspects is prominent is that of fault, which plays an essential role in respect of failure to perform or failure in timely performance of the agreement.

Finally, the connection between the jural aspect and the aspect of faith becomes clear if one considers that we live in a Christian land where legal conceptions have been influenced in great measure by Christian ideas. Completely independent of the question whether the contracting parties personally adhere to Christian beliefs, the agreement which they conclude is thoroughly bound to this connection between law and faith.

So, for example, the principle of contractual freedom, with the simultaneous binding of every contract to a lawful cause, stems from the canon law of the Roman Catholic Church which based this principle on the Holy Scriptures. The interpretation of such concepts as "good morals" and "good faith," etc. has also undoubtedly been strongly influenced by Christian conceptions and concerns.

The above summary examination of the various connections of the legal pattern of the sale agreement in question with all the other aspects of this transaction may be sufficient for now to demonstrate that the theoretical idea of encyclopedia cannot simply be thrust aside in the manner in which it is generally done at the present time.

In any case, quite apart from the question whether the speculative doctrines of science of Fichte, Schelling, or Hegel are acceptable, it is impossible to deny that the structure of law itself demands that scientific thinking, in respect of juridical investigation, proceeds according to an idea of the interconnection of the legal[1] with the other aspects of reality. In this regard, it is of little consequence how this idea is more precisely expressed and whether scientific jurists are aware of the fact that they maintain it. Provisionally, it is sufficient to establish that the idea in question is a necessary presupposition for investigation within the special sciences.

If this can be established, then the encyclopedia of the science of law, which aims to acquaint us with the internal structure of the science of law by pointing out its place within the coherence of the special sciences, can no longer be rejected as aprioristic speculation. On the contrary, it would then appear that this encyclopedia, as itself a philosophical theory of science, must be considered to be utterly essential for bringing to light the foundations of the science of law.

If it is the case that the jural aspect of reality can only exist in unbreakable connection with the remaining aspects of reality, then legal science can only operate theoretically in a responsible fashion if it also proceeds governed by a proper insight into the place of the legal within the universal coherence of aspects.

This insight ought to be expressed, first of all, in jural concept-forming. To be more precise, the basic concepts of the science of law can only be formed in a fruitful manner if they are understood in their proper relationship to, and in their connection with, the basic concepts in which the remaining aspects of reality are theoretically captured. As we shall later observe, entirely incorrect formulations of problems arise from a lack of in-

---

[1] *Editor's note:* By "the legal" (*het recht*) Dooyeweerd clearly means what he refers to as the normative "jural aspect" (*juridische aspect*) of concrete law and not concrete (positive) law itself.

sight into the true relationship and interconnections between the jural and the other aspects of reality.

If it is the task of an introduction to the science of law, first of all, to introduce the aspiring jurist to the nature of the science of law and the basic concepts which the jurist handles, then, on the view presented here, it is also absolutely necessary that such an introduction is based upon a philosophical encyclopedia of the science of law in the sense provisionally outlined.

Such an encyclopedia of the science of law is in reality a philosophy of law. And the philosophy of law thus conceived cannot be divorced from the science of law as a special science.

It is not a hobby for speculatively inclined souls who feel the need for an idealistic conception of law divorced from reality. The encyclopedia, on the contrary, brings to light the necessary foundations and presuppositions of the science of law. It holds up to the science of law the mirror of self-criticism.

1.2   Science and Reality

This self-criticism is indeed indispensable to the science of law. It is also of great importance for aspiring jurists to know, as they make their entrance into its noble edifice, that there is within it no peaceful atmosphere of agreement. It must be realized that they are entering a veritable battlefield of opposing opinions in which, lacking a legal-philosophical orientation, they are bound to end up on the wrong track.

One might try to put their minds at rest, perhaps, with the statement that it is not the task of the science of law as a special science to intrude upon the battle of the philosophical theories of law, but that it ought to restrict itself to the positive law, that is, actually valid law. But what is positive law?

There are widely differing views even on this question. By positive law is one only to understand – as the positivistic approach within legal philosophy taught – the complex of rules of conduct which have been set down in the legislation, and of those (arising from some other source) to which that law refers? Or is there, in addition, positive law which does not derive its validity from the legislator?

If the first standpoint is adopted, then is it the form of law that is alone sufficient to guarantee the positive validity of a legal prescription? Or is it, in the final analysis, determined by the question whether this prescription is really controlled in its application by the organs of state charged with its application? If this latter position is adopted, how then can the science of law come to a decision if, in its estimation, there is a clear discrepancy between, for example, the declaration of a court of law and the legislation itself?

Are there also provisions in the law which can be characterized as not binding, and if so, what is the criterion according to which we distinguish between binding and nonbinding provisions of the law, when the law itself has great difficulty in offering a criterion?

Is the provision in our law containing the General Provisions that custom, unless derived from law itself, does not establish law to be understood as positive law? But if there is the formation of an established jurisprudence *contra legem*, is this then customary law? And if so, given the possibility of an established jurisprudence *contra legem* is difficult to deny, what then is the positive law – a legal rule which has become a dead letter or a rule which is applied outside of, and in conflict with, the law actually in effect?

Furthermore, if in the final analysis everything depends upon the question whether a mandatory rule of behavior is actually applied, is the actual course of conduct of the societal institutions charged with the administration of law alone decisive, or is the common attitude of the legal participants also a factor?

And, finally, is positive law only a factual datum, or does it also bear the character of a "norm," of rules with which one ought to comply?

Here I have deliberately formulated a number of questions which present themselves inescapably even to those who believe that in positive law they have an unproblematic given. This "naive-positivistic" attitude has now been widely recognized as unscientific.

Even though positive law as such may not be dependent on the view one has of it (a proposition that, incidentally, is contested), within the science, it is precisely this view on which depends the answer to the most difficult question as to what must be understood by positive law.

What we have revealed in this difference of opinion that has emerged is a fundamental disagreement affecting the entire investigation of law.

How profoundly legal theory is influenced by the difference in viewpoint concerning the structure of reality appears when we become better acquainted with the basic concepts and the general doctrines of the science of law. We have to commence with the remark that calling upon reality in the elucidation of a particular theoretical conception can never be neutral vis-à-vis philosophy. In order to elucidate this we for a moment have to give a closer account of the relationship between science and reality.

In part 1.1, we showed by way of an illustration of a simple sale agreement how great is the diversity of aspects which reality displays. In the meantime, it is indeed clear that in the ordinary experiences of daily life one does not arrive at an articulated distinguishing of reality into separate aspects.

In daily life, events, acts, things, etc., are experienced as individual, temporal totalities of which the different aspects are never experienced explicitly and individually, but only implicitly and in an unbroken mutual coherence of this particular act, this particular thing, etc.

So in naive, that is, "nonscientific" experience of reality, an individual thing, such as the chestnut tree in my garden, is not separately conceived with respect to its mathematical aspects of quantitative multiplicity and spatial relationships, its physical aspect of energy-mass, its biotic aspect of organic life, etc. Instead, it is conceived immediately, in its individual unity, as a tree in which all of these aspects are presented as an unbroken coherence but without my analyzing them separately.

It is only in the scientific, theoretical attitude of knowing whereby the aspects of reality are individually analyzed and distinguished from each other that the possibility of the separate special sciences arises.

At the outset of theoretical instruction in mathematics, one is taught to think of the relationships of number and space apart from the things which are perceived by the senses in everyday experience. In their naive way of thinking, children begin to observe these relationships in the context of concrete things; for example, they must use wooden beads on their play pens in order to learn to count, and only gradually do they develop an eye for relationships of number and space as such.

Thus jurists, too, in their scientific speciality, do not direct their attention to the full concrete reality of a thing or event. Instead, they aim to become acquainted with its jural aspect. For just this reason: in the area of scientific investigation, an appeal to naive experience of reality, in order to defend a particular theoretical view of the field of investigation, has no meaning. It is not because this prescientific attitude of experience is wrong or valueless, but simply because knowledge gained by the special sciences is only oriented to aspects of reality which have been theoretically distinguished from each other; about this, naive experience has nothing to teach us.

Astronomers, whose thought is oriented to the physical aspect of movement of the heavenly bodies, will not ascribe to the naive experience of a sunset any power to refute the astronomical theory of the double movement of the earth. And yet, insofar as they remain conscious of the limitation of their special science, they will restrain themselves from asserting that this experience is false.

From a special scientific point of view, that latter assertion is no longer sound. In our naive observing of a sunset, we do not experience the separate aspect of movement of this event but the full concrete reality of it as an individual, total structure. Yet naive experience cannot teach us anything relating to the distinct aspects of this event. To be able to say that it gives us erroneous information about "the true state of affairs" regarding the aspect of movement it is necessary, first, to have ascribed to that mode of experiencing a particular theory about the movements of the sun and the earth. It is this that is false because naive experience is in no way a theory of reality; it is simply naive experiencing of reality without any further refinement. As soon as it is concluded on the basis of sensory experience that the sun moves around the earth, you have already crossed over the boundary into theory. If one says, however, "I observe how the sun is sinking below the horizon," then no theory about the movements of the heavenly bodies has yet been presented.

Therefore when those working in one of the special sciences begin to appeal to "reality," they ought to be aware of the fact that they are appealing to a coherence of reality which they have already broken up into its aspects in order, subsequently, to investigate it in a scientific fashion within one of these theoretically distinguished aspects. As scientists, they must keep in mind that the reality which has been theoretically analyzed in this fashion is no longer the reality which presents itself to them in ordinary experiencing, but is, on the contrary, a theoretical view of reality. This view, if it is truly to be a view of reality, cannot limit itself to theoretical insight into a particular aspect; it must always be a view of reality within the structure of the mutual interrelationships of its aspects.

An illustration may clarify what we have been saying here. In 1929 there appeared the first volume of a remarkable book by the Swedish professor Anders Wilhelm Lundstedt, *Die Unwissenschaftlichkeit der Rechtswissenschaft*. In this work the author attempts to show that all of the current concepts with which the science of law operates, such as those of rights and duties, obligation, legal norm, etc., are nothing more than false speculative constructions without any basis in empirical (experiential) reality.

The Roman jurists taught that an undertaking, an obligation, arises from an agreement in virtue of which one party is obligated to the other to execute a performance and the other party acquires the right to have this performance carried out. That writer, following his colleague Hägerström, maintains this entire view of the matter was merely based on a primitive, magical conception whereby, through the pronouncement of a specific formula, one acquired a mysterious power over the person from whom performance was due and from which the latter could only be freed by performance. The modern science of law has turned this magical power over the person from whom performance is owing into a "right" of the person to whom performance is due, and a corresponding physico-psychical "debt."[1]

---

1 *Editor's note:* "Debt" here has the meaning of one owing a performance, rather than its usual narrower meaning in the (English) common law of one owing a monetary payment (debt).

But according to Lundstedt, there is nothing in reality corresponding to these concepts, any more than there is in reality something corresponding to the primitive magical notion that the "obligation" is a sphere of power to which the person owing a performance is bound. According to him, the unique reality of the "obligation" resides in the factual situation that when a person acts or fails to act (whether prescribed by law, contract or otherwise) whereby the other party suffers damage (prescribed in a specific manner), the former, on the demand of the injured party, can be compulsorily required to give in satisfaction a certain sum of money to cover the trial costs and the damage suffered.

Rights, duties, and norms therefore are not to be found in reality. Science, however, is bound to the limits of experiential reality. Therefore there must be a radical cleaning out in legal science's arsenal of concepts because nothing in empirical reality corresponds to the concepts which are currently employed there.

So much for Lundstedt. His argument is an instructive example of an appeal to reality in justification of a specific theoretical view of legal life. What kind of "reality" is this which is set over against the "scholasticism of the jurists" with such pathos? Certainly not reality as it presents itself in ordinary experience!

Every normally developed person who enters into an agreement, or does something that is forbidden by law, has an implicit awareness of rights and obligations, of that which is proper and that which is improper before the law, even though that person may not possess any theoretical insight into the jural aspect of human society.

As soon as the normative aspects are eliminated, that is to say, those aspects in which reality functions according to rules of what "ought to be done," it is no longer concrete reality to which an appeal is made, but rather a theoretical abstraction from that reality. And the moment that one equates such a theoretical abstraction with "true reality," not only the boundaries of ordinary experience but also those of the special sciences are transgressed. A theoretical view of the structure of reality is simply being presented as the true one, and this theoretical view of reality is of necessity philosophical in character.

Thus Lundstedt's view of reality identifies the abstracted physico-psychical aspects of reality with the concrete reality of experience and is thereby obliged, in a theoretical fashion, to locate legal life within these physico-psychical aspects. Legal life is thereby entirely deprived of its normative meaning.

That writer is being very consistent in maintaining this naturalistic view of law when he correctly observes of his own standpoint that, in the nature of the case, it is impossible to speak any longer of "compensation" because "reality" does not know this phenomenon.

But reflecting on the argument set forth in the preceding paragraph, one might remark: Does such a theoretical, essentially philosophical view of the structure of reality not have any higher standards of evaluation than the subjective conviction of the scientific inquirer?

If this were so, every appeal to reality ("the facts") would be without scientific value, and a boundless theoretical arbitrariness would, in the last analysis, take the place of scientific truth.

Happily, science is not in such an abominable state! The "facts" to which it appeals must indeed make themselves accessible to naive experience in which reality presents itself structurally just as it is. Furthermore, the theoretical view of the structure of reality is not simply surrendered to the subjective arbitrariness of the thinker. It must be able to give a proper theoretical account of the nontheoretical experience of reality; otherwise it builds upon speculative quicksand. There is a further criterion for the scientific truth of that view, about which I shall later speak when considering the so-called antinomies.

An appeal to reality for theoretical purposes is completely unjustified if reality, as it presents itself in ordinary experience, is identified in an aprioristic manner with a theoretical abstraction of particular aspects of that experiential reality. The danger which this brings with it is the impression left with the student who is philosophically unschooled that such a theoretical view of reality is not dependent upon a particular philosophical standpoint and this uncritical way of thinking is also urged upon the neophyte jurist "in the name of simplicity" because the intention is to reproduce only what is the "ordinary, everyday conception" of reality.

In opposition to this view, I require as a demand of scientific honesty that a jurist-in-the-making must be taught to recognize the unbreakable connection between a view of the structure of positive law and the philosophic vision of the structure of reality in its entirety. This is because the theoretical view of reality is always of a philosophical character.

In order to render a satisfactory account of this state of affairs it is necessary to examine in more detail the question as to the relationship in which philosophy stands to the knowledge of the special sciences, on the one hand, and to naive, nontheoretical experience of reality, on the other.

1.3 Philosophy, the Special Sciences, and Naive Experience of Reality. Cosmic Time and the First Transcendental Basic Problem of Any Conceivable Philosophic System

In part 1.2 we saw that in the naive, that is to say, nontheoretical approach of everyday life, the various aspects of reality are neither individually distinguished, nor theoretically analyzed. In this approach our vision is directed not to abstract relationships of number, to abstract figures of space, abstract movements of matter, abstract interrelationships of feeling, abstract forms of language and social intercourse, abstract legal relationships, etc. Instead, we experience reality here in the concrete totality structures of individual things, events, acts, and of concrete forms of social life, such as the family, the state, the business enterprise, the church, etc.

These structures, which we shall call individuality-structures of reality, embrace in principle all aspects of reality without exception. But in such structures, the aspects are grouped in a typical manner within an individual totality. In naive experience attention is oriented not to the distinct aspects of this totality but to the individual totality itself.

Nevertheless, in the attitude of naive experience, we do have an implicit awareness of the richness of aspects in which reality presents itself within these totality structures.

If a theoretician, for example, would like to set me straight by informing me that this little table, this tree, this chair are in reality nothing more than complexes of atoms, and that only physics and chemistry are able to give us any insight into their true structure and nature, then my naive awareness of reality reacts intuitively against this pretension of scientific theory to restrict the full reality of these things, which are familiar to me in my everyday experience, to their physico-chemical aspect (that is to say, the aspect of movement).

I sense that such a theory deprives me of the many-sided richness of things as I experience them. Actually, it eliminates them altogether. And, even if I cannot refute it in a scientific fashion with my naive experience, I am nevertheless deeply convinced that it cannot be right.

This is because the full temporal reality of the things which I experience in daily life is only given to me in an unbreakable coherence of all the aspects, of the "natural sides" (namely, the mathematical, physical, biotic, and psychical aspects) in which reality is subject to natural laws, as well as the "normative sides" (namely, the logical, historical, lingual, social, economic, aesthetic, jural, moral, and faith aspects) in which reality is subject to rules of what ought to be.

For my untheorized conception of reality, this little table is no longer this little table as soon as theory attempts to reduce what is given to a system of abstract physico-chemical formulas. The full reality of the thing as we experience it in everyday reality also has its objective-sensory form, its objective coherence of logical attributes by which it is differentiated from other things, its objective meaning in language, its function in social intercourse and interaction, its economic value (I can immediately observe whether it is an expensive or a cheap article), its objective beauty or ugliness, its function as a legal object (it belongs either to me or to someone else), etc.

Insofar as a thing also functions in the normative aspects of reality, naive experience subjects it without objection to norms, not as a responsible subject, but as an object, as a thing. The table, for example, is well or poorly formed, pretty or ugly, nice or not nice, expensive or cheap, etc.

The peculiarity of naive experience reveals itself in the fact that our thought does not set its logical-analytical aspect over against the distinguished nonlogical aspects of reality; it does not make an aspect into a problem – into a *Gegenstand*, as the Germans call it – of knowledge, but reveals itself in the fact that our thought instead remains naively incorporated into full temporal reality, that is to say, it experiences the psychical, logical, and the remaining normative functions of things as indissoluble constituents of and in reality.

Wherever, in some fashion or other, we abstract in our thinking a *Gegenstand* out of concrete reality, we are not dealing with the naive but with the theoretical attitude of thought. This is the source of the error in the view which seeks a kind of theory of knowledge in naive experience, such as, for example, the "copy theory." Epistemology understands this to be the view that a (physical) thing-reality, enclosed within itself, is reproduced in our consciousness like a photographic image. As if all of temporal reality could be reduced to sensory impressions!

It is scientific thought that initially separates temporal reality into its various aspects and sets the nonlogical aspects as a *Gegenstand*, as a problem, over against the logical function of concept-forming. To this end it must abstract these aspects out of their given indissoluble coherence by way of theoretico-logical analysis. It should certainly be clear that theoretical thought is indeed thought that subtracts something from full reality. The special sciences have broken up reality into compartments; but all of the special sciences together, in their mutual complementing of one another, cannot bring us to a knowledge of reality in its unbroken unity. Piecing together the slices cut from an apple does not give us back the original piece of fruit.

The first question now is this, What is abstracted by theoretical thought from the fullness of given reality? Of what is the abstraction made?[1]

---

1 *Editor's note:* The same question is stated in two ways. The answer that would be expected is "the modal aspects" (see *A New Critique*, vol. 1, 38 ff). However, the actual answer given does not refer to the aspects but to (cosmic) time. The reason for this is that Dooyeweerd does not clearly distinguish here two different but closely related questions: 1. What is abstracted in the theoretical act of thought (*Gegenstand*-relation)? and; 2. From what is the abstraction made? Cosmic time, in which the aspects are embedded, and which ensures their inter-modal coherence, is the answer to the second question only. The relationship between time and the aspects is more clearly explained, and the questions more clearly formulated, in *A New Critique*, vol. 1, 22 ff. More complicated internal inconsistencies in Dooyeweerd's

With this question we introduce the so-called transcendental critique of theoretical thought which, through exploring the nontheoretical presuppositions of theoretical thought, initiates an investigation into that which, from the outset, makes philosophic thought, as theoretical thought, possible. This critical question makes it impossible for us to proceed from the abstract theoretical *Gegenstand*-relation as an unproblematical datum and thus to seek our starting point within the theoretical attitude of thought itself.

The answer to this question we have posed must be the following: In the first place, theoretical thought abstracts from time, which holds all aspects of reality in an unbroken coherence, and within which the logical aspect is bound together with all the nonlogical aspects.

Time, in this universal, cosmic sense, must indeed be distinguished from the particular aspects of time in which it expresses itself, for example, from clock time, insofar as this simply presents a measurement of time in the aspect of movement. In every aspect of reality, cosmic time, which embraces all of the aspects, expresses itself in a specific sense within a particular modality. A few illustrations make this clear.

In the aspect of number, time functions in the particular sense (modality) of how much (discrete quantity). If I say that 2 precedes 3 and 4 in the series of numbers, I have in mind a temporal relationship amongst the numbers which may not, however, be confused with the consecutive moments of my subjective act of counting. In this series, the number 2 precedes the numbers 3 and 4 and has a quantitative temporal sense: $2 < 3 < 4$. This is a fact that is not dependent upon my subjective act of counting but is founded in the temporal order of numbers.

In the spatial aspect of reality, time functions in the particular sense of spatial simultaneity, and within that spatial simultaneity, in the sense of spatially greater or smaller. A particular geometrical plane figure, for example, can only exist in the simultaneous extension of its spatial parts and not in the succession characteristic of movement in which one point disappears as the following one appears. If I take a triangle and divide one of its sides (A–B) down the middle, then I have point M. Even though the lines AB and AM are simultaneous in their extendedness, nevertheless, figuring from point A, point M is spatially earlier than point B because the latter is situated further from point A than is point M. Here the time relationships clearly bear the particular sense of the spatial relationship with respect to the length of the lines AM and AB.

In the aspect of movement, time functions in the particular sense of the relationships of movement. As we have said, clock time, in its merely

---

understanding of the *Gegenstand*-relation are extensively discussed in D.F.M. Strauss, "An Analysis of the Structure of Analysis (The Gegenstand-relation in discussion)," *Philosophia Reformata* 49, no. 1 (1984): 35-56.

physical aspect, is nothing more than the measure of movement. In the meaning of movement there is no static simultaneity, but only a dynamic one dependent upon movement itself.

In the biotic aspect of reality, time functions in the particular sense of the time of the organic development of life, of birth, maturation, and death. The question as to when a living individual is born is clearly a question of biological[1] time which can only be answered in a biological sense.

In the aspect of feeling, time functions in the particular sense of feeling time in which the moments of feeling interpenetrate each other qualitatively in a continuous stream, which does not allow for a mechanical isolation of moments. In the duration of a feeling of emotional tension or anxiety there is a quality of intensity which does not lend itself to being measured in purely extensional terms. If a person is aroused emotionally, time just flies; if one is bored and depressed, time simply crawls along.

In the logical aspect, time functions in the particular sense of logical priority and posteriority as this temporal relationship expresses itself significantly in the logical principle of sufficient ground. What serves as a logical premise is prior in logical time: in the logical syllogism the logical grounds (premises) logically precede the consequent (conclusion). So, for example, the basic concept of law is also anterior in the logical order of time to the concept of a concrete legal phenomenon such as a sale agreement.

In the historical aspect, time functions in the specific sense of cultural development with its internal interpenetration of past, present, and future. The historical period, bounded as it is by important transitional points in cultural development, is a temporal configuration in the particular sense of history, as is the case for a historical moment.

In the lingual aspect of reality, time functions in the particular sense of symbolical meaning. One need only think, for example, of the symbolic pause between two spoken sentences, of the significance of the slow movement of a conductor's baton to indicate to the orchestra the beginning of an *adagio*.

In the aspect of social intercourse, time functions in the particular sense of politeness, courtesy, tact, conviviality. One need only think of the special social significance of allowing someone to go first who has a higher position in society, of greeting a hostess first, of choosing what is the precise moment for making a visit as a matter of tact.

---

1 *General Editor's note:* Dooyeweerd's philosophy is sensitive to the distinction between what is *ontically given* and what is the result of human intervention – be it through reflection or through giving positive form to ontic possibilities. Dooyeweerd's own language use is not consistent, however, and in most cases throughout this text, biological, ontological, and psychological should read biotic, ontic, and psychical. On pages 125 and 130 below Dooyeweerd employs the correct terms.

In the economic aspect, time functions in the particular sense of economic value, which always presupposes a relative scarcity of serviceable economic goods and an avoidance of too great a cost to obtain and use them. Thus the economic phenomenon of interest depends upon a higher economic valuation of the immediate over the future utility of the same economic goods, or of the abstract value of the money, by which they may be procured. Consider also the English expression, "time is money."

In the aesthetic aspect of reality, time functions in the particular aspect of beautiful harmony. One need only think of the Aristotelian rule for drama: unity of time, place, and action. The difference in principle between historical and aesthetic time reveals itself prominently in a historical drama or a historical novel. If their authors simply follow the historical order of occurrence of the events, then they mistake the requirements of a work of art. Aesthetic time should not be aesthetically empty. A historical course of events, as such, does not follow any aesthetic order of time.

In the jural aspect of reality, time functions in the particular sense of law which we have yet to investigate more closely. For example, in the extinguishment of ownership, or of a claim through being statute-barred because of the expiry of a specified period during which the right-holder does not give any indication from conduct that the right will be exercised, time does not display a mathematical, physical, logical, or historical sense but a very definite jural sense which is governed by jural norms.

For example, the Civil Code stipulates that the period of limitation for claims in general is 30 years. In this fixed period of time there is an expression of a normative legal requirement, namely, that of securing legal certainty in intercourse. In determining the period of validity of legal norms, as well as that of the period of time in which a legal fact (that is, a fact to which legal consequences attach) occurred, the juridical sense of time which we have in mind comes to expression. Consider the question as to when a commercial agreement has taken place, for example, if, between the offer to sell and the acceptance, a period of a week has elapsed, and if the written reply to the offer made by the offeror, for example, is received a week after it has been sent. Consider also the question as to whether a law has "retrospective force," whether it will hold for legal facts which occurred before the law comes into effect but whose legal consequences are yet to be manifested. Such would be the case, for example, for someone who, at the point of reaching the age of twenty-one, has attained majority under civil legislation, but who in the meantime is faced with a new law which only allows it to commence at the age of twenty-three. Finally, think of the legal consequences of not fulfilling one's legal obligations on time.

In the moral aspect of reality, time functions according to the particular sense of the moral obligation of love. In the moral order of time, every lost moment means an omission morally speaking. "Time is pressing" is an expression which, used in a moral sense, brings this situation sharply into focus.

Finally, in the faith aspect of reality, time takes on a specific meaning of the revelation of the supra-temporal, of what lies hidden beyond time. It is in this sense that the opening words of the Book of Genesis, "In the beginning God created the heavens and the earth," should be understood. It is in this sense also, as I see it, that one should understand the "days" of creation, in which God's creative work – not subject to time as such – is related in faith to human work days in order that we might always view our temporal work in the light of God's supra-temporal work of creation. And it is also in this sense that the confession that rebirth precedes faith is to be understood.

All the mentioned aspects are merely particular modalities, particular ways in which cosmic time–which overarches the aspects in a cosmic continuity expresses itself. This cosmic time, considered as to its law-side, is a time-order which gives to the various aspects their established place and structure. Considered as to its subject-side, it is a cosmic time-duration which differs according to various things, acts, events, and temporal human existence and which expresses itself in all of the aspects of reality as well. In naive experience, time is not experienced according to its particular abstracted aspects but in the continuity of its temporal coherence in which all the aspects of time are inseparably joined together. When a house catches fire this event is not experienced in its separate abstracted aspects but in the continuity of its coherence in time within which all aspects of time are indissolubly connected. When in everyday life I look at my watch, I do not consider time simply in its abstract aspect of movement, but also in its aspect of feeling, its symbolic, its social, and its jural aspect, etc. Clock time continually reminds me of my social responsibilities.

It is precisely because naive experience remains enmeshed in this continuity of cosmic time that the aspects of reality do not come to my awareness in an articulated fashion, in the discontinuous way characteristic of theory. The continuity of cosmic time conceals the various aspects of our cosmos from naive awareness.

It is not possible to form a concept of cosmic time as such. The fact is that every concept presupposes time. We can only form for ourselves a theoretical idea or "limiting concept" of time as a cosmic presupposition of every concept toward which theoretical thought also points in its restlessness. Theoretical thought, however, must begin by abstracting from cosmic time which, in its continuity, spans the various aspects of reality in order to be able to grasp these aspects themselves in a logical discontinuity.

For this reason the special sciences remain oriented to the investigation of the changeable phenomena within a particular aspect of reality. They do not in any way direct their attention to the nature of the aspects themselves. By contrast, it is the inescapable task of theoretical thought to grasp the theoretically differentiated aspects according to their constant structure which lies at the basis of all changeable phenomena, that is to say, to understand the aspects in their mutual coherence out of their root-unity.

What we have already said entails the idea that the philosophical idea of totality must be something completely different from the natural-scientific idea of the cosmos or the "universe." By its very nature, astronomy only views the cosmos according to its mathematical and physico-chemical aspects, with a conscious elimination of all the rest. It does not consider the fundamental nature or structure of the above aspects as a theoretical problem, but it only investigates the variable reality within these aspects.

Contrastingly, it is philosophy which initially must subject the internal structure and nature of the aspects of reality themselves to an investigation within a view of totality, not the variable phenomena which come to expression within them. None of these aspects can be left out of consideration. Attention must be directed theoretically to the totality, the entirety of aspects, in terms of their deeper root-unity.

This eliminates as a matter of course the positivistic position which asserts that philosophy has nothing to offer other than a synthesis of what the various special sciences have provided for us by way of theoretical results.

This root-unity cannot itself be given in time because there we only encounter the aspects in their irreducible diversity. On the one hand, philosophy cannot be allowed to fall back into the attitude of naive experience. It must maintain the theoretical, the scientific attitude of thought and retain a theoretical distance over against naive experience, if it is to remain true science. On the other hand, however, if it truly wishes to embrace temporal reality in the theoretical view of totality, it cannot stay focused on the disconnected multiplicity of scientifically abstracted aspects; instead, it must grasp these in their deeper unity and in their mutual coherence.

Only in this fashion is a theoretical conception of temporal reality possible which presents itself in its many-sidedness within naive experience. Naive experience cannot itself give a theoretical account of the structure of the reality which is experienced by it. The special sciences, as such, are in no better position to do this because they only take into view the variable phenomena within particular aspects.

To philosophy alone falls the task in question. And above all it is the philosophical encyclopedia which is in a position to perform it.

1.4 The Second Transcendental Basic Problem of Philosophy: The Archimedean Point

As a science of totality in this sense, however, encyclopedia, in its intrinsically philosophic character, is in need of a point of departure, an Archimedean point, as we shall call it,[1] from the standpoint of which it is possible to grasp the various aspects of reality in the theoretical view of totality.

If, to employ a metaphor, a traveller wishes to obtain a panorama of the surrounding landscape, that person must ascend an observation point which towers above the various points of this landscape. Remaining at ground level, the traveller can only obtain an impression of the landscape from a particular optic angle.

Thus philosophy, too, needs an observation point that stands above the various aspects of temporal reality. The structure of theoretical thought itself, which holds universally, impresses upon us, in accordance with our critical investigation, the necessity of such an Archimedean point.

In part 1.3 we observed that the theoretical attitude of thought, differing in principle from the naive or pretheoretical attitude, is characterized by the abstract *Gegenstand*-relation in which the logical aspect of thought is intentionally set over against the nonlogical aspects of reality presented for investigation.

In this *Gegenstand*-relationship there arises a true antithesis, a setting over against each other of the logical and the nonlogical. Now if we are to truly arrive at a concept of the *Gegenstand*, however, theoretical thought cannot remain within this antithesis. It must arrive at a true synthesis, an epistemological connection of the logical, analytical aspect of thought and the nonlogical *Gegenstand*. If I am to obtain a genuinely logical concept of law, then I cannot stop at the theoretical problem, which is posed for thought in the nonlogical character of law, but I must orient logical analysis to this nonlogical *Gegenstand* and bring into being a true connection between my analysis and the modal meaning of law. By "modal meaning" is to be understood the "how-ness" (modus = the manner of being) of law.

The possibility of this synthesis depends, in the first place, on the fact that in reality the aspects are not distinguished and set over against each other but find themselves within an unbreakable underlying coherence which, as we saw in the previous paragraph, is preserved by the cosmic or-

---

[1] Archimedes, the well-known Greek natural scientist, sought an immovable position beyond the world from which he could move the world. Thus philosophy seeks a firm standpoint above the temporal diversity of meaning of the aspects in order to understand their deeper unity and totality.

der of time. Therefore that from which the theoretical attitude of thought must abstract is indeed the presupposition of every theoretical concept. But this given temporal coherence is not able to account totally for the possibility of the synthesis. Synthesis also presupposes an idea of the deeper root-unity of the distinguished aspects, an idea which can be obtained only if we choose our standpoint above the theoretical diversity.

Here, however, the second basic problem of the transcendental criticism of thought arises, which can be formulated as follows: From what standpoint can the aspects, which have been distinguished and set over against each other in the theoretical *Gegenstand*-relation, be united again in a theoretical view of totality?

It is clear that this standpoint, which we have called the Archimedean point of theoretical thought, cannot be discovered in any one of the aspects which have been articulated theoretically, and therefore not in the logical aspect, in particular. Within the logical aspect, the opposition between the logical aspect of thought and the nonlogical *Gegenstand* cannot be bridged. The Archimedean point, which makes the theoretical synthesis initially possible, must lie, as a starting point, above the aspects which have been theoretically set apart if the intrinsic diversity of the latter is not to be eliminated in an uncritical fashion by reducing the nonlogical to the logical, or the logical to the nonlogical.

The structure of theoretical synthesis demands that the theoretical *Gegenstand*-relation, with which the theoretical attitude of thought stands or falls, be allowed to remain intact. Even in their theoretical reconciliation, the logical aspect of thought and the nonlogical *Gegenstand* aspect should not be allowed to transgress each other's boundary, theoretically, but must remain mutually distinct.

Therefore the second transcendental basic problem of every conceivable philosophy is the problem of its starting point.

By making this problem the subject of our transcendental critique, we view the starting point of any conceivable philosophical system in light of the transcendental critique. Every dogmatic beginning with theoretical thought as a self-sufficient and unproblematic datum is branded here, in the most fundamental way, as unscientific because the true starting point of a thinker is thereby camouflaged under an arbitrary dogmatic assertion.

We want now to show, first of all, that this dogmatic standpoint necessarily leads philosophy into an impasse. Without any further proof, the following has been set forth as an axiom: a philosophy which desires to remain truly scientific must choose its starting point in theoretical thinking and in theoretical thinking alone. Those who make theoretical thought dependent upon prescientific presuppositions confuse faith with science and exclude themselves automatically from the scientific community.

So it is assumed! But those who believe that they can find their starting point within theoretical thought must immediately indicate more precisely what they mean by this starting point.

We have observed that the theoretical attitude of thought is bound to the *Gegenstand*-relation, and according to its inner structure is necessarily dependent upon theoretical synthesis. This synthesis always exists, as we have seen, in a theoretical connecting of the logical aspect of thought with the nonlogical aspect delimiting the field of investigation. The synthetic character it adopts depends upon the aspect of reality to which theoretical thought directs itself as a field of investigation. Is it, for example, mathematical, physical, biological, psychological, historical, or juridical thought?

In which of these synthetic specifications of theoretical thought should the starting point of philosophy now be located? Irrespective of where the starting point is chosen, the elevation of such a standpoint – which remains, in essence, simply the standpoint of a special science – to the starting point of philosophy must result in the absolutization of a special-scientific aspect of reality. There arises then mathematicism, or physicalism, or biologism, or pyschologism, or historicism, etc.

This procedure is certainly not a scientifically sound one. But it is also indefensible with reference to so-called purely theoretical philosophy because it seeks to eliminate the fundamental diversity of the set-apart and opposed aspects of reality which are implied in the *Gegenstand*-relation by a dogmatic absolutization of one of these aspects.

The above "isms," after all, are very prevalent in contemporary philosophy, and the special sciences become the victim of them as soon as they place such an uncritical philosophic vision of reality at the foundation of their special scientific interpretations of what is given in experience. Nevertheless, so long as a starting point is sought within theoretical thought itself, it appears that such an uncritical absolutization of a special scientific point of view cannot be avoided.

From this point on we shall call those who defend this current point of view the advocates of the "immanence standpoint" because they consider the Archimedean point of philosophy to be immanent with respect to philosophic theoretical thought. And we shall call contemporary philosophy which embraces this point of view "immanence philosophy."

There is, however, a movement within this immanence standpoint which has come to a definite awareness of the uncritical nature of the absolutization of a special scientific point of view and of making it the starting point of philosophy. This movement holds, nonetheless, that a starting point can be discovered entirely within the bounds of theoretical thought, while fully retaining the dogma of the so-called autonomy of science. This starting point is purported to be elevated above the diversity of the particular synthetic points of view of the special sciences and therefore maintained as an all-embracing standpoint.

We need first of all to subject this critical direction within immanence philosophy to closer investigation.

1.5 The Christian Transcendence Standpoint and the Critical Immanence Standpoint in Philosophy. The Third Transcendental Basic Problem of Philosophy

In part 1.4 we saw that the starting point, the Archimedean point of philosophy, from which we have to grasp the theoretically analyzed diversity of aspects of temporal reality in a view of totality, can only be of service if it itself is elevated above this diversity. The question is simply where within human consciousness this point can be found. The question demands critical self-reflection within philosophic thought.

So long as our thought remains oriented only to the diversity of theoretically analyzed *gegenständliche* aspects, it lacks concentration upon the deeper unity of the aspects. In critical self-reflection, by contrast, thought obtains its orientation to the I-ness which is operative in thought. Now our "I-ness" is not merely operative in its logical function of thought; it functions in all aspects of temporal reality without exception. It is the undivided center of all temporal human existence. In every case, philosophical reflection will thus have to direct itself to this undivided center in order to discover an Archimedean point for a philosophical encyclopedia.

Even in immanence philosophy, which seeks to discover its starting point within theoretical thought itself, the insight that a truly philosophical orientation of thought must begin with reflection on one's self was attained relatively early. The saying of the Delphic oracle, "Know thyself," was already placed at the gateway of philosophy by Socrates.

But immanence philosophy throughout has not reached this insight. That is the case, for instance, with the modern naturalistic movements. They seek to reduce the entire cosmos to a natural-scientific system of thought and also conceive of humanity as merely a complicated system of physico-chemical relationships which are able to be investigated by means of the natural-scientific method.

In modern times, it was Immanuel Kant who, following the path of critical self-reflection, thought he could discover an Archimedean point within the logical aspect of theoretical thought itself, which would be elevated above the diversity of the synthetic points of view of the special sciences.

Now it must be kept in mind that the concrete act of thought, as a real act proceeding from the "I," can never be totally exhausted by its logical aspect. Instead, as a real act, it functions in all the aspects of reality without exception,[1] even in the aspect of faith, just as does, for instance, an act of imagination or an act of will.

In the theoretical attitude of thought, however, as we saw earlier, we set the logical aspect of thought theoretically over against the nonlogical aspects. Kant proceeds from this *Gegenstand*-relation as an epistemological datum, and searches for the epistemological subject of the activity of thought, which he believes he can discover by way of a complete abstraction, from the concrete, real activity of thought. According to him, the thinking ego must lie as a presupposition at the foundation of every conceivable special scientific synthetic act of thought because it is the ego that makes the latter possible in the first place. It must then be sought in the logical aspect because, according to him, all of empirical reality, including the concrete activity of thought, is in principle the *Gegenstand* of the logical subject of thought. The thinking ego, as an epistemological subject, is then to be viewed as a subjective-logical pole of thought over against which all of empirical reality stands in polar opposition as the *Gegenstand*. All of experiential reality is a *Gegenstand* for possible experience, which is related to the epistemological subject. The latter itself, however, can never become a *Gegenstand* of thought because, in the *Gegenstand*-relation, the "I think" always remains in the subjective-logical pole of thought. It is not able to become a *Gegenstand* because the thinking ego must always direct itself to every possible *Gegenstand*. Indeed, according to Kant, the "empirical ego," in the sense of this individual person who is bound to time and place, can become a *Gegenstand* of the epistemological subject. But from this it merely appears that the latter can only be discovered by way of a total theoretical abstraction from all "empirical reality" which, according to Kant, coincides with the entire range of physico-psychical phenomena as the *Gegenstand* of the science of mathematics.

The concept of the "thinking ego," which is acquired by way of epistemological abstraction, is called in Kantian circles the transcendental ego, or the "transcendental subject of thought."[2] Here "transcendental" is understood as a generally valid presupposition. It makes human expe-

---

[1] Including the pre-logical aspects! This is immediately apparent when we consider that the activity of thought is confined to the cerebral cortex, and that it can therefore be shown that in every act of thought there is a dimension of emotional perception, a biotic (physiological) side, an aspect of movement (a physico-chemical aspect). So, for example, it is possible to measure the electrical current that is induced in the cerebrum by each act of thought. The living nerve cells of the cerebrum are also in action during every act of thought.

[2] As a matter of fact, he calls it the "transcendental-logical unity of apperception." Apperception is discriminating experience, in contrast to the purely sensory

rience possible in the first place and underlies it as a presupposition without itself being empirical in character (that is to say, for Kant, a possible *Gegenstand* of universally valid experience).

According to Kant, this transcendental-logical subject of thought must of necessity be a logical unity above all the possible diversity of synthetic acts of thought insofar as all theoretical distinguishing and connecting proceed from it. So Kant believed that he had overcome the dogmatic absolutizing of the particular synthetic points of view of the special sciences via the so-called critique of knowledge (see his famous *Critique of Pure Reason*).

This entire "critical" method of thought established by Kant, which is emphatically opposed by the Kantians to the dogmatic or uncritical positions, in the meantime, has itself taken up a truly dogmatic position, as has been established in my own transcendental critique of thought. It still proceeds from the theoretical *Gegenstand*-relation as an unproblematical datum and thus eliminates in a dogmatic fashion the first transcendental basic problem of any conceivable philosophy, which has been proposed by us (namely, what is to be taken away, abstracted, in the theoretical *Gegenstand*-relation, from full, concrete reality as it is given to us, and how is this abstraction possible?) (See note on p. 28.)

The result of this dogmatic starting-out with the theoretical *Gegenstand*-relation is a wholesale theorizing of experiential reality and, by implication also, the naive (nontheoretical) manner of experiencing. According to Kant, all of empirical reality is a *Gegenstand* of the logical subject of thought. We know, however, that this is incorrect per se because the *Gegenstand* can only arise by a theoretico-logical abstraction, by abstracting something from reality as given.

According to the "critical," Kantian way of thinking, naive experience is itself nothing more than a totality of synthetic activities of consciousness by which the *Gegenstand* of experience is initially created. By themselves, the "syntheses" of naive experience are not yet scientific and therefore lack "general validity" or "objectivity." One then does not have to reckon with it further in epistemology because it has been thoroughly refuted in this manner.

In the meantime, we know that naive experience does not have a *Gegenstand*-relation at all and that, in its acts of knowing, it does not establish any "theoretical synthesis," any more than organic materials, as they appear in nature, are a product of an artificial synthesis in the chemical laboratory. Neither is it therefore a kind of theory about reality which can be fundamentally refuted by a critique of knowledge. On the contrary, it is the very basis for a critique of knowledge, which can never be denied by the critique with impunity.

What is truly inherent in naive experience is the nonabstract subject-object relation which is founded in reality itself. This relationship, which also plays such a fundamental role in the jural aspect, we will return to consider in detail later on.

In the present context, we content ourselves with making the observation that, if in naive experience we ascribe to a rose sensory-psychical characteristics, such as a red color, a sensory form, etc., we remain very much aware that this flower is not a psychical subject and thus cannot itself perceive in a sensory fashion, but that, in this aspect, it is only an object of possible subjective perception. The same holds for the logical, the cultural, the aesthetic, and other normative characteristics which we ascribe to the rose. The rose indeed lives as a biotic subject, but in all later aspects we experience it only in an object-function which is related structurally not to the individual experiencing of any one person but to every possible subjective experiencing.

It is precisely by means of this subject-object relation that we experience temporal reality, not abstractly, that is to say, only in one or more theoretically isolated aspects, but as a totality in the given coherence of all of its aspects. This relationship is therefore diametrically opposed to that of the *Gegenstand*-relation. The subject-object relation leaves given reality intact; the *Gegenstand*-relation, by contrast, introduces abstraction. The subject-object relation leaves the unity of reality undisturbed. It even conceives the logical aspect of thought as being incorporated into concrete reality. Contrastingly, the *Gegenstand*-relation sets reality theoretically apart and puts the logical aspect of thought over against the nonlogical aspects.

The immediate result of proceeding from the *Gegenstand*-relation as from an unproblematical datum is the fundamental mistake of identifying the two relationships. Even for Kant *Gegenstand* and object are one and the same.

It is easy to see that in this manner the entire view of empirical reality is in principle distorted. This appears immediately from the fact that Kant identifies "empirical reality" with the theoretical abstraction by means of which the natural science of mathematics conceives it. He thus arrives at the identification of "empirical" reality with the reality of "nature."

In this theoretical abstraction, all of the normative aspects of the reality of experience are eliminated, even though they nonetheless comprise, in naive experience, an inseparable part of the things which only participate in these aspects within an object-function.

We have still not laid bare, however, the most dangerous trap in Kant's epistemological argument, namely, the conception of the transcendental-logical subject of thought as a logical unity above the diversity of the special scientific syntheses. The possibility of discovering, in an epistemological way, the starting point or Archimedean point in theoretical thought itself stands or falls with the question as to whether or not this is correct.

Kant's transcendental-logical subject of thought cannot transcend the *Gegenstand*-relationship with its theoretical antithesis. Indeed it is only the subjective logical pole of thought in opposition to which all empirical reality is supposed to stand as a *Gegenstand*. However, if the transcendental subject of thought itself does not transcend the *Gegenstand*-relation, then neither can it transcend the theoretical antithesis between the logical aspect and the nonlogical aspects. By implication, then, it is out of the question that the theoretical synthesis intended by Kant could proceed from this abstract subject of thought. For, as we saw in part 1.4, this synthesis (which may never eliminate the *Gegenstand*-relation if the theoretical attitude of thought is to be maintained) requires a standpoint itself elevated above the diversity of the aspects which have been theoretically set apart, and over against, each other.

It is undoubtedly true that the thinking "I" stands above, transcends this diversity. But the proposition that this can be accomplished by the ego in its logical-theoretical function of thought is incorrect. The immediate consequence of this false conception is that Kant, in an uncritical fashion, makes the synthesis itself into a transcendental-logical activity. And this conception has immediate consequences for the entire theory of science.

What we have called the aspects of reality, in Kant's way of thinking – insofar as they are even recognized by it – can only be transcendental-logical categories, or fundamental concepts, which lie at the foundation of all possible experience. According to him, these possess a synthetic character because they are related at the outset (a priori) to potential sensory experience.

According to Kant, nothing of reality is given to us other than as a chaos of as-yet-unordered, sensory-psychical impressions (*Empfindungen*) which form only the "material" or "stuff" of our experience.[1] These impressions are then conceived by human consciousness in the so-called transcendental forms of sensory perception, namely, space and time, and are reduced by the transcendental-logical forms of thought, or categories, into real *Gegenstände* (natural things).

Kant therefore conceives of "space and time" as a priori, transcendental presuppositions of sensory (psychical) perception – transcendental in the

---

[1] That this cannot be the case at all is apparent from the fact that sensory-psychical impressions can only be isolated from the full datum of experience via theoretical abstraction. A theoretical abstraction is, however, never given in experience; it is first the product of an artificial disjunction, or theoretical analysis, which is never carried out in naive experiencing.

sense that they lie at the foundation of all possible experience. And he calls them "sensory forms of perception" because they give an initial form to the chaotic sensory material of experience.

But it is only the logical forms of thought or categories, according to him, that introduce essential determinations into the sensory impressions in space and time. What we have called the mathematical aspect and the physical aspect of movement (these are just the aspects which mathematical natural science abstracts from concrete reality) become in Kant a system of logical categories of thought which are related synthetically to the forms of perception (space and time) of psychical-sensory perception, and in this synthetic function are called by him mathematical and dynamic categories.

That Kant acknowledges no other logical categories than that of mathematics and physics has its explanation in his dogmatic identification of empirical reality with theoretical abstractions of the latter via the natural science of mathematics.

For this reason he does not acknowledge any other aspects of empirical reality with the exception of the sensory (the psychical, in our sense of the word) and the logical aspect. Only the sensory-psychical, with its forms of perception of space and time, is not reduced by him to synthetic logical categories.

Kant refuses to do this, as we shall see later, in order to be able to put a stop to the natural sciences' method of investigation at that time, which sought to determine all events in a closed chain of mechanical cause and effect, before it transgresses into the normative sphere of the supra-sensory, moral life (the moral aspect, in our sense of the word). According to Kant, within this moral sphere the freedom and autonomy of human personality must be accepted.[1]

To this end he maintained that the categories of natural science are in principle limited in their applicability to the phenomena of sense perception.

For this reason the sensory could not be reduced to the logical aspect, and Kant maintained the true *Gegenstand*-relation, at least between the logical and the sensory (psychical) aspects. But here the problem of theoretical synthesis becomes very acute in his system. How is it possible, Kant asks himself, to have an a priori (lying at the foundation of possible

---

[1] Kant did not seek the root of human personality in the logical function of thought at all but in the moral function of will which, according to him, was free and autonomous. That the human person, however, at the root of its being, is a free and autonomous moral personality which posits the norm for itself is, according to Kant, unable to be established by science; it is a matter of rational faith. He desires, however, to separate faith and science and to maintain the autonomy of science. Therefore Kant must seek the starting point of theoretical science in theoretical thought itself.

experience) synthesis between logical categories of thought and the sensory material of experience?

He answers by appealing to the intermediary of time in which we construct an a priori sensory image (schema) out of our logical categories.

In time we also discovered the first transcendental presupposition that lies at the foundation of the possibility of synthesis. In doing this we conceived of time in the universal sense in which it embraces all the aspects. By contrast, Kant is required by his starting point to view time only in its psychical-sensory aspect as a form of sense perception. And it is clear that the psychical aspect of time, which is always restricted to the sensory sphere, can never explain a theoretical synthesis or connection between the logical and the psychical aspect. Kant therefore is prevented from offering a solution to the problem of synthesis.

In the twentieth century, contrary to his own conception according to which the categories of thought only relate to natural-scientific knowledge, Kant's epistemological method was also applied to the science of law by some jurists such as Kelsen and others who belonged to the so-called Marburg School of neo-Kantians. Rudolf Stammler, who did not himself belong to this school, began to explain the jural aspect as a system of synthetic-logical categories of thought, the categories of law, comprised in the transcendental concept of law,[1] in which we can order the content of experience. He thought that he was thereby remaining true to Kant's own approach which this great philosopher was supposed to have abandoned in his own philosophy of law.

How Stammler conceived of the role of these categories of thought in experience is possibly best made clear by the use of the following illustration. Suppose that you had been the witness of an accident in which a railroad gate had struck a passer-by in the neck resulting in that person's immediate death. Suppose also that you subsequently observe the lawful execution of a death sentence in which the condemned person dies by means of the guillotine. In what respect do these experiences differ from each other?

As the material of sense experience they do not differ, according to Stammler, except in the manner which that material is organized by consciousness in forms of thought – in the first instance, within the category of mechanics (movement), in the second instance within the category of law, which organizes the material of experience according to the scheme of means and end. The jural aspect of reality, according to him, is nothing more than a logical form of thought in which our consciousness orders the in-themselves-completely-unformed impressions of sense experience.

---

[1] Again called transcendental because it is viewed as a generally valid presupposition of all jural experiencing.

Everyone senses that in such a conception of the nature of law the jural aspect is torn from its meaning coherence with all the other aspects and that the door is opened for the greatest arbitrariness in forming the basic jural concepts.

Kant's attempt to discover the true Archimedean point by following the path of critical self-reflection in the theoretico-logical aspect of thought must therefore be regarded as having completely failed.

In the question as to where this Archimedean point for theoretical thought may indeed be found, we encounter the third transcendental basic problem of all possible philosophy, which we can formulate as follows, How is the choice of the Archimedean point, from which the theoretical synthesis can be accomplished, possible?

The answer to this question can only be given if, employing the truly critical method of self-reflection with which we have begun, we give an account of the nature of the human ego. In the latter the individual center, or concentration point of all our functions that diverge into the various aspects of temporal reality, is discovered.

How is it possible to have an essential concentration of all the aspects of temporal reality on their deeper unity, aspects which have been theoretically distinguished and set over against each other? What is the nature of this concentric direction of our thinking?

The answer must be: We can only discover the Archimedean point for theoretical thought from which the theoretical synthesis is initially made possible by relating all of the aspects to their absolute origin. And it is not an abstract epistemological subject but only our ego, as the individual undivided concentration point of all our temporal existence, that is able to give thought this concentric orientation.

Now this concentric relating of all temporal diversity to the absolute origin of all things is an act of an unmistakably religious character. In religion, our ego, as the individual center, stands in immediate relationship to God as the absolute origin of all things.[1] Human beings come to know themselves in this basic religious relationship. The ego is nothing else than the religious root, the religious concentration point, of our entire temporal existence.

And humankind's self-knowledge is completely dependent on its knowledge of God. It is the divine Word-revelation, together with the self-revelation of God to humanity, which discloses humankind to itself. Even in apostasy from this Word-revelation, it remains a firm principle of human nature that self-knowledge is completely dependent on the knowl-

---

[1] Religion is not an aspect of temporal reality, such as, for instance, the logical aspect or even the aspect of faith. It does not add any new aspect to reality but concentrates all temporality on its true, or supposed, absolute origin. For that reason it is impossible to speak of an absolutization of religion. Only religion, according to its nature, is immediately related to the absolute origin.

edge which humankind has concerning its god (or god-substitute). We can call this law the "law of religious concentration."

When, for example, the Greek philosopher Aristotle seeks the center of human nature, which distinguishes a human being from an animal, in the theoretical activity of thought, this conception is totally dependent upon his idea of deity as "the absolute and pure (no longer bound to sense) thought," which has itself for an object (the *noēsis noēseoos*).

When in the modern period the German philosopher Leibniz seeks the center of human nature in exact mathematical thought, this conception also is completely dependent upon his idea of deity as creative mathematical thought, the "great geometer" (*intellectus archetypus*).

And when Kant seeks the deepest being and center of human nature in the supra-sensory, autonomous moral function, in which the will orients itself purely and exclusively to the moral law, and which it sets up completely independent of all natural causes, then this conception is entirely dependent upon Kant's idea of God which is essentially moralistic.

But even outside philosophy as a science, the law of religious concentration holds universally. When many so-called primitive heathen peoples conceive of the deity impersonally as a mysterious power (*mana*) which reveals itself in as-yet-incomprehensible phenomena of nature, we notice that these same peoples have a lack of insight into human personality, a lack of any conception of its transcendence above the animals, plants, and inorganic things. In the sphere of mana-belief there also flourishes so-called totemism in which an entire people or tribe honors an animal, plant, or even an inorganic thing as the divine tribal father or tribal mother, and the members of the community identify themselves with this totem. They are storks, or eagles, or palm trees.

Impressed by this data, the German professor Ernst Cassirer, once a leading figure of the previously mentioned Marburg School of neo-Kantians,[1] declared, "So again it becomes evident that humankind grasps and knows its own being only insofar as it is able to make itself visible in the images of its gods."[2]

In none of its branches was immanence philosophy able to rise above that phase of self-reflection in which the heart of human personality is sought within one of the temporal functions of consciousness (be it the logical function of thought, the moral function of will, the function of feeling, or the historical function, etc.).

---

1 Its founder was Hermann Cohen. The other major figure along with Ernst Cassirer was Paul Natorp.
2 Ernst Cassirer, *Philosophie der symbolischen Formen*, vol. 2, *Das mythische Denken* (Berlin: Bruno Cassirer, 1925), 269. English trans. *Philosophy of Symbolic Forms*, vol. 2, *Mythical Thought*, trans. Ralph Manheim (New Haven: Yale University Press, 1955), 211.

It is in the divine Word-revelation, which has its fulfillment in Christ Jesus as the incarnate word, that humankind first truly comes to an understanding of itself. The words of the Scriptures, "out of the heart are the issues of life," [Proverbs 4:23, KJV] is the pregnant summary of the consistent witness of God's word concerning the religious root of all human existence. The latter transcends all of the temporal functions of human nature in the various aspects of reality because here they all come to a focus in the religious basic relationship to God as the absolute origin and creator of the cosmos.[1]

Humanity functions in all the aspects of temporal reality without exception. But human existence finds its deeper unity, its true supra-temporal center, in the "heart" which is also called by the Scriptures the "soul" or the "spirit" of a person (which, however, has nothing in common with the concepts "spirit" and "soul" in immanence philosophy). Whether in the service of God or an idol, all the temporal functions, including thought, take their point of departure out of, and are focused in, the heart.

Every elevation of a theoretically isolated aspect to the root-unity of all the others, as we have discovered in the various "isms" of immanence philosophy, is in truth a religious choice of position of the human ego over against the absolute origin. Such an absolutization can never be explained in a purely theoretical manner because the theoretical *Gegenstand*-relationship as such does not provide any scientific foundation for the absolutization of a particular synthesis (in a theoretical concept). In such an absolutization there is revealed the ineradicable inner religious tendency of the human heart toward the origin, which does not discover any resting place in what is relative and does not rest until it has referred everything relative to an absolute ground.

Have we now discovered in the human ego, in the transcendent religious sense of the individual religious root of all temporal human existence, the true Archimedean point of philosophy?

No, because in the true point of departure there must be focused not only individual human existence but the meaning of the entire temporal cosmos. The theoretically differentiated aspects and individuality-structures of temporal reality are not simply the possession of the individual person; they form the fundamental structural framework in which all temporal creatures, relationships, and events are included, even the animal realm, the plant realm, and the realm of inorganic things. For that reason

---

[1] From this it is evident that the "heart," in this pregnant, scriptural sense, may not be identified with the temporal function of thought or the temporal function of feeling. Those who read the Holy Scriptures in this way utterly fail to understand the radical significance of the fall into sin and redemption in Christ Jesus – in relation to themselves.

we have simply described true knowledge of oneself as the necessary way to the discovery of the Archimedean point of philosophy.

The latter must possess a supra-individual character but, at the same time, it must embrace the human ego, in the sense that the latter participates in it. For it is always the human ego that thinks philosophically. If it did not participate in the Archimedean point, in which the entire meaning of our temporal cosmos is concentrated, then the starting point of its thought would remain extrinsic to it. But the latter would be an impossible situation. The starting point that we choose must give a religious direction to all of our immanent theoretical activity of thought. How would this be possible if we ourselves did not participate in this starting point?

In his epistemology, Kant saw clearly that it is not the individual thinking ego that can be the starting point of theoretical synthesis. But in the interests of the dogma of the autonomy of science over against faith, he thought that he could discover a universally valid starting point in the theoretical abstraction of a "transcendental-logical subject of thought" from which all individual reality was theoretically abstracted.

As we have seen, this was an uncritical conception. Once we have perceived that the true Archimedean point of theoretical thought, according to the immanent structure of that thought itself, must be of a transcendent-religious nature, then there remains only one possibility for a supra-individual starting point in which the full individual ego participates. This is the religious root-community of the human race. An individual person indeed participates in this community, even though it has a supra-individual character.

The Bible has revealed to us that humankind has been created in such a root-community, so that along with Adam, the first head, the entire human race fell away from God into sin. And the Bible has revealed to us at the same time that the full meaning of the entire temporal cosmos was focused in this religious root-community. Because of humankind's fall into sin the entire temporal world has been cursed. The other creatures, which are included with humanity in the same temporal order of the world, do not themselves have a religious root to their existence. Humanity's task was to disclose the entire temporal creation in the service of God. When humankind, in its radical fall into sin, becomes disobedient with respect to this task, it takes with it, in this fall, the entire temporal world. Apart from humanity, the latter could not independently relate itself to God and develop its inherent potentialities in the service of God.

The Fall, the radical (that is, concerning-the-root) apostasy from God, involved the human heart elevating itself above its divine origin. Humankind, thinking that it was something in itself and that it was therefore like God, began to seek both itself and its god also within that which is temporal. This was the service of idols in apostasy from the true God as He has revealed himself in the human heart by his Word.

The religious root-community of humanity can only reveal itself in a communal religious spirit which, as a *dunamis*, a "spiritual power," drives all temporal human activity forward and sets its direction, even though the individual may not be at all conscious of it. We can call this *dunamis* the religious community-motive, if we take the word "motive" in its original, pregnant sense (Latin: *movere*, to move, to propel).

Since humanity's fall and the promise in paradise of the coming redemption in Christ Jesus, there are active in the religious root-community of humanity two kinds of *dunamis*, and these two fundamental motives stand over against each other in an irreconcilable religious (thus not simply theoretical) antithesis.[1] The first basic motive is of an idolatrous nature; the second is the *dunamis* of the divine Word-revelation, which operates through the Spirit of God in the hearts of those who have been reborn in Christ as the restored humanity.

The first ground-motive can express itself in various forms because the idolatrous direction of the religious communal spirit orients itself in an absolutizing fashion to what is temporal with all its intrinsic diversity.

The second ground-motive, in the nature of the case, can only have a single, integral form because it cannot be anything else than the ground-motive of the divine Word-revelation itself. If, in the history of the human race, it begins to display various forms, that can only be attributed to the tendency of the human heart to seek an impossible religious synthesis between the ground-motive of the Word-revelation and the motives of idolatrous religion which stand in a radical antithesis to the former.

1.6   The Four Religious Ground Motives of Western Thought

Our transcendental critique of theoretical thought initiated an investigation into the necessary presuppositions of philosophy as the science of totality, that is, into those presuppositions required by the internal structure of this thought itself. It has now reached its final stage. Because of the direction which our investigation took in part 1.5, we are now in a position to expose the disguise of a supposedly scientific neutrality with respect to faith and religion, and to uncover the true starting points of theoretical systems. We now know that they are actually rooted in religious ground-motives which have an inherently communal character, and

---

[1] Theoretical antithesis is bridged over by theoretical synthesis. This can occur because it is not radical. Religious antithesis, by contrast, has to do with the spiritual root of the temporal cosmos and can never be bridged theoretically. More about this in the text below.

are therefore elevated above the personal viewpoint and conviction of the individual thinker.

Now we want to take stock of the ground-motives which have governed the development of Western philosophical thought. By these means, it follows that our insight into the development of legal philosophy and, by implication, the science of law will also be deepened. The traditional conception of this developmental process, to be specific, was burdened with the dogmatic prejudice that, at most, philosophy and science in general are involved with religion in the primitive stage of their development, but that they have gradually disengaged from this connection in order to pursue their own purely theoretical course. The truth appears to be, however, that it was the religious ground-motive that first made philosophic thought possible, because it is only there that the true starting point of theoretical thought can be discovered.

Exceedingly faulty interpretations of earlier philosophical systems have been produced as the result of the supposedly "purely theoretical" point of view. Because a purely theoretical conception, as a matter of fact, cannot exist, we find that a religious ground-motive, which served as a starting point, has been placed at the foundation of theoretical systems which were controlled by a very different ground-motive.

Our transcendental criticism therefore also requires us to search out new pathways with regard to the science of the history of philosophy. Even in a scientific sense, these promise to do greater justice to the systems which have been developed.

In the main there are four religious ground-motives which have controlled the history of Western thought. In fact, as the deepest driving forces of its dynamism, they lie at the foundation of the entire cultural development of the West.

The four ground-motives we have in mind are the following: (1) the form-matter motive of Greek antiquity; (ii) the scriptural motive of creation, fall into sin, and redemption by Jesus Christ; (iii) the Romanistic religious synthesis-motive (introduced by Roman Catholicism) of nature and grace that tries to reconcile (i) and (ii); (iv) the modern, humanistic ground-motive of nature and freedom in which there is an attempt to bring all of the preceding motives into a "this-worldly" synthesis concentrated on humankind.

The first and the fourth ground-motives have a polar character; they are torn by an internal dualism. They contain a religious and therefore absolute antithesis which does not allow for any synthesis. In this respect, a religious antithesis differs in principle from a theoretical antithesis, of which we have earlier spoken. The latter, as we have seen, allows for a theoretical synthesis on the basis of a religious starting point because this starting point remains elevated above the aspects which are set over against each other theoretically. But if the religious starting point itself is torn by a polar opposition, no higher point of departure can be found that is able to reconcile this religious antithesis.

If theoretical thought takes its point of departure from such a dualistic ground-motive, theoretical concept-formation of necessity will have to suffer its consequences. It must now be clear that theoretical thought is not in a position to eliminate such a religious conflict by a theoretical synthesis. Nevertheless, we shall see how philosophy has repeatedly attempted to accomplish this, which can only be explained as a result of a lack of a transcendental critique of theoretical thought.

Where it is not possible to obtain a genuine synthesis transcending the religious antithesis, the only possible solution is to ascribe religious primacy to one of the two motives opposing each other in the ground-motive. In addition, the opposing motive will be de-divinized and demoted.

The polarity of the first and fourth religious ground-motives is caused by the religious absolutizing of a temporal aspect, or a complex of temporal aspects of created reality. These aspects, however, stand in unbreakable relation to the others. The absolutizing of the former by an inner necessity evokes their counterparts which assert themselves with the same religious absoluteness against the former. However, the opposing motives determine each other mutually.

So the meaning of the Greek motive of form can never be conceived apart from the motive of matter, and vice versa. Nor can the meaning of the humanistic motive of nature be understood apart from the humanistic freedom motive, and vice versa. With respect to the ground-motive of nature and grace introduced by Roman Catholicism, the situation is somewhat different because here a dualism of foreign origin is introduced into the Christian ground-motive of creation, fall, and redemption by the attempt to reconcile the motive of creation religiously with the Greek form-matter motive. Therefore we get a double religious antithesis: (i) between the ground-motive of the Christian religion and that of Greek religion; and (ii) between form and matter within the motive of nature. Yet here also the motive of nature and the motive of grace mutually determine each other's meaning.

1.6.1 The Form-Matter Motive

The first motive, given this name (*morphē/hulē*) by Aristotle, dominated Greek thought from its very inception. It had its origin in an irreconcilable conflict between the ground-motive of the older telluric and ouranic religions of nature[1] and that of the more recent religion of culture, the religion of the Olympic pantheon.

---
1 The telluric religions are oriented to the earth as the origin of life; the ouranic are oriented to heaven and later also to the sea.

The above religions of nature, whose construction is to a great extent conjectural because of the lack of adequate source material, manifested strong local variations in their cultic forms and in their particular faith representations. In these religions it is still possible to establish as the common ground-motive the divinization of what is flowing, the periodical flowing away of earthly, or heavenly, or marine forms of nature in birth and death, in coming into being and destruction, in which the working of a rational order is not discernible but that of *Ananke̅* or *tuche̅*, of blind, unpredictable fate. The godhead was not conceived therefore in a fixed form and as a personal figure, but was conceived of as an eternal, formless stream (for example, the stream of life, which continuously brings forth new life in individual forms from mother earth, according to the changing of the seasons – the cycle of birth – and again takes it back into its womb). The existence of individual forms was conceived of more or less as an "injustice" for which retribution had to be made to *Ananke̅* in the stream of time.

The new religion of culture had been embodied in the official religion of the Greek polis from the eighth century before Christ. At the same time, it provided at Mount Olympus a focal point of national religious life. By contrast with the older religions, it was a religion of form measure, and harmony. The Olympic gods leave the earth and become immortal gods of form, they are in personal shape idealized and absolutized cultural powers. Their form and likeness is superterrestrial, invisible to the physical eye, exalted above the world of sensorily perceptible forms which are subject to *Ananke̅*, to the ever changing cycle of births.

Similar to the way in which the old matter motive of the religion of nature absolutized the organic aspect of life of temporal reality, within the new form motive of the cultural religion the (historical|) cultural aspect is deified. Culture is[1] giving form to a material according to a free, rational design, in opposition to the form-giving discernable within nature.

Since the form motive of the culture religion immediately set itself in absolute, that is to say, religious, antithesis to the matter motive of the old religion of life, it was also completely divorced in Greek religious consciousness from the moment of historical development in which the historical aspect of culture is unbreakably connected with the organic aspect of life. The divine form is conceived of as immortal and invisible and thus elevated above the historical.

The newer religion of culture tries to adapt the older religion of life to itself. The Greek poet-theologians Hesiod and Homer go to all sorts of lengths to make clear to the Greek people that the inhabitants of Olympus had come into being out of the formless nature divinities. But all these at-

---

1 This core moment will be investigated later on.

tempts at synthesis were doomed to failure. The major reason for this failure was that, owing to its basic motive, the religion of the Olympic pantheon negated the deepest problems of life and death.

The blind *Ananke* of the nature religion remains the independent counterpole to the rational power of the effulgent gods of form or culture. The rational form motive of the culture religion evokes again as its polar opposite the somber matter motive in the religion of life. The matter motive itself has a role in the religion of culture as *Moira* which has a more ancient claim than the Olympic gods have. Insofar as this *Moira* appears as humankind's fate which is to die, it corresponds exactly with the ancient *Anangke*.

For these reasons it is understandable that in their private lives the Greeks held to the ancient religion of nature, even though they worshipped the inhabitants of Olympus as the public gods of the polis. It is also understandable that the deeper religious impulses in the people turned first of all to the so-called mystery worship in which the problems of life and death occupied center-stage. In the transitional period between the time of the Mycenaean heroes (celebrated in Homer's epics) and the Persian wars, falls the great religious crisis in Greek thought. The old and the new religion openly express themselves through the violent emergence of the old religion of life in the Dionysian movement and in Orphism.

This conflict is anthropologically expressed in Orphism, a religious reform movement of this time, which revered the legendary poetic singer Orpheus as its founder, and which obtained a profound hold on Greek philosophy. Humankind has a dual origin; it has an immortal rational soul, which stems from the bright firmament of the heavens in which form, measure, and harmony rule. The soul, however, has fallen on the dark earth, where, wrapped in a material body, it is subject to the "wheel of birth," to the *Ananke* of the eternally flowing stream of life. This material body is a "tomb" or "prison" for the soul, which, during its journey on earth, according to the cycles of the stream of life, is obliged to transmutate constantly into other bodies, even those of animals, until, by means of an ascetic way of life, it has purified itself of contamination by the natural body. Only in this way may it return to its true habitation, the firmament of life.

In this anthropological conception, the motive of immortality and form of the culture religion fuses with the old ouranic motive of reverence for the heavens. It recurs in Greek philosophy in various forms, for example, in the Pythagorean school, Empedocles, and Plato.

Hesiod and Homer gave a mythological form to the religion of culture. But even after that mythological form had been undermined in the consciousness of the people, the actual religious ground-motive that emerged out of its encounter with the ancient religion of life continued to dominate the entire attitude of life and thought of the Greeks. And in philosophic circles it could deck itself out in new forms of faith which better fulfilled the needs of the time. From its inception, Greek philosophy was involved in the inner conflict between the form motive and the matter motive that drove it in opposing directions.

The Greek conception of "nature" (*physis*) is also completely dominated by this polar ground-motive. In book 5, chapter 4 of his *Metaphysics*, Aristotle summarizes the various meanings of the word *physis*. Now it had the meaning of the process of birth (*phuesthai*) out of the formless stream of life which – often in the flowing form of a changeable element such as water, air, or fire – was conceived of as the origin of all things. In addition, one must take into consideration that for the Greeks these "elements" originally had a mythological-religious meaning. Again, nature meant the form of being which expressed unchangeable essence.

In his concept of "nature," Aristotle attempted to unite the motives of form and matter. "Nature" is therefore the essential form of things which have a principle of movement in themselves and are thus composed of "form" and "matter."

Greek *theoria* is proclaimed the true way to knowledge as soon as it attempts to penetrate behind the forms of reality perceptible to the senses into the absolute ground of things, as soon as it desires therefore to become meta-physics.[1] Not faith (*pistis*) but the theoretical activity of thought leads us to know absolute truth. From the very inception of Greek philosophy, the function of faith is debased to the lower sphere of sensory representation to which the great mass of humankind remains bound because they do not know how to raise themselves to the level of theoretical thinking.

Furthermore, for the Greeks it was characteristic of *theoria*, insofar as it concerned the supra-sensory forms of being, that it possessed a "spiritual contemplation" which transcended the logical concept. From Plato on, these eternal forms are called *eidē*, and the word *eidos* – just like the word *idea* – comes from a root that means seeing or intuiting. All this can only be understood in terms of the Greek form-matter motive.

Originally, in the Greek philosophy of nature, the matter motive of the nature religion gets the upper hand in an obvious reaction to the form motive of the culture religion. *Hulē*, as an unformed and always moving but "spirited" power (*rheuston*), becomes divinized, often in the image of a fluid element such as water, air, or fire, and it is accepted as the divine origin (*archē*) of all individual forms, which, however, according to *Anankē*

---

[1] *General Editor's note*: The original text contains this hyphen.

are periodically taken back again into the womb of the unbounded and eternally flowing *hulē*.[1]

The Ionian thinker Anaximander (6th century before Christ) sees a law of justice *(Anankē = dikē)* at work in this process.[2] The nature philosophy only attempts to rationalize the incalculable *Anankē* in order to make the matter motif useful for a kind of natural-scientific explanation of the genesis of material things.

Heraclitus, who according to Plato makes the statement, "Everything flows and nothing remains unchanged," and characterizes the process of the eternal flow of life as divine through the opposites of the visible forms, sees a *Logos*, a cosmic law, at work in this process which maintains a constant equilibrium, a measure, and harmony between coming into being and perishing. Anaximander also accepted a principle of equilibrium, the law of justice (*dikē*), which, according to him, controlled all nature. This principle of equilibrium, that is supposed to introduce measure and harmony into the process of the flow of matter, again undoubtedly originated in the fundamental motive of the culture religion. It cannot be explained in terms of the principle of matter itself. The pre-Socratic philosophy, however, already comes up against the inner conflict between the motives of form and matter, which receives its philosophical expression in the problem concerning the relationship of being and becoming.

Parmenides (6th century before Christ), the founder of the so-called Eleatic School, puts this problem in a truly antithetical way. In reality, according to him, being exists as eternal, unchangeable, and indivisible. Theoretical logical thought can conceptually grasp being in the logical principle of identity, the "is." However, no true reality can then be ascribed to becoming with its oppositions because "becoming" does not possess any identity, it does not have a set form but passes through opposing forms. According to Parmenides, "being" encloses everything in an undifferentiated unity. Partly depending on Orphism, he thinks of this unity as being in a static form, as the "all-encompassing round firmament," which encloses everything in its purely mathematical configuration. From the time of the philosophic contest between Parmenides and

---

[1] It is clear that the Greek conception of matter (*hulē*) is quite different from that of modern natural science. The Greek *hulē* can only be conceived in its polar opposition to unchanging form. In itself it is altogether flowing and indeterminate, chaotic. The modern concept of matter in mathematical natural science, by contrast, is completely determined by physical-chemical causes.

[2] Making a truly Greek emendation to the statement of Mephisto in Goethe's *Faust*, it could be said: "Denn alles, was entsteht,/Ist wert, dass es zugrunde geht."
General Editor's note: "For all that comes to be/Deserves to perish wretchedly." *Goethe's Faust*, trans. and intro. Walter Kaufmann, bilingual ed. (Garden City, New York: Doubleday & Company, 1961), 1339-1340.

Heraclitus, it became no longer scientifically possible to trace the form principle back to the matter principle as the origin (*archē*).

However, even in the final stage of development of the Ionian philosophy of nature, the form principle of the culture religion begins to attain primacy. In the meantime, under the influence of religion, it is purified by philosophy of the polytheistic tendencies and the motives which are at odds with the ethical standards of the people's mores.

Anaxagoras of Clazomenae is the first Greek thinker who elevates the *nous* as "thinking spirit" to the divine principle of form and thinks of divine formative thought as purified of any confusion with "matter."[1] "Matter," as an independent polar opposite of *nous* (the divine demiurge), is completely dedivinized by him. It is even deprived of "movement" which, in the earlier philosophy of nature, was revered as the divine principle of life of *hulē*. It was degraded to the status of a static chaos in which everything is mixed up with everything else, while the form-giving movement, which makes a cosmos out of chaos, issues exclusively from *nous*, from "divine thought." Anaxagoras begins an approach to the principle of form in the culture religion in which an attempt is made to ethically purify the latter in an allegorical-ethical explanation of mythology.

In the thought of Protagoras of Abdera (5th century before Christ), the founder of Sophism, the primacy is exclusively given to the culture-motive. Without hesitation, he applies to epistemology the principle of matter according to the Heraclitean conception of the eternal flowing of all things. In so doing he put to one side the *logos*-idea, which for Heraclitus created a counterweight to the principle of matter by binding the stream of becoming to a constant law of proportion. In this way Protagoras also denied the possibility of universally valid concepts which would be faithful to reality, and so precipitated a severe crisis in Greek science. He declared science to be without value, and underneath this depreciation of theoretical science lay the depreciation of the principle of matter. His famous *homo mensura* rule (that man is the measure of all things) has nothing at all to do with modern humanistic conceptions, but is no more than a consistent application of the Greek principle of matter to the terrain of human knowledge, with the aim of denying to the latter any kind of foundation. Human nature, according to him, does not possess any constant, universally valid form. Therefore he declares that the individual person, in the complete fluidity of subjective, sensory perception and states of feeling, is the measure of all things; the measure is not a universal, "rational human nature," which is bound to constant standards. Under the domination of the principle of matter, he views human nature as being submerged in unrestrained and limitless ferocity.

---
[1] Even Parmenides continued to think of *nous* in a material form as being identical with eternal being, as a spherical body.

This is also the source of his rejection of a so-called natural law which, without any positive realization, would be given along with human nature. Boundless "nature" receives true "form" only by means of "culture," by way of the free forming which proceeds from the *polis* as the bearer of this religion of culture. According to him, the *polis*, the city state, by its positive rules, is what brings law, morality, and religion into being. In these areas it is not the individual but the opinion of the state that sets the standard.

So it appears that even the founder of Sophism, who is usually thought to be the father of the Greek "Enlightenment" which is supposed to have liberated philosophy entirely from religion, is also completely dominated in his theory by the motive of form and matter as a religious communal motive.

With Socrates there is a decisive reorientation to the primacy of the rational principle of form over the principle of matter. It is he who for the first time places the polar ground-motive of Greek philosophy under the searchlight of self-reflection. The Delphic oracle, "Know thyself," is placed by him at the center of philosophy.

According to Plato (*Phaidrus*, 230A), Socrates desires to know whether, at the center of his being, he is related to Typhon, the nature god of destructive storms – a pregnant symbol of the principle of matter – who takes on many forms, and is inflated with pride and wild, or whether he possesses a simple, clear, "Appollonian" nature.

Pure *nous*, which Anaxagoras proclaimed to be the divine origin of all cosmic form, was conceived by Socrates, in an ethico-religious deepening, as the origin of the *kalokagathon*, the "good and the beautiful." The entire Socratic method of dialectical reasoning, which aimed to checkmate the sophistic nihilism in epistemology by laying bare its internal contradictions and to bring it under control by means of the rational concept, acquires a truly religious orientation to the divine power of the form of the *kalokagathon*. The Greek idea of theory (theoretical knowledge) here again betrays its undeniably religious tendency. In contrast to *pistis* (faith), which bases itself upon subjective opinion (*doxa*), theoretical thought becomes the religious organ of knowledge par excellence by which the human spirit comes into immediate contact with the divinity as pure *nous*. According to Socrates, a concept that does not lead us on the path of discovery of the divine power relating to the form of the good and the beautiful, which therefore does not teach us for what a thing is "good," what is its goal, is altogether lacking in value.

From this critical turning point, Greek philosophy runs its course to the classical form "idealism" of Plato and Aristotle. The principle of matter has now definitely shed all its divinity. For these thinkers divinity in its entirety is now concentrated in the absolutized *nous* as the rational principle of form of the *One*, the *True*, the *Good*, and the *Beautiful* (these are the so-called four transcendental determinations of "being" as a metaphysical basic concept; one discerns them throughout scholastic philosophy).

But the dualism inherent in their idea of the origin was not to be eliminated even by these great thinkers. Especially in the initial phase of the development of Plato's doctrine of ideas (the doctrine of the eternal forms of being, which are supposed to lie at the foundation of all transitory sensory forms), it becomes exaggerated into an almost unbearable religious tension between the principle of form and the principle of matter. The world of ideas becomes completely separated from the material world of sensory things.

At this time the dualism also influences Plato's view of human nature. Under the influence of Orphism, a sharp theoretical dichotomy is made between the "simple" "immortal" soul, which is elevated above the stream of becoming and identified with the theoretical function of thought, and the "composite," impure "material body," in which the soul is shut up as in a prison, and from whose corrupting influence the divine soul must increasingly free itself (Plato in his dialogue *Phaedo*).

But when in his later development Plato attempts to bridge this absolute dualism, and to reconcile the principle of form and the principle of matter in his thinking, there remains, nevertheless, a polar opposition between these two fundamental principles of origin which dominate his thinking. Even in the *Timaeus*, a dialogue concerning the origin of the cosmos, which belongs to Plato's penultimate period, the divine *nous* as the demiurge (the giver of form to chaotic material) has as an eternal counterpart, the necessity (*Ananke̅*) of the matter principle. *Nous* does not have any power over this *Ananke̅*, which has a chaotic influence on the transitory world; it can only try to bring it under control by reasoning with it.

In the trilogy *Orestea* of the great tragedian Aeschylus, one discovers the surprising equivalent of this persuasion of *Ananke̅* by the divine principle of form. The tragedy ends with the persuasion by Athena, the goddess of wisdom, of the wild goddesses of destruction (the daughters of *Ananke̅*), who are persecuting Orestes. The tragedy concludes with the triumphant cry, "So Zeus and *Ananke̅* were reconciled." From this is clearly revealed how the religious ground-motive makes itself felt far outside the limits of science.

Finally, in his mature period, Aristotle attempts to bridge over the dualism of the ground-motive by abandoning the Platonic doctrine of ideas, with its sharp distinction between the "eternally existing forms" and the temporal sensory-material things which are subject to becoming. He conceives the "form" as being immanent in sensory things which are composed of "form" and "matter."

According to him, form becomes "substantial form," which first gives to things substantial (that is, independent) existence; and he denies that "matter" can really (actually) exist in itself (without form). It is only a potentiality, a possibility which initially comes into actuality (reality) by way of the form, as marble possesses in itself the potential for becoming a statue. As immanent, teleological principles, the substantial forms are ordered according to lower and higher stages of perfection (the lowest are the forms of organic things, the next are the forms of plants and animals, and the highest step is the "rational soul" as the "substantial form" of a human being). But at the same time the lower form, in its turn, becomes "matter" of the higher.

In the temporal cosmos, no "form" exists without "matter." But the original dualism of the ground-motive returns in both poles of Aristotle's doctrine of being (metaphysics): the divinity as pure form and as the *nous* which thinks itself absolutely, on the one side, and pure matter (*proote hulē*) as the principle of becoming and incompleteness, which is as yet deprived of all form, on the other side.

According to Aristotle, as with Plato, the *Anankē* of the matter principle is the independently potent cause of all failure to attain form, the cause of everything that is monstrous in the world.

1.6.2 The Motive of Creation, Fall, and Redemption

The second ground-motive is that of creation, fall into sin, and redemption through Christ Jesus in the communion of the Holy Spirit. It was introduced into the thought of the West by the Christian religion in combination with the Old Testament Jewish religion as a new religious communal motive. In its revelation concerning the creation, it immediately sets itself in a radical antithesis against the form-matter motive of ancient philosophy. The quintessence of Greek wisdom was *ex nihilo nihil fit* (nothing can come from nothing). And in the Greek idea of origin the dualistic form-matter principle was preserved.

By direct contrast, God reveals himself in his Word as the integral and absolute origin, the creator of heaven and earth. The revelation of humankind to itself in the integral religious root of its entire temporal existence is directly related to this self-revelation of God to humankind.

God created humankind in God's own image. As God reveals himself as creator, as the absolute and integral origin of all things, so he concentrates all temporal functions and structures of human existence in a religious root-unity, in which all of temporal life is supposed to be oriented to the service of God. This is the radical character of the scriptural motive of creation that penetrates to the religious root of what is created. It reveals humanity to itself, at the center of its entire existence.

The center of humanity's existence must not be sought in one of its temporal functions; as the integral, indivisible root of all temporal functions, it lies at the foundation of all temporal life – even at the foundation of human thought. This is the "heart," the soul or spirit, of human nature in the pregnant religious sense found in the Word-revelation.

Greek philosophy, in terms of its form-matter motive, seeks the human soul, at one time, in the flowing *hulē*, and then, at another time, in the abstract complex of the function of feeling, the theoretical function of thought and the moral function of will, which is then supposed to be qualified by *nous* as immortal "form." However, dualism of any kind in human existence is nowhere to be found in Holy Scripture. Greek philosophy's conception of an immortal *anima rationalis* was not able to be understood as the integral root-unity of human nature. It was simply a theoretical abstraction from the temporal (bodily) existence of humankind which continually found the "material body" as a second theoretical abstraction over against itself (think of the *Gegenstand*-relation).

However, according to the divine Word-revelation, the soul of a person is not a theoretical abstraction but the full, concrete, individual root-unity of human existence, the "inner person" in the Pauline sense, which comes to outward expression in temporal, bodily life. The revelation concerning the fall into sin as the radical corruption of humanity has an unbreakable connection with this revelation of humankind to itself. Because sin affects the religious root of human nature, not a single temporal function of humankind can escape its grasp. And the same is also true of redemption in Christ Jesus, which regenerates the heart and thus must reveal its renewing influence in all temporal expressions of life, even in the theoretical activity of thought.

As soon as it entered into the Hellenistic world of thought, the Christian religion was immediately threatened because, in cooperation with those of the Persian and other eastern religions, the Greek religious ground-motive began to get the upper hand in the theological-philosophical reflection on the content of the divine revelation.

Thus "Christian Gnosticism," under Greek and eastern influence, fell back into the acceptance of a dual origin of the creation. It made a distinction between the inferior creator-God and lawgiver of the Old Testament which, as a demiurge in giving form to chaos, had to come into contact with "impure matter" (and therefore could not be perfect) and the higher redeemer-God of the New Testament. And in the same way that Greek philosophy elevated philosophical theory as the true way to the knowledge of God far above faith, so Gnosticism set gnosis as the contemplative theory about God above the scriptural faith of the Christian community.

One encounters the same dualism in the second century after Christ in Marcion of Sinope. He only took Paul's doctrine of justification by faith as a point of contact to make a sharp separation between the legalistic Jewish religion of Jehovah, the creator of heaven and earth, and the Christian religion of redemption of the God of love, who revealed himself in Jesus Christ.

The Greek ground-motive had great influence in the first centuries of the Christian church amongst various Church Fathers who set themselves to defend the Christian faith over against pagan thinkers. In the Alexandrian school of the Greek church fathers (Clement, Origen, 2nd century AD), gnosis, as the contemplative knowledge of God, is again elevated above the faith of the community, and the Divine Word (the *Logos*, by whom all things are created) is conceived under the influence of the Greek-Jewish *logos* speculation (Philo) as the mediator between the Divine Unity and the world that is dispersed in "matter."

So in the first centuries of the church fathers, the Christian religion was deprived of its integral and radical character owing to the influence of the Greek ground-motive. Under the pretence of a higher gnosis, which especially amongst the Alexandrians involved allegorical exegesis, there arose among many of the apologetes, in reaction to the antinomianism of Gnosticism, a theological view that denatured the Word-revelation into a "higher moral teaching" and that no longer understood the creation, the Fall, or redemption in a scriptural manner.

Even after the Christian church had established the doctrine of the Trinity at the councils of Nicea (325) and Constantinople (381), the influence of the Greek religious ground-motive continued to manifest itself in the thought of the church fathers. Philosophical thought within the orthodox camp reached its high point in Aurelius Augustine (4th century, AD), who was destined to put his stamp on Christian thought up to the 13th century and continued to have a powerful influence afterwards.

The ground-motive of the Christian religion is undoubtedly understood here in a scriptural way, and from the time of his conversion, Augustine's powerful, sanctified spirit was more and more deeply influenced by it. Augustine maintained in a powerful fashion both the integral and radical character of this motive. He accepted the absolute creativity of God and the radical meaning of the Fall and of redemption. At those points where this scriptural ground-motive penetrates his philosophical thought, it can be seen that, for the most part, he heads in new directions opposed to ancient philosophy. This is the case, for example, with the Christian philosophy of history which was developed in his famous *City of God*.

Yet he does not truly reform his theoretical view of reality. Precisely at this point, the Greek form-matter motive continues to dominate his view, even to the extent of affecting his interpretation of chapter one of the book of Genesis. The "earth" in Genesis 1:1 is supposed to mean the "first yet formless matter" and the creation is supposed to have taken place according to eternal "ideas" or "forms" in the Divine *Logos*. His view of the divine order of the world is strongly influenced by Neoplatonism.

This fundamental lack of a truly scriptural view of reality also typifies the entire scholastic movement following in Augustine's footsteps until Thomas Aquinas and his teacher Albertus Magnus. At this point in particular there is a great deal of vagueness concerning the relationship of philosophy to dogmatic theology. The Christian character of philosophy in general is sought in its relation of subservience to Christian theology (*philosophia ancilla theologiae christianae*). At the same time as the rejection of the autonomy of philosophy with respect to Christian faith, there was a denial of its autonomy with respect to dogmatic theology. As a result Christian thought and theological thought become identified.

In addition there is no objection to dependence, at important points, on ancient philosophy whose ground-motive is not clearly understood in its pagan-religious character. As a result there is a great deal of uncritical acceptance of pagan thought patterns, more specifically, Neoplatonism.[1] Nevertheless, even here the scriptural ground-motive is generally retained in its purity. The autonomy of theoretical thought was rejected, for example, by Augustine in a decisive manner and with clear insight into the relationship of religion and science. It is impossible then to speak here of a truly religious synthesis-standpoint.

1.6.3 The Nature-Grace Motive

At the high point of the so-called medieval synthesis, the conscious attempt to reconcile the mutually opposed religious ground-motives of the Christian religion and Greek philosophy, particularly that of Aristotle, led in the 12th and 13th centuries AD to the introduction of a truly religious pattern of synthesis, that of nature and grace. This gave a typically Roman Catholic stamp to the scholasticism of the Middle Ages and of modern times.

Its unreconciled internal dualism continues, to a great extent, to influence even reformational thinking, Lutheran in particular. This is so, in spite of the fact that the Reformation had in principle vanquished it by its return to the scriptural, Augustinian doctrine of the radical significance for human nature of the fall into sin, its rejection of the autonomy of the "natural light of reason" and the natural meritoriousness of good works, and its confession of justification by faith alone.

In this fundamentally religious attempt at synthesis was concealed the dualistic motive of "nature" and "grace." The attempt was made to effect a synthesis between the Greek conception of the nature (*physis*) of temporal beings (a conception that was completely dominated by the dualistic form-matter motive and excluded any conception of creation in a scriptural sense) with the Christian, scriptural doctrine of creation. Thus, according to the Aristotelian model, "human nature" was conceived of as a

---

[1] Particularly, the Neoplatonic doctrine of ideas, accommodated to the creation, the Greek dichotomy of the *anima rationalis* and the material body, and the confusing of original sin with sexual libido as the effect of the sensory principle of matter in conflict with the form-giving principle of reason, all of this under Platonic influence.

"rational nature" composed of the material body and the *anima rationalis* as a substantial form.[1] Nature was now conceived by Roman Catholicism as an autonomous preparation for "supernatural grace." Grace was placed above "nature" as a higher stage of perfection and, by means of the temporal church institution's sacramental grace, would become infused into "nature."

In this conception there was no longer any place for the radical significance of the fall into sin and redemption. According to the Roman Catholic doctrine, the Fall has not radically corrupted "nature" but has only deprived it of the "supernatural gift of grace" (*donum superadditum*).

As long as the religious ground-motive of nature and grace rules philosophy, it leads to typical expressions of a polar tension within Christian thought. At one point, Christian thinking was being driven in a dangerous pagan direction by giving the primacy to the "nature-motive," and at another point, in a no less dangerous mystical direction which, along with a denial of creation, identifies "nature" and "sin" and desires to escape "nature" in a mystical experience of grace. It also comes to expression in a clear dualism that gives full rein to the autonomy of nature and that wants to separate "nature" and "grace" in a radical way. So there were, for example, the nominalistic orientations in late scholasticism (14th century).

In the framework of this ground-motive, the only way of maintaining the religious synthesis was for the ecclesiastical authorities to condemn the "heresies" in philosophy. It found major support for its attempt to do this in the dominant figure of scholasticism in the high Middle Ages, the Dominican "Pater Angelicus," Thomas Aquinas (13th century). He posited "nature," according to its Aristotelian conception, as the autonomous but subsidiary step preceding "grace." In this scheme the mutual relationship between the two was construed as that of "matter" and "form." "Nature" becomes matter for the higher "form" of grace. In other words, there is an appeal for help to the same schema that had already been required to render service in Greek thought in order to reconcile two antagonistic religious motives.

In the meantime, we may observe that the nature-motive is no longer conceived of in a purely Aristotelian way according to the form-matter theme. In conformity with the religious attempt at synthesis, it is accommodated to the church doctrine concerning grace. So Thomas attempts first of all to reconcile the form-matter theme by also including "matter"

---

[1] This Aristotelian view even received ecclesiastical sanction at the Council of Vienna.

under what has been created. Matter has not been created independently but along with material substances.[1]

In Thomas, autonomy of reason means something entirely different from its meaning among the Greeks. This is despite the fact that Thomas, in sharp disagreement with Augustine, maintains the autonomy of natural reason in the domain of philosophy and even though, in conformity with the school of Aristotle, he develops a natural theology as the crown of his metaphysical doctrine of being which is supposed to be constructed quite independently of revelation. And in Thomas, autonomy of reason means something entirely different again from its meaning in modern humanism.

His conception is that natural theoretical reason, being limited to the natural realm, cannot rise to the supernatural mysteries of grace – they can only be known by "revelation" – and therefore cannot teach anything that would be in conflict with these mysteries.

The consequence of this standpoint is that there is a continual attempt at the accommodation of philosophy, which, via Thomas mainly, follows the Aristotelian approach accompanied by an admixture of Augustinian/Neoplatonic ideas, with the ecclesiastical interpretation of the Holy Scriptures.

Within the framework of the nature-grace scheme there is, by its very nature, no opportunity for intrinsic Christian philosophical thinking that follows the lead of the ground-motive of the divine Word-revelation with respect to the internal concerns of science as well as those of church confession.

1.6.4 The Motive of Nature and Freedom

The fourth great fundamental motive is that of nature and freedom. It stems from the modern humanistic religion of personality and science that arose at the time of the Renaissance. It gradually absorbs the three older ground-motives within itself by making them undergo a fundamental metamorphosis. This motive is rooted in a religion of human personality in which the Christian ground-motive of creation, fall, and redemption becomes secularized.

In the idea of human personality resides the idea of a creative freedom that can accept no law other than that which freedom itself has posed autonomously by its reason. This new personality-motive has been pitted with a revolutionary passion against the medieval idea of the subordination of the individual in all spheres of life to the authority of the church.

At this point, momentarily, the paths of the great historical movement of the Reformation and that of humanism join, so long as the latter, as a so-called Christian humanism, is prepared to orient itself to the Holy

---

[1] It may also be remarked that this was not a novel discovery of Thomas. Patristic thinkers (for example, Augustine) had already worked with the idea of *prima materia* which they attempted to ascribe to God's creative sovereignty.

Scripture and to advocate free inquiry into the Bible. But it was not long before the paths of the Reformation and humanism radically diverged. This occurred as soon as humanism, rejecting the idea that human personality should be subjected to a suprarational revelation, brought every truth-claim, or every assertion of a norm of action, before the tribunal of autonomous human reason.

It was at the time of the Enlightenment (during the latter part of the 17th century and throughout the 18th century) that this humanistic religion of reason emancipated itself completely from the Holy Scriptures. Since then it has proceeded to considerably deepen itself in the freedom idealism preached by Kant and the post-Kantian idealists.

Residing in the new religious idea of personality from the outset, however, were two mutually antagonistic tendencies. At the time of the Renaissance, along with the depths of the creative freedom of his autonomous personality, the modern person discovered the field of nature as the terrain upon which sovereign reason would be able to unfold itself.

By means of Copernicus' discovery of the double movement of the earth around the sun, the ancient geocentric (Aristotelian-Ptolemaic) world-view, in which the earth functioned as the static center of the universe, underwent a complete transformation. The church for a long while continued to hold fast to the old world-view, which it thought, quite erroneously, was founded in the Holy Scriptures but which, in point of fact, only agreed with the Scriptures insofar as the earth is the center of the history of salvation. Hence the new astronomical discovery was regarded as a kind of new gospel over against the authoritative teaching of the church.

An entirely new conception of nature was developed by the famous Italian Renaissance philosopher and former monk, Giordano Bruno (16th century). The idea of the spatial infinity of the universe was placed over against the classical Greek and scholastic doctrine of the limitation of form and the finitude of the universe. It was glorified as the expression of the divine infinitude.[1]

In this infinite universe, full of creative life-force and beauty, modern humanity discovered infinite possibilities for the expression of its free personality. Nature was conceived as the territory that had to be dominated by the free personality with its "sovereign reason."

Giordano Bruno apotheosized reason in a pantheistic sense. Infinite nature (*natura naturata*) became the macrocosmic reflection of individual,

---

[1] In classical Greek philosophy the *apeiron* was identified with "evil," the principle of matter that is not limited by any "form." This was the case, for example, in Plato's thought. In Leibniz (17th century), with his discovery of the infinitesimal calculus, the ground of evil was sought precisely in "finitude." Nothing proves in a more convincing way the internal break of humanism with the Greek principle of form.

free personality as the microcosmos. In the art of the Renaissance, this new conception of nature comes to poignant expression over against that of the Middle Ages which was ecclesiastically confined. Thus from the very beginning there existed an inner religious connection between the modern conception of nature and that of personal freedom.

Therefore, when the foundations of the classical mathematical sciences of nature were laid by Galileo and Newton, in which the scientific method for controlling of the physical forces of nature was demonstrated by tracing the physical laws that hold within the movement aspect of reality, this new method of science was immediately absolutized and made into a new ideal of science. It was claimed that this ideal should be accepted as a guide for every area of science. It was supposed to provide the key for the entire philosophic view of reality.

The modern personality-ideal of autonomy no longer made room for reality given in naive experience. Nor did it permit a basis to be found in given forms of being, as found in classical Greek philosophy. The new motive of creation had been borrowed from the Christian ground-motive but had also been reconstructed along humanistic lines. It demanded a theoretical reconstruction of the temporal cosmos with the aid of exact, mathematically qualified basic elements, such as movement and matter, in the physically qualified sense of "density of mass" subjected to the law of gravity. The latter had to cohere rationally, precluding the intrusion of hidden causes and *qualitates occultae*.

Hence the English philosopher Thomas Hobbes (17th century), in a clear allusion to the story of creation, gives an indication of his philosophy of nature by the thought-experiment of entirely demolishing given reality, the latter being scientifically unreliable. Afterwards, mathematical thought lights the flame of reason and is obliged to theoretically re-create reality piece by piece with the most simple elements of exact thinking, until, as a closed chain of mechanical cause and effect, it has become completely controllable.

The analysis of reality into its most simple, precisely determined elements, and the synthesis of these elements into a theoretical totality, became a fundamental requirement of the new ideal of science. That requirement was worked out by the French philosopher Descartes, the famous founder of modern humanistic philosophy, in what have become classic rules of the scientific method.

This ideal of science had been brought into being by the new ideal of personality itself. In the humanistic ground-motive, nature and freedom belonged indissolubly together. But as soon as the new nature-motive, as a dominant motive, began to make itself felt consistently in humanistic philosophy, so that the entire extent of reality from top to bottom was construed as a closed chain of mechanical cause and effect, there was no longer a place in any part of reality for the "free autonomous personality." "Nature" showed itself to be a dangerous enemy of "freedom."

Until the time of Rousseau and Kant (the latter half of the 18th century), the modern motive of nature almost went unchallenged in humanistic philosophy. Within the framework of the new ideal of science, thinkers such as Descartes and Leibniz attempted to save human freedom by seeking that freedom itself in exact mathematical thought that was supposed to give direction to the will.

In his metaphysics (philosophic doctrine of being), Descartes allowed for two substances: the *res extensiva*, that is, material, spatially extended body, and the *res cogitans*, that is, the thinking soul. The latter was supposed to be viewed by philosophy as if the "body" did not exist, and the former as if no "soul" existed. The actual religious impulse behind this dualistic metaphysics was the ideal of free personality which in its supposed center – mathematical thought – could not be allowed to fall victim to mechanical determination.

By contrast, Thomas Hobbes did not wish to acknowledge this limitation in the application of the humanistic ideal of science. Reality in its entirety, including human thought-life, was brought by him, in a methodical way, under the mechanistic common denominator of "moving body." And without any qualms he also sacrifices the freedom of will to the ideal of mechanistic explanation. It no longer needs to be argued that this humanistic "materialism" has nothing in common with Greek "materialism" which was dependent upon an entirely different ground-motive, that of flowing matter unlimited by forms.

The fundamental reorientation within humanistic philosophy arrives with Rousseau and Kant. By way of a critical self-reflection, humanism begins to discern that the motive of the freedom and autonomy of human personality, the deepest impulse of its philosophic theories, is not able to be realized within the framework of the deterministic ideal of science, and that thinking oriented to mathematics and the natural sciences is never in a position to establish what is the center of human personality.

This insight resulted in Rousseau's depreciation of theoretical science, his challenge to the basic idea of the Enlightenment that humankind is made free primarily by science and is put on the path of gradual progress. Rousseau proclaimed, with the passion of religious conviction, the freedom and autonomy of human personality which he considered was not rooted in theoretical thought but in the function of feeling. For Rousseau the sense of moral freedom is decisive; according to him, it is in that sense, and not in theoretical thought, that the seat of human personality lies. In opposition to the deterministic results of the science-ideal, he seeks a refuge for the freedom of personality in a religion of feeling. This does not prevent him, however, from constructing a philosophic doctrine of natural rights in which the freedom and autonomy of the individual are again supposed to be founded theoretically by way of a mathematical, constructive method.

Almost contemporaneously with Rousseau, David Hume, the Scottish thinker, was undermining the foundations of mathematics and natural science by a psychologically oriented critique of knowledge. He sought to demonstrate that the logical concepts of relation have their psychological origin in sense impressions, which are subject to the psychical laws of association, but which do not allow for any universally valid statements about reality outside of ourselves. Thereby the natural-scientific concept of causality was denied any real epistemological value.

In agreement with Rousseau, Kant ascribes absolute primacy to the humanistic ideal of personality. However, in contrast to Hume and Rousseau, because he also wants to save the ideal of science, he rejects Rousseau's religion of feeling. To this end he desires to establish a sharp boundary between the claims of science and those of the free personality. His criticism of knowledge was intended, in the first place, to strike at the very foundations of theoretical metaphysics. By means of theoretical thought, this metaphysics had attempted to establish, in a scientific fashion, both the essence of things as they exist "in themselves" (apart from sense perception) and also the essence of human personality. Kant maintains, however, that science (for him, mathematical natural science) is always limited to the phenomena of sense and can never give us an account of "things in themselves" or of supra-sensory reality.

In this way, he denied the possibility of a metaphysical natural philosophy, a metaphysical psychology, and a "natural" (metaphysical) theology. The autonomous freedom of human personality, as well as the existence of God, are for Kant unable to be proved in a theoretical fashion, but are only necessary postulates of "rational faith." They are "ideas" of so-called practical reason which do not present us with scientific knowledge but only with guidelines, with norms for practical action. There is no real bridge between "theoretical" and "practical" reason, between science and faith, between nature and freedom.

Science, for Kant, must view human activity as being completely determined in a mechanical fashion; but it embraces only "empirical" reality, that is, the totality of sensory (psychical) perceptions of reality, which are conceived of in space and time as they are determined by the categories of thought, and which are brought into a synthetic unity by the "epistemological subject." Beyond this, however, human consciousness is required, by the practical faith of reason, to accept the existence of supra-sensory normative ideas – in pride of place is the idea of the freedom and autonomy of human personality. Above the merely theoretical knowledge of theoretical reason, Kant gave primacy (practical priority) to these practical ideas of reason, which are nothing more that a summary of the humanistic ideal of personality and the correlated idea of God.

In part 1.6.1 we observed how the form-matter motive, which arose out of Greek philosophy, plays an essential role in Kant's critique of knowledge. The forms of thought of the "understanding" (the logical-analytical function) are restricted in their epistemological value to sensory material, but they do not have their origin, as Hume had taught, in the impressions of sense experience. In contrast to the sense-based knowledge, scientific thought has an autonomy, a "spontaneity," and a creative freedom through which it arbitrarily prescribes the law for its *Gegenstand* in its logico-synthetic imparting of form. But this logical forming remains bound to a sense-material which the understanding itself has not created but which it receives.

So in Kant's critique of knowledge, the Greek theme of form and matter receives an entirely new meaning. It now serves to limit the claims of the humanistic science-ideal in the interests of the humanistic ideal of personality and, at the same time, rescues the autonomy of natural-scientific thought from Hume's psychologistic critique of knowledge.

It is the forms of thought that make the experience of nature possible in the first place. They are the transcendental presuppositions of the latter, and thus they cannot have their origin in the material of sense experience. But science has no say outside the limits of sense experience. The category of natural-scientific causality, through which theoretical thought seeks a complete determination and domination of "natural phenomena," has no validity at all outside the domain of sensory perception. For this reason it cannot dominate the core of human personality, its autonomous freedom.

Kant's view establishes an unbridgeable gulf between the natural laws which are determined by the ideal of science and the norms for human action which are set by the ideal of personality. In other words, the theme of form and matter is completely absorbed by Kant in the religious ground-motive of modern humanism, that of nature and freedom, just as Thomas Aquinas had absorbed it into the Roman Catholic ground-motive of nature and grace.

Even the latter ground-motive was given a new meaning by humanistic philosophy within the framework of the religious ground-motive of nature and freedom. Leibniz declared that the "realm of grace" was identical with the "realm of free rationality," the love-community of the rational God with the rational creatures as a fruit of clear and distinct insight into the rational order of the world, while the "realm of nature" comprised the remaining, mechanically determined things. And at the end of his life, Kant worked out in detail the absorption of the nature-grace scheme within that of nature and freedom in his celebrated lectures on "The Conflict of the Faculties" (1796).

So we observe how the humanistic ground-motive gradually absorbed within itself all the other religious ground-motives and attempted to bring them into a religious synthesis. But this was only possible by way of a fundamental reinterpretation of their original meaning.

The boundary that was set by Kant between nature and freedom could not satisfy post-Kantian idealism (Fichte, Schelling, and Hegel). It also wished to push back, on its own ground, the deterministic ideal of science, the investigation of the phenomena of nature, in the interests of a consistent application of the idea of freedom. Only then does the idea of freedom acquire such absoluteness with regard to the conception of reality that it apparently no longer needs to fear any opposition from the old ideal of science. Kant's "critical" idealism, with its boundary between "nature" and "freedom," is transformed into an absolute idealism in which "nature" itself is interpenetrated by the idea of freedom.

Because of the polar structure of the humanistic ground-motive, the ideal of science returns in this new form, absolute freedom-idealism, coming into tension again with the personality-ideal. The attempt to interpenetrate theoretical thought itself with the idea of freedom and to think of nature and freedom as a dialectical[1] unity now leads to a new conception of science which is no longer oriented to the mathematical science of nature but to the science of history.

At the foundation of this development lay a new conception of the personality-ideal. Kant's conception of autonomous freedom was individualistic and rationalistic. According to him, the *autos*, the human self-hood, lies in the *nomos*, the general rule of the moral law. In this fashion there was no place for individuality with regard to talents and gifts. According to Kant, every human being, in respect of its moral nature, is an autonomous free personality who establishes its will according to the same formal general rule, the so-called categorical imperative. The individual person, considered in an idealistic fashion, is only an individual instance of the autonomous law of morality. In this rationalistic conception of human personality, the humanistic ideal of science, with its natural-scientific orientation, still retains its influence. It was only in the domain of aesthetics that for Kant there was a place for the individuality of genius. For this reason he did not develop a true idea of community, an idea of a "spiritual-moral realm" in which individual personalities are bound together in-

---

1 The dialectical method of this idealism, in which there is a search for a higher synthesis beyond the antithesis, is a covert religious attempt at synthesis. It attempts to eliminate the polar tension between nature and freedom in a theoretical way, as if it were simply a question of bridging a purely theoretical antithesis in a theoretical synthesis.

wardly into a higher unity, each according to his or her own disposition and individual gifts.

The new form which the absolute freedom-idealism gave to the humanistic ideal of personality, by contrast, proceeded in an irrationalistic direction. Early romanticism had already begun to ridicule Kant's "bourgeois morality of law," and set over against the latter its "morality of genius" according to which the brilliant personality does not fall within the sphere of a general rule that relates to the masses, but discovers the pointer for its activity in its own unique individual disposition. It was no longer possible to deduce the *autos* from the *nomos*. On the contrary, the *nomos* was supposed to spring from the individual *autos*.

So a polar opposition between the rationalistic and the irrationalistic conceptions came to expression within the humanistic ideal of personality itself. The first sought to exhaust the subjective individuality of personality in the law, the general rule; the latter, on the contrary, sought to reduce the law to an individual revelation of subjective individuality.

This overemphasis of subjective individuality led, in the nature of the case, to an overemphasis on the idea of community. If, on this standpoint, one did not wish to fall into a complete anarchism in the spheres of morality and law, which early romanticism defended, for instance, in Friedrich Schlegel's novel *Lucinde*, there had to be accepted above the individual personality, at least, a supra-individual community of personalities that, as an *Überperson*, would be able to elevate its communal will as a course of conduct for the individual's actions ("transpersonalism").

It was also possible to conceive this *Überperson* in an irrationalistic way. Its "general will" was not a *volonté générale*, which was construed by way of the mathematical method from the autonomous wills of individuals, in the sense of the earlier humanistic doctrine of natural law; it was only a concrete result of its individual communal nature.

It was thought that the "autonomy of the individual personality" was being maintained because the communal will was conceived as the true individual moral will of all the members of the community. It is only in the community that individuality attains its legitimacy. It can only be conceived within the community, just as in a living organism the individual functions of the organs can only be understood in their significance for the individual totality.

To this extent, certain representatives of absolute idealism (among the jurists in particular) still recognized an individual sphere of personality outside the community, which was then placed in dialectical relationship over against the community. But this was simply the result of a compromise with the individualistic conception of the personality-ideal.

In such a conception of the idea of freedom, natural-scientific thought was doomed to lose all of its allure as a universal method of science. This was the natural-scientific thought that had expressed itself within classical physics in an individualistic reduction of complex phenomena to their most simple elements, whose interrelationships were determined in a rigid causal fashion. Absolute freedom-idealism only saw in it the residual influence of the individualistic and rationalistic thinking of the "Enlightenment." Even science had to be interpenetrated by the new spirit of the freedom-idealism. Furthermore, it was thought that in the discipline of history the field of investigation had been discovered in which the law of existence for the irrationalistic and supra-personal way of thinking was revealed most pregnantly.

Although during the Enlightenment, the ideal for the historical field of study was also pursued in the uncovering of universal laws of historical development according to the model of natural science, this conception was abandoned by the new historical form of thinking that emerged under the influence of freedom-idealism.

The historian cannot be preoccupied with the discovery of general laws that determine individual events and the actions of individuals. Such a specialist is concerned with what is "once and for all" and individual as such: the battle of Waterloo, the historically unique figure of Napoleon, the Renaissance as an individual period of culture, etc.

Here it is no longer a matter of a conceptual natural-scientific understanding of "lawful" relationships between simple elements, but concerns a spiritual-scientific understanding of individual interconnections in a supra-individual totality of relations that never repeat themselves in the same way.

At the end of the 18th century, Herder had already discovered among the peoples and nations individual historical totalities which determine the nature of their members.

In his last period, Fichte had developed an entire methodology of historical science according to which he set the historical as the "lawless" sharply over against the field of investigation of natural phenomena, even though he recognized in the development of culture a "hidden law of providence."

Friedrich Julius Stahl, (1802-1861) the founder of the German anti-revolutionary doctrine of the state, in agreement with this new historical manner of thought, would soon identify the "hidden law-conformity" with "God's guidance in history." In this way, an irrationalistic and by no means harmless tendency was introduced into the anti-revolutionary conception of history.

The doctrine of the "individual spirit of the people" made its entrance. It was prompted by the Historical School of Law against the rationalistic doctrine of natural law that had been entertained from the time of Hugo Grotius. The latter doctrine, under the influence of the mathematical science-ideal, thought it could deduce from universal, rational human nature an eternal order of natural law and an eternal natural morality that would be applicable to every people and to every period. The Historical School, however, under the direction of Friedrich Carl von Savigny, taught that every order of law is the historical product of the individual nature of a people, an individual *folk* spirit. The latter has brought forth the entire national culture, of which law, language, social forms, art, etc., are merely dependent "aspects." Nature and freedom are united in a dialectical fashion in this individual spirit. It is indeed true that every people brings forth its "culture" in "freedom," but in the historical process of development a regulating role is performed by the supra-individual tradition of this folk. This tradition originally dominates the people in an unconscious way. It operates as the individual national spirit of a folk with an inner necessity which is transformed into freedom because culture is consciously formed with a knowledge of its connection with the past, with the separating out of what has vitality, and what is defunct in the tradition, and is therefore within the course of historical continuity. Thus in the historical manner of thinking, "nature," through the course of development, becomes freedom. In this way, Schelling had attempted to infuse natural science with the idealistic notion of freedom by way of his doctrine of the higher and lower potencies.

According to Schelling, in the process of development, these "potencies" disclose, even in natural phenomena, an individual creative freedom for which the earlier mechanistic mode of explanation had no place. In support, even at this time, he could point to the phenomena of electro-magnetism, which did not permit itself to be fitted into the mechanistic notion. Above all, he pointed to the development of the living organism, in which the potency of a "free power of creation" expresses itself according to a plan appropriate for the purpose. History, in the sense of the free development of culture, thus came to be viewed as the higher level (potency) of natural evolution, so-called natural history. In the development of its "potencies" nature itself is a dialectical synthesis of necessity and freedom.

So scientific speculation came under the influence of the growing historicism which, however, born out of freedom-idealism, appeared very soon to harbor within itself a dangerous tendency for the humanistic personality-ideal. So long as it was restrained by the idea of humanity, so long as the "individual spirit of the people" was only regarded as a temporal historical manifestation of the "eternal idea of free autonomous human community," as "the spiritual realm of free personalities" (Fichte), this dangerous tendency could not yet reveal itself fully.

Indeed, in the Germanic wing of the historical school of jurisprudence (which studied German legal history), it had already resulted in revolutionary opposition to the fundamental principles of civil law as they had developed in the Roman *jus gentium*, which functioned as a world law in the emancipation of the individual from the national community. Through the influence of the humanistic doctrine of natural law in the doctrine of human rights, these fundamental principles were also incorporated into the modern codifications.

Historicism originally led to an exaltation of Germanic folk law, which tied the entire legal position of the individual to membership in the community. But Otto Gierke, one of the leaders of the Germanic school, soon observed the danger of the historicistic exaltation of "*volk*." He effected a compromise with the idea of natural law that was supposed to proceed from the universal rational nature of the human person and that accorded to the person inalienable (civil) rights – rights of individuals in their capacity as human beings – even outside their connection with the community.

To the degree that historicism began to dominate scientific thought, it was also clear that freedom-idealism could not hold its own against the relativisitic tendencies which came to expression in this historical way of thinking.

Were not the supposedly "eternal" ideas of freedom, autonomy, natural law and natural morality themselves historically determined? How could anyone thinking scientifically abandon themselves to idealistic speculations and suppose that they could elevate themselves above the historical stream of evolution which includes all empirical reality, *Natur und Geschichte*? The new historical ideal of science wished to understand everything in a historical way and no longer had any appreciation for faith in an eternal idea of humanity, for the humanistic personality-ideal in its idealistic conceptions.

Darwinism, through its doctrine of the evolution of the species, in combination with Marxism, through its doctrine of class conflict and the conditioning of all the ideologies of law, morals, and religion by the historical-economic development of society, undermined faith in the unchangeable, rational nature of the human being.

Nietzsche wanted to view the human being only as a *noch nicht festgestellte Tier* – an as yet undetermined animal – which is differentiated from the other animals only by the fact that it is not yet equipped with unchangeable instincts and an unchangeably circumscribed *Umwelt*. But in the course of the development of culture, the human being has taken the determinion of its destiny into its own hands and therefore manifests, not an eternal, unchangeable nature, but an absolutely dynamic one.

He wants to build his doctrine of humankind exclusively on the data of science in *Natur und Geschichte*. He fulminates against the hubris of the human being's overestimation of itself, which thinks that the entire cosmos is related to itself as a goal, and which has the illusion that, in its "free personality" and its "reason," it is radically exalted above the animal. The human being is an "imaginative animal" that from time to time needs to reflect upon the purpose of its own existence, and then, in religious and idealistic fantasies, decrees a conception of "eternal human nature" to be an indisputable truth for a specific period of time. This is the situation until the conception has again declined in a later historical period. It then preaches new "eternal truths" about human nature, which again in turn must make way for other conceptions.

Since Copernicus' revolution in astronomy, science has now advanced so far that humankind has killed its "gods" and in the course of historical development, can strive towards expanding its power, which is not subject to the standards of eternal morality or religion, but is oriented only to the ideal of the "superman" (*Übermensch*). Rising to still higher pinnacles of historical power, the "will to power" is the only possible meaning of the never-ending process of historical development.

So Nietzsche – and from an entirely different (semi-Christian) standpoint, the Danish philosopher Srren Kierkegaard – served the death warrant on German idealism. The great religious process of degeneration of humanism was ushered in. Most recently, the process has led to a radical crisis of Western culture. This is the end phase of the truly dialectical process of development in which the humanistic ground-motive has insinuated itself into the world-and-life-view of modern humanity.

Since the suppression of Roman Catholicism and the Reformation, humanism had for three centuries assumed the unchallenged leadership in the development of Western culture. By reason of this process of inner degeneration, it has now lost its monopolistic historical position of power. At the same time, a chaotic struggle for the leadership of the future development of the West has broken out. Here the older cultural powers, Roman Catholicism and the Reformation, have also now freed themselves from their isolation in the backwaters of Western culture, and have begun to participate in the great conflict over the spiritual future of humankind with new scientific weapons.

Humanism's process of inner decay as a religiously rooted world-and-life-view even revealed itself in thinkers who tried to revive the Kantian or the Hegelian philosophy in the twentieth century (neo-Kantianism and neo-Hegelianism). Historicist thinking, however, did not appear to allow for any retreat to the idealistic metaphysics of the personality-ideal. Insofar as ideas were still allowed in philosophy (for instance, an idea of right), they were only allowed as rigid, empty forms or merely formal indicators, the content of which was supposed to be completely historically conditioned.

Anti-humanistic spiritual movements (fascism, national socialism, etc.) emerged from modern relativistic historicism. These replaced the eternal ideas of the personality-ideal by myth. The latter does not lay claim to being eternal truth but is simply in a position to activate the spirit of a national community in the course of historical development by seizing upon its folk instincts.

The trancendental critique of philosophic thought introduced here has been completely ignored through the influence of the dogma of the autonomy of science. Yet it is only in the light of the entire course of development of thought examined above that this critique acquires such significance and becomes so necessary. When one considers that the foundations upon which it was thought possible to build have been completely demolished by the upheavals of a period of tremendous transition, and also that the spiritual struggle has shown itself across the board to be one of religious convictions, it is no longer adequate, in the old dogmatic fashion, to parade the "autonomy of reason" as a scientific axiom. During the time in which the dominant theme of humanism had almost unchallenged sway over philosophic thought, this might have been understandable. Those who think, however, that they can still beat a retreat to this dogmatic standpoint within the present spiritual crisis in the interest of barring the way to radical critical self-reflection, by that very strategy, betray their failure to understand the deeper roots of this crisis.

1.7 The Cosmonomic Idea[1] as the Transcendental Ground-idea of Philosophy: The Transcendental Critique of Theoretical Thought and "Metaphysics"

In the course of an investigation of the structure of the theoretical attitude of thought with its *Gegenstand*-relation, the trancendental critique of theoretical thought has laid bare a triad of fundamental problems that hold for philosophy of any kind. They are briefly summarized below.

The structure of the theoretical *Gegenstand*-relation, with its antithesis between the logical aspect of thought and the nonlogical aspects of the fields of investigation, presented the first problem: (1) What is abstracted in the theoretical *Gegenstand*-relation from the structure of concrete reality as it is presented in naive experience, and how is this abstraction possible?

The structure of theoretical synthesis and its theoretical connection of the logical aspect with the nonlogical aspects led us subsequently to the second problem: (2) From what standpoint can the aspects, which have

---

[1] *Editor's note:* Dooyeweerd uses the term *wetsidee* (lit. "law-idea"). However, he himself expressed a preference for translating this term as "cosmonomic idea" to avoid it mistakenly being given a specifically juridical sense rather than its intended cosmic meaning. See *A New Critique*, vol. 1, 93.

been distinguished and set over against each other in the theoretical *Gegenstand*-relation, be united in a theoretical view of totality? This is the problem of the Archimedean or starting point of philosophy.

Finally, the question concerning the nature of the choice of the starting point brought us to the third fundamental problem: (3) How is the choice of the Archimedean point for theoretical synthesis possible?

By way of these three fundamental questions, which are imposed upon us by the internal structure of the theoretical attitude of thought itself, we orient theoretical thought to its three fundamental presuppositions.

These presuppositions, which lie at the foundation of the possibility of theoretical thought, appeared in the course of our investigation to be:

(i) The given unbreakable coherence and fixed place of the aspects in the cosmic order of time;
(ii) The "I" as the individual religious concentration-point of human existence from which the act of theoretical thought proceeds, as well as the supra-individual religious root-community of humankind in which our ego participates, and which, by its religious ground-motives, determines the choice of the Archimedean point for theoretical synthesis;
(iii) The absolute origin (*archē*) in respect of which the thinking ego necessarily takes a position when it relates the theoretically distinguished aspects to their deeper root-unity (their Archimedean point).

Now it appeared that the religious ground-motives of form and matter, nature and grace, and nature and freedom were of an inner dialectical character. That is to say, they appeared to be founded in a religious dualism, wherein what was conceived to be the origin (deity) could never be the integral, truly absolute origin of the temporal cosmos. Therefore it always discovered over against itself another independent principle of origin (irrespective of whether one ascribed divine character to it or whether it had been radically de-divinized).

This fundamental dualism appeared to be caused by a completely, or (in the case of Roman Catholicism) a partially, apostate orientation of the religious ground-motive. This involved the absolutizing and divinizing of something within the created reality, while in opposition, other parts of the cosmos, which had not been included, made the same absolute claims for themselves. For this reason it appeared that each polar motive of the fundamental dialectical theme mutually determined the other. In order to know what the Greeks understood by the principle of matter, it is necessary to penetrate into the religious sense of their principle of form, and vice versa. In order to know what the Roman Catholic scholastic philosophy understands by nature, it is necessary to delve into its conception of grace as the supernatural, and vice versa. In order to know what humanism understands by nature, it is necessary to inquire into the religious sense of its motive of freedom, and vice versa.

Since the choice of the Archimedean point of philosophy is conditioned by a religious motive, it should not be thought strange that in systems where there is no longer the attempt to reduce one of the polar factors of the ground-motive to the other (for instance, form to matter or nature to freedom, or vice versa), but where the dualism is openly acknowledged, philosophical thought does not manifest any unity of starting point. Instead it proceeds from two Archimedean points which it refuses to reduce to one another. (Thus, for example, Kant reserved the transcendental-logical subject of thought for the theoretical philosophy of nature, and the idea of the free, autonomous personality for so-called practical philosophy and ethics.) In truth, however, these antagonistic starting points continue to mutually determine each other.

At the same time, the polarly opposed directions in philosophy, which proceed from the same ground-motive,[1] discover their deeper unity and coherence in the ground-motive itself because the latter is a communal religious motive. To be precise, one should say that the religious ground-motive itself is the true starting point of philosophy.

It is now easy to observe that the three basic transcendental problems which we have formulated are unbreakably connected with one another, and that it is simply impossible to answer any one of the critical boundary questions apart from the others.

This is even more clearly expressed if we formulate them as follows:

(i) What is the mutual relationship and coherence of the aspects which have been distinguished and set over against each other in the theoretical *Gegenstand*-relation?

(ii) What is their deeper root-unity from which we can grasp them in a theoretical view of totality?

(iii) What is their ultimate origin?

It would appear therefore, in the course of our transcendental critique, that the view taken of the mutual relationship and coherence of the aspects is determined by the starting point that is chosen, and in which it is thought the root-unity of the aspects can be grasped, whether integrally or in part. Further, it appears that the choice of this starting point itself depends on the religious conception of the origin.

No philosophy can escape giving an answer to these three critical ground-, and boundary-questions, either expressly or by implication, because without such an answer theoretical thought is impossible. Providing

---

[1] For instance, the "materialism" of Hobbes, which is entirely rooted in the deterministic ideal of science, and the "idealism" of Fichte, Schelling, or Hegel, which consistently carries through the freedom-motive of the humanistic personality-ideal.

an answer from within the confines of philosophy, as we have already seen, cannot mean anything other than rendering a critical-theoretical account of the necessary presuppositions of theoretical thought which are already included in the structure of this thought. I speak intentionally of presuppositions and not of what is presupposed. The former, in contrast to the latter, have a subjective character. There is no prior guarantee that they are directed towards what is truly presupposed.

So the three dialectical ground-motives of Western thought that we have investigated will never direct theoretical thought to the true origin, the true Archimedean point, and the true order and coherence in the aspects of experience which have been distinguished from each other in the *Gegenstand*-relation. Nevertheless, they will all be related to these states of affairs which are presupposed, even though they present, in principle, a distorted view of them. The presuppositions of theoretical thought therefore may be true or false in an absolute sense, but they always relate to those states of affairs which are presupposed and which are founded in reality.

Theoretical thinking and knowing are always of a subjective character. Hence the theoretical synthesis discussed above has a subjective character. In theoretical synthesis, we form a logical concept of the nonlogical aspect of the field investigated which we have set over against it. Such a concept can be true or false and thus may never be regarded, as Kant attempted to view it, as the true creator of the *Gegenstand,* whether it is restricted to the form, or whether it also includes the ordering of a given experiential matter.

Kant looked for a priori, synthetic categories of thought which were supposed to be given before all experience as its necessary conditions. Thus, in an uncritical fashion, he identified the subjective presuppositions with that which is presupposed in the given structure of reality and so did not allow for the critical question as to whether his presuppositions were in agreement with that which is actually presupposed in the theoretical synthesis.

In the meantime, it has been shown that Kant's presuppositions, which were rooted in the religious ground-motive of nature and freedom, led him to fundamentally misconceive the structure of theoretical synthesis, whereby his entire doctrine of the a priori conditions of experience was also rendered unacceptable in principle. Therefore the first truly critical requirement of thought to be set forth is that the subjective starting point and the subjective presuppositions ought not to be confused with that which is presupposed, but theorists must be constantly prepared to confront their presuppositions with these states of affairs which are presupposed.

When we are concerned with the supra-temporal presupposed conditions (the Archimedean point and the origin), which can only be conceived through true knowledge of self and of God, there is no criterion of truth other than the agreement of our subjective religious presuppositions with the self-revelation of God in his Word.

When it is a matter of what it is that is presupposed, which is founded within the order of cosmic time (the pre-established mutual interrelationship and coherence of the aspects, which are set apart in the *Gegenstand*-relation), the presuppositions related to them can only appeal to the structural states of affairs within temporal reality itself. By means of its investigations, philosophical thought must give a satisfactory account of these states of affairs without eliminating the problem of the *Gegenstand*-relation with its antithesis by way of a dogmatic absolutization of a synthetically conceived aspect.

What was meant by the earlier observation that the solution of the three critical ground- and boundary-questions of philosophical thought must take place within the theoretical limits of philosophical thought itself when giving a self-critical theoretical account of its necessary presuppositions? How can we remain within the theoretical limits of philosophy when we give our account of presuppositions that transcend theoretical thought and also therefore the theoretical concept?

It is only possible to gain insight into this problem by recognizing that at the foundation of every synthetic concept that is formed of a field of investigation, for example, the jural sphere, there necessarily lies a theoretical idea of the mutual interrelationship and coherence of the aspects, their deeper root-unity, and their origin, even though a critical account of this idea may not have been given.

This idea itself is of a theoretical character, that is to say, it remains bound to the abstract *Gegenstand*-relation and may therefore never take the place of the supra-theoretical presuppositions that condition it. It has the sole function of focusing the presuppositions in question on the theoretical *Gegenstand*-relation.

And if we take the time to account for the way in which the synthesis between the logical aspect of thought and the jural aspect is carried out, it becomes immediately apparent that such a theoretical idea, of necessity, is foundational to the formation of the concept of law, for example, as the basic concept of the science of law.

If, for instance, the above mentioned Historical School declares law to be a historical product of the historical spirit of a people (*Volksgeist*), then it is easy to see that the jural aspect is thus reduced in a historicist fashion to the historical aspect. Before it is possible, however, to declare that law is a historical phenomenon, it is first necessary to have a synthetic concept of the historical aspect itself.

Such a concept, however, always has the task of logically distinguishing the aspect in question from other aspects. The Historical School's conception is that history is cultural development, in contrast to the development of nature. History itself thereby comes to be viewed as a temporal unfolding of the eternal idea of the community of free people. What we have here is not just a mere conceptual distinction; the concept is only understandable in terms of the humanistic idea of personality.

Note carefully how the Historical School places an idea of the coherence of all normative aspects of temporal reality at the foundation of this concept of history. It always declares that language, social forms, economic life, art, law, morality, etc., are only aspects of the culture of a people and thus find their coherence and deeper unity in the historical development of a particular folk character.

This idea of history, naturally, extends well beyond the concept of the historical aspect as cultural development. It elevates synthetic theoretical thinking in the field of history to the Archimedean point, and culture to the deeper root-unity, of all the normative aspects. Then, of course, the given coherence of these aspects is sought in historical development. The religious ground-motive in which this idea was rooted appeared to be that of nature and freedom in its absolute idealistic form.

This motive also determined the manner in which the concept of history was formed because, in this concept, culture was simply set over against nature but was not conceived as an actual aspect of reality.

By virtue of its idealistic, historicist starting point, the Historical School was not able to conceive of law other than in a historical fashion. At the foundation of its concept of law lay a historical idea of culture which attempted to give, at least for the normative aspects, a theoretical answer to the three fundamental questions of philosophy formulated above.

Because it is the case that the aspects unbreakably relate to each other according to their inner nature and structure, it is not possible to form a concept of a particular aspect without having this concept led by an idea of their mutual coherence and deeper root-unity.

The theoretical idea is always a philosophic idea of the totality and unity of the aspects which have been set apart in the (*Gegenstand-*) relation. By contrast, the theoretical concept is oriented to the theoretical distinguishing of the various aspects. The theoretical idea is not able to eliminate this conceptual distinguishing; it simply relates the latter to the coherence, the root-unity, and the origin of the distinguished aspect. And theoretical distinguishing is only possible on the foundation of such a theoretical idea, for a concept of the parts is not possible without an idea of the whole.

Therefore by maintaining the *Gegenstand*-relation, the theoretical Idea relates the theoretical concept to the presuppositions of all theoretical thought, but itself remains theoretical in nature, thus within the bounds of philosophic thought. In the theoretical nature of the idea resides what I have called its transcendental character. This is because in science everything that lies at the foundation of the possibility of theoretical thought is transcendental. For in theoretical thought, the transcendental is everything that, by means of the inner (immanent) structure of the theoretical mode of thought first makes theoretical thought itself possible; it is everything that stands at the basis of every theoretical conceptual distinction as its theoretical presupposition.

The transcendental ground-idea of philosophic thought, which has to provide the theoretical answer to the three fundamental problems of all possible philosophy, is oriented to religious presuppositions that are transcendent to philosophy, without itself assuming such a transcendent and thus supra-theoretical character.

The truly religious presuppositions, the religious ground-motive of thought, is never of a theoretical character. But the religious ground-motive is only able to influence theoretical thought because it determines the direction and content of the transcendental ground-idea of philosophy which makes philosophical thought at all possible. This is so because the entire method of the theoretical or scientific forming of concepts and, in a deeper sense, our entire vision of the structure of empirical reality, depends upon this fundamental idea.

I want now to give a critical account of the cosmonomic idea that lies at the foundation of the entire *Encyclopedia of the Science of Law*. As we have seen, the cosmonomic idea consists of a three-step process of critical, theoretical self-reflection upon what is presupposed in philosophic thought. The cosmonomic idea is nothing other than the theoretical encapsulation of the three transcendental ideas with respect to the origin, the root-unity, and the mutual relationship and coherence of the aspects of temporal reality that have been set over against each other in the *Gegenstand*-relation.

(1) As the idea of the origin, our Christian cosmonomic idea relates the theoretically distinguished aspects to God's sovereign creative will.

(2) As the idea of the root-unity, and thus of the Archimedean point of theoretical synthesis, this idea relates the above mentioned diversity of the aspects to the root-community of humanity as it has been reborn in Christ, in which the religious ground-motive of the divine Word-revelation operates as a spiritual *dunamis*.

(3) As the idea of the mutual relationship and coherence of the theoretically distinguished aspects, the cosmonomic idea relates these

aspects to the cosmic order of time in which all of the aspects, with their mutual irreducibility or modal sphere sovereignty preserved, are intertwined with each other in an unbreakable coherence.

From our earlier demonstration it must be clear that this idea of law, which is rooted in the scriptural ground-motive of the Word-revelation, must indeed bring with it a radical reversal of the entire theoretic-philosophical vision of the structure of temporal reality.

The idea of a cosmic order of time, with the accompanying idea of the modal sphere sovereignty of the aspects which are founded in that order, is directly dependent upon the idea of the Archimedean point from which the synthetic formation of concepts is carried out.

If the deeper unity of the aspects which have been distinguished in the *Gegenstand*-relation is no longer to be sought within theoretical synthesis itself (which is always involved in uniting a particular analyzed aspect with the logical aspect of thought), but is sought instead in the true center of the temporal cosmos in which all the aspects, without exception, converge in a religious concentration, then we are freed once again to view their mutual irreducibility, their modal sphere sovereignty. We are also then armed against Kant's critical doctrine according to which all differentiation and determination in the *Gegenstand* should find its ground in transcendental-logical concepts which are supposed to proceed from a transcendental-logical subject.

Furthermore, because we have broken with the dogma of the autonomy of science and thus no longer take our starting point from within the theoretical attitude of thought, we have also become free to view the cosmic order of time in its universal meaning, in the sense that it embraces all aspects. Indeed theoretical investigation should enable insight to be attained into the sequence of these aspects within this order of time, revealing a fixed place for each one of them. This is precisely the basic task which a philosophical encyclopedia of the science of law must fulfill.

The transcendental critique of philosophy has established that theoretical thought is not autonomous. The cosmonomic idea expounded here renders an account of this state of affairs by directing theoretical thought to its necessary supra-theoretical presuppositions and implicitly to that which is presupposed.

In immanence philosophy before Kant, theoretical metaphysics took the place of transcendental criticism. Metaphysics proceeded from the dogma concerning the autonomy of theoretical thought, even though, as observed earlier, autonomy was always interpreted in different senses according to the religious ground-motive that lay at the foundation of theoretical thinking.

This metaphysics always included the three following components:

(i) a metaphysical doctrine relating to unchanging "being" that is concealed behind the transitory, sensorily perceptible phenomena and which only obtains a more exact definition in the metaphysical concept of substance as the concept of the thing itself, that is, the thing as it is in itself, apart from human consciousness;
(ii) a metaphysical psychology, as the doctrine of the human soul or spirit;
(iii) a metaphysical theology (*theologia naturalis*), or a metaphysical doctrine concerning the being of God, as the Origin and First Cause of the temporal cosmos.

It is not difficult to see that this metaphysics, by way of "autonomous" theoretical thought, attempted to arrive at a concept of the unity of the aspects, a concept of the individual center, the soul of temporal human existence, and a concept of the origin. Since Greek philosophy, the metaphysical concept of being has served in this respect to reduce the theoretically distinguished aspects to a theoretical unity.

At the same time, this concept of being was unable to grasp the true root-unity, the religious center, of all the aspects. This is clearly expressed in Aristotelian-Thomistic metaphysics in which the concept of being, as the most fundamental concept of philosophy, is expressly called an "analogical" concept. What was meant by this was that "being" is not attributable to all beings in the same fashion. So, for example, there is a fundamental difference between the being of God and the being of the creatures, between the being of a substance, a thing that can exist in itself, independently of another thing, and the being of the attributes of this substance, its so-called accidents, which cannot exist independently but only by inhering in a "substance" that bears them. Being can only be predicated of all these realities (entia) by way of (analogical) resemblance.

In this fashion, however, the concept of being, as the fundamental concept of this metaphysics, became to a high degree unstructured. Its unity is only a unity of analogy, not true root-unity. Merely analogical concepts that are not further defined remain valueless from a scientific point of view and set thought on a wrong path. Later on, as we proceed to develop our own doctrine with respect to modal analogies,[1] this will become quite clear.

The transcendental critique has demonstrated that pure theoretical metaphysics does no more than proclaim religious presuppositions as autonomous scientific conclusions. It is rejected for that reason as being impossible in principle. It stands or falls with the autonomy of science.

As we have seen, Kant rejected theoretical metaphysics for entirely different reasons. He only did it in order to restrict the humanistic sci-

---
1 *Editor's note:* See *analogy* in glossary.

ence-ideal to the sensory phenomena of nature with the object of calling a halt to natural science's attempt to view everything in a deterministic fashion and so as to retain independence for the supra-sensory sphere of free personality. He wished to separate faith and science for the distinct purpose of preserving the autonomy of the latter.

We believe it to have been demonstrated that Kant's critique of theoretical thought is, in great measure, burdened by dogmatism and is thus not a true transcendental criticism of philosophic thought.

The course of our argument is now interrupted for a brief discussion of the theoretical and nontheoretical presuppositions of philosophy.

The entire argument to this point may well have convinced the reader that, lying at the foundation of the theoretical judgments of scientific thought, there are necessary presuppositions of a nontheoretical, or rather, supra-theoretical character, of which the thinker – in the theoretical ground-idea – may or may not be conscious.

Immanence philosophy proceeds on the foundation of the dogma of the self-sufficiency of theoretical thought and has outgrown the naive positivistic standpoint. For that reason it is unable to recognize anything other than theoretical presuppositions (a prioris) as legitimate. All the necessary presuppositions of science that make scientific activity at all possible are viewed on this standpoint as being of an immanent-theoretical character. In contrast, all nontheoretical presuppositions in science are declared forbidden. In the interests of the "objectivity" of scientific knowledge the scientific investigator is obliged to be free of them.

Now as we have seen, the special sciences are of necessity based upon philosophic, therefore theoretical, presuppositions. But philosophy itself also has necessary presuppositions which cannot be of a philosophic-theoretical character. Philosophy cannot deny the supra-theoretical character of these presuppositions without paying the price of falling into theoretical dogmatism.

However, the dogma of the autonomy of theoretical thought is now advanced by its proponents as a legitimate immanent theoretical prejudice that is supposed to possess general validity insofar as it makes true science possible, or so it is alleged. According to this point of view, the autonomy of science belongs to the essence of science.

But as we have shown, the dogma in question is indeed of a supra-theoretical character. This uncritical identification of theoretical and supra-theoretical presuppositions of the immanence standpoint leads to an unscientific attitude with respect to those who reject the dogma of the self-sufficiency of theoretical thought. It also leads to a spiritual tyranny, consisting of the imposition of one's own view of science upon others on pain of exclusion from the scientific community.

Only by making a sharp distinction between the necessary supra-theoretical and the theoretical presuppositions is there protection against making the scientific character of a theory dependent upon anything other than the strictly internal demands of scientific investigation itself.

The demands of science are violated if a nontheoretical presupposition is put in the place of immanent scientific investigation, with the pretence of solving, or with the effect of eliminating, questions which themselves have an internally theoretical character. This criterion holds for science that proceeds from a Christian basis just as much as for science bound to the immanence standpoint.

However, the misunderstanding of the supra-theoretical character of the ultimate presuppositions of philosophy and the claims of scientific monopoly for a dogma, such as that of the self-sufficiency of science, is especially unscientific.

The standard of scientific investigation must be kept unsullied and may never be misused for the spiritual suppression of those with whom one refuses to combat with truly scientific weapons because they do not want to accept the dogma in question.

1.8 The Cosmonomic Idea and the Method of Concept-Formation in the Science of Law

From our preceding discussions we can draw the following conclusions: the science of law cannot proceed as a special science without philosophical presuppositions, more specifically, legal-philosophical presuppositions; philosophy, in particular, the philosophy of law, cannot operate as a theoretical totality-science without supra-theoretical presuppositions.

Whenever one purports to have disengaged the special jural science from philosophy, it is bound to have fateful consequences for both. It is fateful for the special science because, in a completely uncritical manner it proceeds to advance presuppositions of a philosophical character as if they were judgments belonging to it as a special science. It thereby embraces a positivistic theory of reality, which it then proceeds to impose upon all of its practitioners as the nonphilosophical conception of reality concerning everyday life. It is fateful for philosophy because the latter can only give direction to a special science in direct contact with the questions arising out of it as a special science. Without this contact, it loses touch with reality.

For the special jural science, the entire method of theoretical concept-formation is dependent upon the philosophic ground-idea from which it takes its point of departure. It is customary to say that the basic concept of law is a matter for the philosophy of law. This is undoubtedly correct insofar as the constant nature and structure of the jural aspect must be grasped by this conception in a synthetic manner, after there has been an analysis of the various characteristic moments which are bound within this structure into an unbreakable unity.

A concept of law that truly wishes to grasp this structure of the jural aspect can never be found apart from a philosophic idea of the mutual relationship and coherence of the jural aspect with the remaining aspects of reality. In this concept of law the special jural science has its philosophical presupposition. One should not believe, however, that a special science can disregard this philosophical presupposition. As an academic discipline the science of law continually finds itself confronted by the given coherence of the jural aspect with the nonjural aspects of reality. Indeed, it finds itself presented with a relationship which, in a remarkable way that must be further investigated, manifests itself within the structure of the jural aspect itself. In this respect, it is first and foremost a matter of not losing sight of the internal limits of law.

A jurisprudential example may explain this. Since the famous 1926 decision *The Builder of Gouda* (Hoge Raad [Supreme Court], March 12, 1926, NJ. 1926, 777; W.11488), the Hoge Raad has accepted as established jurisprudence that the obligations of morality and propriety create a natural binding commitment. The facts were as follows:

> In contravention of what he had been instructed to do, an architect employed by the municipality of Gouda accepted 35,000 guilders from a contractor. When this came to light he asked for honorable dismissal and made a deposit into the account of the municipality equivalent to the amount illegally acquired by him. He hoped that by doing this he would ensure that his dismissal would indeed be honorable. When it turned out that this was not the case, he claimed back the 35,000 guilders as an unowed payment. His claim was dismissed with the observation that by his payment he had met a natural obligation and therefore, by virtue of paragraph 2, in article 1395 of the Civil Code (the only place where a natural obligation is mentioned), he was not entitled to recovery. On appeal, the Hoge Raad held in respect of this provision "that it not only considered it to apply to cases where, according to a positive legal rule, there is an existing debt owed, yet the right to claim was either unfounded from the start or through later intervening circumstances having occurred, but similarly applies where the person concerned fulfills an obligation owed to another which merely rests upon the precepts of morality and decency."

This first decision by the Hoge Raad on this point is already very instructive. Note that the architect had enriched himself unlawfully (contrary to instructions). If, having acquired the payment in this manner, and after depositing that amount in the municipal account, it had been possible for him to recover on account of the unowed payment, then the unlawful enrichment would have been sanctioned by the judge in the civil court. Thus, in this case, we had here at issue not merely a question of morality or propriety but without doubt a legal principle!

Incidentally, not all cases of natural obligation are concerned with redress for a wrong. Thus, in the case of a natural duty of alimony in respect of a mistress, for example, one certainly may assume a positive, morally qualified legal duty flowing from the very nature of the relationship that exists between a person and his mistress.[1]

Therefore duties of morality and propriety can generate natural obligations. That is to say, it creates a jural bond between the one who, on the basis of such a duty, has to act for the benefit of another, on the one hand, and the beneficiary, on the other. This performance, however, cannot be demanded by right and claiming back the benefit of what has already been given is also out of the question. Furthermore, a natural obligation can, in some circumstances, provide a valid legal basis for converting it into an actionable obligation (which does not require a *causa* for its creation).

The adoption of this stance by the Hoge Raad has extremely important consequences. Gift agreements, for example, according to our civil law, are bound by the formal requirement that they must be embodied in a notarial document. If this requirement is not satisfied, they are nullities and therefore cannot, as a general rule, have legal consequences. But at this point the jurisprudence of the Hoge Raad now applies with its concept of a natural obligation. If the gift is given out of a natural duty of morality and decency, then, according to our highest legal tribunal, it is conveyed in virtue of a natural obligation, and an amount paid under the agreement cannot therefore be recovered. It is of even greater importance that this natural obligation can be converted by agreement into an obligation in respect of which a claim may be made. Without this basis it would have to be viewed as lacking a cause and would therefore be a nullity (see *inter alia* Hoge Raad, May 4, 1932, NJ 1933; W 12442). This is particularly relevant for gifts made by a man to a woman with whom he is living in an extra-marital relationship; for financial obligations set out in divorce agreements or a separation from bed and board, in which case these agreements are not to be regarded as legally valid; and for retirement agreements be-

---

1 *Editor's note:* In the Dutch text this sentence immediately followed: "This concept of a morally qualified legal duty will be explained below in part 4 of this Introduction." This appears to be an error and has been omitted to avoid confusion because part 4 of this Introduction does not explain the concept mentioned, whereas the discussion immediately following the omitted sentence contains an extended discussion of the said concept. The omitted sentence had the following footnote reference: See also *Harms-De Visser* (Hoge Raad, November 30, 1945, NJ. 1946, 62) in which the Hoge Raad held that a life insurance payment to a surviving spouse is not a gift, but the fulfillment of a natural obligation.

tween employers and employees, in the sense of converting a natural obligation into one that is enforceable.

Juristic practice shows us here that at its very heart is the requirement of an acceptable criterion to distinguish, for legal purposes, the demands of law, morality, and propriety. What, in this context, is to be understood by the requirements of morality and propriety? If they were to be conceived according to their original characteristic sense of the moral and the social aspects of reality, then the boundaries marking off law, morality, and propriety would indeed be eliminated and a practically untenable situation would be created that would render illusory many mandatory provisions of the Civil Code.

It is not a question, for example, of designating all gifts given out of affection (an intrinsically moral figure) as the fulfilling of the demands of a "natural relationship." This has been established repeatedly by the jurisprudence. Even less is it a question of legally requiring from someone a moral sacrifice because of a natural relationship, which the person has to make in order to carry out an obligation that arises from love but which, according to a jural standard, exceeds even the limits of a natural relationship.

On the other hand, propriety, in the sense of a social obligation, is also not a pattern that allows itself simply to be transplanted into legal life, precisely because, in its original sense, it does not have a jural character and does not possess a jural configuration.

In the jurisprudence an appeal has been made to criteria which only consist of an inadequate formulation of a practical intuition with respect to the scope of law. But these practical intuitions, even though they may offer nothing more than a general formula, saying little if anything, cannot always be said to be satisfactory even from a practical point of view.

Thus it appears that the Hoge Raad, in its decision of April 22, 1937, (*The Sister-in-Law Case*, NJ. 1937,1108), wished to confine the natural obligation to "a moral duty aimed at redressing a moral or material wrong or to recompense services rendered." This criterion was sharply attacked by Professor P. Scholten who maintained that in this case various maintenance-related moral duties would fall outside the concept of natural obligation.

In the decision of February 18, 1938 (*The 17 Year-Old Marriage Case*, NJ. 1938, 323), concerning a wife separated from bed and board, the Hoge Raad was already prepared to depart from the criterion stated in *The Sister-in-Law Case*.

The general formula that has been introduced by Dutch jurisprudence in order to delimit, for legal purposes, a natural relationship, conveys no meaning if taken at face value. According to the formula, the relationship is only present for legal purposes if a moral obligation, which is obligatory according to an objective standard, is assumed. Nothing can be understood by an "objective standard" other than a universally valid rule (norm) of propriety. But the issue on which everything depends concerns precisely what kind of norm this is. It cannot be moral, in the original sense of the word, because it is then lacking any jural delimitation. If, however, the objective standard is not moral in character, then neither can the obligation that creates a natural relationship be a truly moral obligation. Apparently, the administration of justice then employs a concept of moral obligation which must be understood, not in the original sense of "moral," but in a juristic sense that has not been subjected to a more precise definition.

A judge should not be blamed for such lack of clarity in the use of these concepts. The judge's task is not scientific, but of a practical-juridical nature. And insofar as a judge requires the help of legal science in his deliberations, he is never obliged to give scientific pronouncements but practical-juridical decisions that satisfy, to the greatest possible degree, the requirements of legal life.

In contrast, the science of law ought not to allow itself to be satisfied with such purely practical criteria if it is to continue making the claim of being scientific. The basic concept of law ought to be conceived in such a fashion that it indeed gives a theoretical account of the relationship and mutual coherence of the legal with the nonjural aspects of reality, and for this purpose, as we have seen, a philosophical ground-idea is a prerequisite.

We should not be surprised that the dominant schools of legal philosophy have not been able, from the standpoint of immanence philosophy, to present a concept of law that can offer to the special science of law a reliable approach. Kant's statement, "The jurists are still searching for their concept of law," (though it has a different meaning for him) involves an acknowledgment that there is still lacking an encyclopedic account of the place of the jural aspect within the coherence of the aspects of reality. And so long as this has not been accomplished, the concept of law actually remains suspended in mid-air, and theoretical arbitrariness takes the place of exact investigation into the structure of reality in which the jural aspect is embedded.

The principal reason why it has not been possible, on the immanence standpoint, to establish the encyclopedic position of law within the coherence of the aspects of reality must be sought in the fact that on this standpoint it was repeatedly necessary to reduce the jural to another aspect in order to arrive at a concept of law.

This point is directly connected with what we observed earlier concerning the relationship of the concept of law to the transcendental basic idea of philosophy. The theoretical concept of law, so it appeared, allows us, first to theoretically distinguish the jural aspect from the nonjural aspects of reality. But for this theoretical distinguishing there is required a basis of comparison, a kind of denominator on the basis of which the aspects interconnect and by means of which they can be compared with each other. If they had no mutual point of contact with each other at all, they would be completely incommensurable and it would be impossible, in principle, to discern in what respect they differ from each other.

This state of affairs can be made clear to a certain extent by using the analogy of fractions. Each has a prime number (a number that cannot be further divided) as a denominator, for example, 1/2, 1/3, 1/5, and 1/7. Such fractions first must be brought under a common denominator in order to be able to calculate their mutual relation in whole numbers.

In theoretically distinguishing the aspects, we also require, as it were, a denominator in terms of which they may be compared. During our discussion of the second basic problem of philosophy, that of theoretical synthesis, we identified this as the problem of the Archimedean point. Without an Archimedean point on the basis of which we can conceive the aspects in their deeper root-unity, theoretical analysis and synthesis is impossible. If the choice of the Archimedean point is now immanent to theoretical thought, then the basic denominator[1] of the aspects must be sought within a theoretical synthesis. And because this synthesis itself is always of a specific character – depending on the aspect towards which it directs theoretical thought with its logical concept-forming – a particular synthetically conceived aspect will be elevated to be the basic denominator for all the rest. We have seen how this was the source of all the "isms" in philosophy.

These "isms" are echoed in the different conceptions of law which have been constructed by the various schools of immanence-philosophy, and

---

1   *Editor's note:* There is potential confusion for the reader in Dooyeweerd's treatment of the second basic problem of theoretical thought. This might arise especially for those familiar with his definitive treatment of these problems in *A New Critique*, vol. 1. There he refers to time as the "common" or "basic denominator" that guarantees the inter-modal coherence of the aspects (p. 47). It is therefore confusing when he uses the same analogy of the denominator in explaining the second basic problem of the Archimedean point. Here, not time, but the Archimedean point itself is referred to as the "basic denominator." Arguably, this is a less apt analogy for describing the Archimedean point than for time, because the Archimedean point is not so much a common basis for the synthetic act of thought as the point from which every theoretical synthesis is performed. It must be admitted, however, even after this and earlier clarification (see note on p. 28), and taking account of a clearer treatment in his mature analysis contained in *A New Critique*, there still remains unresolved difficulties in Dooyeweerd's account of the basic transcendental problems of theoretical thought. (See D.F.M. Strauss, "An Analysis of the Structure of Analysis [The Gegenstand-relation in discussion]," *Philosophia Reformata* 49, no. 1 [1984]: 35-56).

which have been transposed from the philosophy of law into the jural special science.

Thus the conception of Krabbe, the former professor in constitutional law and the philosophy of law at Leiden, is that law has an intrinsically psychical character and that all positive law – law posited in a binding form – has its only source in the legal sensibilities of the members of the nation. This conception is the result of a psychologistic view of law, at the basis of which there is a psychologistic cosmonomic idea.

Hence the conception of Kelsen, the German neo-Kantian legal theorist and philosopher of law, is that the jural aspect has its origin in a transcendental-logical form of thought. This view is the result of a formalist-logicistic view of law which has, at its foundation, a logicistic cosmonomic idea, which in turn is actually dependent upon mathematical thought.

And the previously discussed conception of the Historical School, founded in 1814 by the German legal theorist von Savigny, views law as a phenomenon of historical development, which has its only source in the national historical spirit of a people. This was itself the result of a historicist view of law, and this has its source in an idealistic-historicist cosmonomic idea.

It is impossible, on the immanence standpoint, to conceive of the various aspects of temporal reality in their sphere sovereignty and their mutual irreducibility. Of course, there is also here an attempt to make some kind of theoretical distinction between law, morality, and the rules of social intercourse; but only based on an aspect that has been absolutized beforehand in a transcendental ground-idea.

Thus we observed that the Historical School only regarded law as an aspect of a people's cultural development which is able to be isolated by theoretical thought. Forms of social intercourse, language, economics, art, etc., were also accepted as aspects of culture. Hence the Historical School's concept of law is that of a modality (a special revelation) of the historical folk culture. On the basis of this denominator, law is supposed to be distinguished from forms of commerce, language, economics, morality, etc.

It is also impossible to escape the religiously determined theoretical corroding of the sphere sovereignty of the aspects of reality by forsaking a material denominator in favour of delimiting the aspects from each other in an exclusively formal-logical way. In the latter case, for example, the attempt is made to distinguish law, morality, and social forms from each other by subsuming all of these aspects under a purely formal general concept, a *genus proximum*. The concept "norm of action" has been introduced as such a *genus proximum*. The attempt is then made to distinguish the three normative-aspects we have mentioned from each other by establishing their specific attributes (*differentia specifica*). In addition, the legal and social norms are grouped together as communal norms of "external" behavior. The moral norm, by contrast, is conceived as the norm that regulates only the internal attitude of the individual. Finally, the legal norm is distinguished from the social norm (the so-called *Konventionalnorm*) through designating the former in contrast to the latter as a compulsory social norm, a specific characteristic of law that is often better described as organized legal compulsion.

This method of determining the concept of law might well be regarded as the prevailing one in legal science. One comes across it in all kinds of juridical texts and introductions to the science of law, which especially do not want to weary the first year student with philosophical explanations.

Now it must be remarked at the outset that every attempt to encompass legal, moral, and social norms under a more general concept, a logical *genus proximum*, leads to a logistic levelling of their inner nature. Here a logical denominator is proposed, and it is assumed in turn that the distinguished aspects have a common logical denominator.

The entire method of concept-formation according to *genus proximum* and *differentia specifica* is taken from Aristotelian logic. Aristotle distinguished sharply between the analogical concepts (see the conclusion of part 1.7) in the metaphysical doctrine of being (ontology) and the generic concepts of the empirical sciences. According to him, the generic concepts are formed by way of a complete abstraction from the experience of individual things that have specific essential characteristics in common. The essential characteristics that are common to a group of things and thus are attributable to them univocally ("simpliciter," says scholasticism) are brought together in a general conception (generic concept) in abstraction from those attributes in respect of which the things differ from each other. The genera are divided into species by the addition of specific attributes that inhere in the essential form, which has a narrower group of genera. Thus it is possible to say that all human beings are rational, because they have the essence of rationality in common. The predicate "rational" is attributed to them univocally (simpliciter).

Thus, according to Aristotle, the concept "living being" is the *genus proximum* of rational living being (*animal rationale*) and animal living being (*animal brutum*). In this fashion, according to Aristotle and Aristotelian scholasticism, it is indeed possible to obtain complete conceptual unity because there is an opportunity here for complete or genuine abstraction.

By contrast, the analogical or transcendental concepts of ontology have contents which are attributable to entities that differ in principle with regard to the nature of their being. Thus they can never say something univocally about these entities. These transcendental concepts are therefore elevated above all generic concepts; they lie at the foundation of all concepts in general. Hence they are called "transcendental" in a metaphysical sense. In this case, being does not allow the possibility of authentic or complete abstraction of the specific characteristics. Here only an incomplete conceptual unity can be obtained by way of incomplete or inauthentic abstraction. This results from the fact that the entities falling under the analogical concept differ in the very respect in which they agree, so that in understanding the element of agreement it is specifically impossible to abstract from the intrinsic difference. Such a concept has the potential for theoretical diversity within itself for the very reason that it is not a complete unity.

These analogical concepts have already been criticized at the end of part 1.7. Regarding the generic concepts, it must be observed that they only have a right to existence within the framework of the mutually irreducible aspects. Thus it is possible to form generic and specific concepts within the science of law itself, provided that all these juridical concepts are considered on the foundation of the basic concept of law, which has to embrace synthetically the irreducible uniqueness of the jural aspect. However, as soon as the method of concept-formation according to *genus proximum* and *differentia specifica* is applied to this basic concept of law, it becomes indeterminate regarding its meaning, bereft of scientific value, and misleading.

Even a brief critical analysis of the concept of law as construed by this method will teach us this. In contradistinction to the moral norm, the legal norm is supposed to be a norm of communal action. But does morality not have any communal norms? Does there not hold, for example, within marriage and the family, a moral norm of love possessing an explicitly communal nature? Or do the moral responsibilities of the parents with respect to their children, and of the husband with respect to his wife, exist on the same footing as moral responsibilities towards an anonymous beggar who happens to cross our path? Furthermore, is it truly the case that all legal norms have a communal character? Is there then no difference in principle between the norms of so-called civil law, and, for example, those of the internal legal relations of the state or the church which, to be sure, do have a communal nature? The internal character of civil law, as we shall see later, resides in the very fact that it ascribes rights and obligations to individual persons as such, regardless of their belonging to a specific community, such as a state, a people, a particular family, or a race. And is it the dimension of community that qualifies law in the sense of actual law of the community, or is it not rather the very opposite, it is law that determines the jural sphere of a community? Does not community possess its social side, its economic side, and its moral side, as well?

Furthermore, the attempt has been made to distinguish law from morality and from social rules as well by means of the criterion of "coercion." But in what sense is coercion understood here? There is coercion of a physical, a psychological, an economic, a conventional social nature, etc. The social obligations of propriety, courtesy, etc., are often much more effective in compelling performance than legal prescriptions, which sometimes are sanctioned, for example, by payment of only nominal monetary compensation or a fine (a traffic ticket, for instance). The economic coercion of lock-out, boycott, etc., often affects interests to a much greater extent than does legal coercion; it is also highly organized. Even when there is an attempt therefore to define law by means of the criterion of "coercion," it is legal coercion, apparently, that is meant. In this case, however, the element that is chosen as the sole qualifying element (viz., law: legal compulsion) is the very thing that is supposed to be defined by it.

From this short critical discussion it can be seen that the definition of a legal norm as a "coercive communal norm" is thoroughly indeterminate, misleading, or even "wrong in principle." That such a definition is easily digested by the beginner student, and is apparently understood without difficulty, is no recommendation at all for this method of concept-formation as a whole. It leaves jurists completely at sea as soon as they begin to involve themselves in the actual study of law. With respect to the underlying concept of law, this is just the very state of affairs that ought not to exist. It must either give direction and support to the entire special scientific investigation of legal life or it is intrinsically worthless. An entirely different method, already implicitly prescribed by our cosmonomic idea, needs to be adopted for the formation of jural concepts.

1.9 The Law-Spheres and their Modal Structures. The Concepts of Law and Subject in the Science of Law

The aspects of reality are modes, particular ways of revealing a religious root-unity that indeed transcends the diversity within the order of time.

Just as the white light of the sun is refracted by a prism into the seven color ranges of the sensorily perceptible spectrum of light, and just as no one of these colors can alone establish the unity of all the others, so the religious root-unity of the temporal cosmos is broken up by the prism of cosmic time into the aspects as its modalities, no one of which comprises the root-unity of the others.

Now, as we have already remarked repeatedly, these aspects are set within constant structures which themselves do not vary in time. By "structure" we understand an architectural plan that is a relative unity in a diversity of moments. The structures of the aspects are thus able to be called the modal structures of reality because the aspects themselves are modalities of a deeper unity.

That they do not have a variable but a constant character must be ascribed to the fact that they are fundamental in nature, so that the possibility of all the variable and transitory phenomena which present themselves within the aspects presupposes these aspects. Therefore, in the Philosophy of the Cosmonomic Idea, they are called "ontic a prioris." They are called "ontic" because, unlike Kant's a priori forms of consciousness, they are not founded merely in subjective consciousness but essentially in temporal reality. They are called "a prioris" because they lie at the foundation of all of the changing phenomena of reality.

If we apply this to the jural aspect, then we can establish the following: A concrete legal configuration, for example, a purchase agreement made between A and B, comes into being at a particular point in time and is discharged after the parties have carried it out. But as a legal configuration this agreement is enclosed in the modal structure of law, which itself cannot originate and expire within time because it is a structural law [in the cosmic sense] for the changing life of law [in the jural sense] that initially gives to it its jural character.[1] Only on this basis, for instance, is it still possible to recognize classical Roman law as law, even though it has long since lost its positive legal force. Of course, in saying this it does not follow that the modal structure of legal life bears a supra-temporal, transcendent character. Instead, as already observed, it is enclosed within the cosmic order of time as an order, as a cosmic law-ordering, and not in respect of its subjective side as individual duration of time.

The modal structure of an aspect delimits a sphere of modal laws to which temporal reality is subjected within this particular aspect. From now on this will be called its "law-sphere." Thus each aspect of reality is set within its own law-sphere, which is delimited from all other law-spheres by a modal structure. Each law-sphere in relation to every other is sovereign within its own sphere because, as already stated, the modal structure of these spheres find their deeper root-unity not within time but above it.

The laws of number are not reducible to spatial laws, nor are the spatial reducible to the laws of motion. The latter cannot be reduced to those of organic life. These in turn are not reducible to laws of feeling and thought.

---

1 *Editor's note:* Dooyeweerd here uses *wet* and *recht* to distinguish, respectively, law in its cosmic sense and law in its jural sense, applicable to positive human law. Because English has only the one word to translate the two Dutch terms, it has been necessary, in order to avoid confusion of the two senses of law, to insert in parentheses, where required, a qualification of "law" in order to distinguish the different senses in the above sentence.

The jural laws are not reducible to the logical, the historical, lingual, social, aesthetic, economic, moral or to the laws of faith.

In every law-sphere temporal reality has a modal function and in this function is subjected (*sujet* or *subjekt*) to the laws of the modal spheres. Therefore every law-sphere has a law-side and a subject-side that are given only in an unbreakable correlation with each other.[1] There is no law without a subject (*sujet*) that is subjected to it, and there is no subject without a law that limits the subject and binds it to an order. Thus the entirety of temporal reality is only presented to us in an unbreakable correlation of its law- and subject-side.

In the law-sphere of number the numerical functions are subjected to the laws for number. In the logical law-sphere thought is subject to the logical norms of thought. And thus, in the jural law-sphere, the legal subject is subjected to legal norms.

Both the law-side and the subject-side of an aspect of reality have a constant modal structure. Within this structure, however, both the subjective (and within the previously discussed subject-object relation, also the objective) modal functions which concrete facts, events, social relationships, and even the individual person have, within the aspect of reality involved, are of an entirely individual character.

On the law-side of a law-sphere, the modal laws will indeed become typified, as we shall see later. That is to say, they will assume a typical character in the various individuality-structures of reality. But, in spite of all its further concretizing, in its orientation to the individuality of the subject, the law-type never attains the actual individuality that is inherent in the subject-side of reality. Law still remains a rule, an ordering, to which the subject in its unique individuality remains subjected. If the law itself were to become wholly individual, it would no longer stand above the subject but would merge into the latter.

If we relate the cosmonomic idea to the theoretically distinguished laws of the various spheres, then, from a Christian point of view, we must see the root-unity of these modal laws in the religious fullness of the divine law. This is the law which has been revealed and fulfilled by Jesus Christ and demands service to God from the heart with all its temporal functions. In this fundamental law the diversity of the temporal ordinances has its religious focus.

If we relate the philosophical ground-idea, in its subjective dimension (thus as the idea of the subject), to the theoretically distinguished modal subject-functions of temporal reality in its various aspects, then, from a Christian standpoint, we arrive at the idea of the religious root-community of humankind – fallen into sin in its first head Adam, and born again in Je-

---

1 *General Editor's note:* Dooyeweerd's mature conception distinguishes between *law-*

sus Christ as the second head – and to the idea of the "heart" (the soul or the spirit) as the individual religious center of human existence that participates in the community. In this religious root-unity of the entire temporal cosmos, law and subject also appear to be unbreakably correlated.

Only if you proceed from the scriptural Christian standpoint is it really possible to penetrate to the radical unity and fullness of meaning of the divine law-giving for the temporal cosmos. According to the divine plan of creation, the modal laws of all the law-spheres without exception are concentrated upon this root-unity.

Under the influence of the Greek motive of form and matter and the humanistic ground-motive of nature and freedom there arose a polar opposition between natural laws for the nonrational creation and norms, or practical laws, for humankind which is qualified by its rational nature. A search was thus made, on the one hand, for a deeper unity of all natural laws (the unity of the natural-scientific world-view, according to the modern humanistic science-ideal) and, on the other hand, for a deeper unity of all laws for human activity. So the moral law came to be identified with the absolute unity of all norms.

Scholastic theology simply took over this conception from Greek philosophy. In the framework of the Romanistic ground-motive of nature and grace, the natural moral law (*lex naturalis*), which was supposed to be imbedded in the autonomous rational nature (essential form) of humankind, was conceived as the only norm of action, and the legal norm was supposed to be only a modality of that moral law. The norms of faith were completely dismissed, along with the religious central commandment of the Christian faith, to the supernatural sphere of grace. There was no place here for irreducible, unique normative laws of a historical, social, linguistic, and economic kind.

It is for this reason that, in modern Roman Catholic scholasticism, a tendency has predominated of incorporating economics (at least in respect of the person as a subject) into ethics. Economics here refers to what the classical school proclaimed to be a natural science which is given the task of tracking down, if only in part, the unchangeable natural laws of economic activity. It was thought that this was the only way to conceive of economic activity under norms, instead of under rigid laws of nature, and once again to place humankind, rather than material things, at the center. But it was not recognized that in this way the unique modal character of the economic law-sphere was completely misconstrued.

---

side and *factual side*. At the *factual side* a further differentiation is made possible by the subject-object relation in all post-arithmetical aspects, making possible the distinction between the *factual subject-side* and the *factual object-side*. Thus the ambiguous use of the term subject – meaning both "being subjected to" and "is correlated with an object" is avoided.

In the economic law-sphere, one is subject to uniquely economic norms governing human actions, not the norms of morality.

The scholastic approach in Protestant theology took over from Roman Catholic scholasticism the conception of the moral law as the unity of norms of practical action. It rejected the autonomy of the natural moral law only with respect to the supernatural norms of faith and maintained a conception of the moral law identified with the Decalogue as unbreakably connected with the basic commandment of the Christian religion. However, it must be emphatically denied that the radical sense of the religious basic commandment could be thus preserved by relating the religious root-unity of the divine law exclusively to the moral law. Merely by pointing to the great cultural mandate that at the creation was given by God to humankind – "Subdue the earth and have dominion over it" (Genesis 1:28) – is enough to show that conceiving the moral law as a unity of norms cannot be scriptural. For this cultural mandate cannot in any way be reduced to the moral law. Instead it undoubtedly refers to the central religious commandment: the demand to serve God out of love, and one's neighbor with the whole heart and with all one's temporal powers. And should not the logical norms of thought, the norms of social intercourse, the norms of language, the economic, and the aesthetic norms also be related to this central commandment?

But we cannot stop with the normative aspects of the divine law-giving if we want to grasp the full radical meaning of the religious central commandment. Natural laws, for that reason, are also already dependent upon the religious central commandment. For they do not exist in themselves but, within the cosmic order of time, are unbreakably intertwined with the normative aspects of the divine law. However, the main point is that these laws of nature do not have a rigid, closed character; humankind is called to disclose them. This will become apparent from our following explorations.

The curse of humanity's fall into sin has permeated the entire cosmos because the religious meaning of the entire cosmos was concentrated in humankind. Yet it is also the case that the central religious commandment cannot be the root-unity merely of the normative aspects of the divine law-giving.

The modal law- and subject-concept, developed above, can only be understood in the light of this radical law- and subject-idea. It cannot be found within immanence philosophy. In particular, those who adopt that standpoint have lost sight of the concept of the subject, as *sujet*, as subjected to the law, because the idea of the Divine Sovereign Creator, in the integral sense of the scriptural ground-motive, does not have any place.

The law as an idea of origin is, at one point (viz., in Aristotelian scholasticism), conceived as an objective principle of reason that presents the essence (substantial form) of things and, at another, as a purely theoretical epistemological judgment concerning the coherence of sensory phenomena (for example, Newton's law of gravitation), or yet again in relation to norms of human action as ordinances that have come into being by human willing (as in the modern humanistic doctrine of science). An illustration of the latter are the positive laws of the state. Here the subject is either identified with metaphysical substance (thing in itself), or is elevated to the position of law-giver, whether in an epistemological sense (as the transcendental subject of thought in Kant), or in a moral sense (the Kantian idea of autonomous personality).

In particular, there is lacking, on the immanence standpoint, the insight that reality is given only in an unbreakable correlation of law- and subject-side, in which neither the subject-side nor the law-side can be reduced to the other.

So there came into being the rationalistic and the irrationalistic conceptions of reality discussed above which, in modern humanistic philosophy in particular, stand diametrically opposed to each other. Both conceptions are also to be found playing themselves off against each other in the science of law.

Rationalism pregnantly manifests itself in the conception that law is nothing more than a set of legal norms, and that the subjective legal fact (a fact with legal consequences), subjective right (as, for example, property right, right of ownership, the right of the buyer to expect delivery of purchased goods, etc.), and all legal patterns that in principle, according to our conception, belong to the subject-side of the jural law-sphere are able to be reduced completely to legal norms. Thus the neo-Kantian professor Hans Kelsen, whom we have already mentioned on several occasions, tells us that a subjective legal personality such as, for example, a corporation which possesses, and which appears in practice to possess, a subjective unity in the multiplicity of its members, occurs within a framework of positive legal rules that define the competence of such a corporation so as to give expression to the general rules of state law in a more concrete form. Incorporating the same approach is his remarkable conception of the state. In reality the state is a subjective community of rulers and subjects and as such functions in all of the aspects of reality. But in Kelsen the state is identical to the logical system of all positive legal rules which are left to the state for legal formation according to international law, and which are amenable to degrees of ordering from the more general to more particular forms whereby a higher law-former authorizes (delegates) a lower for more particularized concretizing of law. This line of approach is also followed in his conception of a subjective right as an authorization (delegation) by the law-giver to the one authorized for further concretizing of the abstract and general positive legal norms that are deposited in the law.

In contrast, a typical irrationalistic conception says that, in itself, the legal norm as general rule is nothing else than a worthless logical generalizing of a concrete, subjective decision in an individual legal contest.[1]

Also irrationalistic is, for example, the earlier mentioned conception of the Historical School, that a legal order is the completely individual product of a subjective, national historical spirit of a people which, originally, unconsciously, without any purposeful human forming, arises from the folk-spirit according to the analogy of a living organism.

Of course, rationalistic and irrationalistic theories of law manifest themselves in any number of varieties, depending on the philosophic denominator to which the jural aspect has been reduced. So in legal theory it is just as possible to have a biologistic, a psychologistic, or a historicist irrationalism as it is to have a psychologistic, mathematistic, or historicist-economistic rationalism.

Later on, as we deal with the basic problems of the theory of law, we shall repeatedly encounter the opposition of rationalistic and irrationalistic concepts. It is apparent even now, however, just how important the law- and subject-concept is for legal theory, as this is rooted in a philosophic ground-idea, whether or not it has become recognized by the scientific jurist.

1.10 The Cosmic Order of the Law-Spheres and the Method of Analysis of the Modal Structures

We have already seen that the law-spheres, in spite of their modal sphere sovereignty, unbreakably cohere with one another in cosmic time. By means of the cosmic order of time they are arranged in an established and irreversible order which irrevocably establishes their place in an order of succession. The question now is, How can theoretical thought trace this temporal order? It has assuredly been established that in this mode of thought we must abstract from the continuity of cosmic time in order to be able to form an articulated scientific concept of the distinguished aspects of reality.

In the meantime, it has become clear that cosmic time expresses itself in every aspect of reality, in a unique modal sense, and that the modal structures of meaning, by which the law-spheres are distinguished from each other, are themselves founded in the cosmic order of time. Thus the cos-

---

[1] The adage of the Roman jurist: *Non ex regula jus sumatur, sed ex iure quod est, regula fiat*, should certainly not be interpreted in this irrationalistic sense. Here *regula* does not mean a legal norm that holds in practice but only one that has been established a priori by theory. This adage correctly warns against attempting to deduce binding law in practice from such a theoretical rule.

mic order of time must express itself distinctly in every modal structure. And so the theoretical analysis of the modal structure of a law-sphere itself necessarily brings to light the place of that sphere in the temporal order of the law-spheres.

In part 1 of this Introduction we presented a provisional but somewhat rudimentary analysis of the complex interconnections of the jural moments of a commercial contract with all the other aspects of reality. This necessitates further clarification as to how the modal structure of the jural aspect expresses its temporal coherence with the structures of all the other aspects. It is indeed true that theoretical analysis of the modal meaning-structures can never give us a concept of the cosmic continuity in which time bridges the boundaries of the modal aspects; but it can acquaint us, albeit in a theoretical discontinuity, with the place that the law-spheres occupy in the temporal order.

We have also seen in part 1 that the science of law works with many basic concepts which also play a fundamental role in other special sciences but which, in their juristic employment, obtain a unique jural sense. So the jurist works with a unique jural concept of unity in multiplicity that apparently refers back to the concept of number in arithmetic (*arithmetica*) without itself taking on an original arithmetical sense. Think of the unity of the sale agreement in the duality of the declaration of will by the two parties. Or think of the unity of the corporate legal person in the multiplicity of its members. The science of law also works with a unique jural concept of space (the area over which legal norms hold, or the place of the legal fact which is subjected to it). It also works with a unique jural concept of cause, (on the law-side of the jural law-sphere, legal ground and legal consequence, and on the subject-side, the idea of the subjective causation of an action). These apparently point to physical causality in the aspect of movement, because cause and effect indeed presuppose movement.[1] It also operates with a unique organ- and life-concept (legal life and legal organ). This apparently points back to the organic concept of life as the basic concept of biological science. It also works with a unique jural concept of will and will-capacity (accountability) that would appear to point back to the basic concepts of psychology as the special science having to do with the emotional sensory-aspect of reality. And so we could go on.

On the other hand, we discovered, for instance, how the internal connection with the moral aspect expresses itself within the jural aspect. The Hoge Raad, for example, employed the concept "moral obligation" as the source of a natural bond. We have already seen that "moral obligation," in that context cannot be meant in the original sense of the moral aspect, but

---

1 *Editor's note:* See note on p.14.

instead must evidently be understood in a unique jural sense that was not further defined by the Court.

It will be clear, at the same time, that within the modal structure of the jural aspect the internal connection with the aspects of quantity, space, movement, organic life, feeling, the logical-analytical, the historical, etc., must be different from, for instance, the internal connection with the moral aspect.

It is indeed easy to conceive of a legal system in which this connection has not yet come to expression. Primitive legal systems account for morality in general as an order distinct from that of law. They are completely formalistic, that is to say, they allow a binding undertaking to arise exclusively from the juristic form of a legal fact. Consider, for example, the words that are used at the time of an agreement or other symbolic forms, which here often have a specifically religious meaning; they bind the parties strictly to these forms. In such a formalistic conception there is, of course, no place for investigation of legal phenomena such as guilt, good faith, good morals, admissible cause, moral obligation etc., that is to say, all those legal configurations in which the internal relationship between law and morality is expressed.

By contrast, one discovers in such primitive legal systems that of necessity the internal connection with the aspects of number, space, movement, organic life, etc., are given jural expression. Primitive criminal law, for instance, is based on the principle of *Erfolgshaftung*, that is to say, it discovers its measure of criminal punishment exclusively in the seriousness of the illegal act's effect. It thus acknowledges of necessity jural causality, but the jural concept of guilt does not have any place here.

If the fundamental concept of law, in which we attempt to understand the modal structure of the jural aspect in a synthetic way, is truly to establish a trustworthy guide for the science of law, then this structural framework must be incorporated theoretically into that concept of law. And it has already been shown that the current methods of juridical concept-formation fall miserably short in this respect.

From the standpoint of my own cosmonomic idea how is it possible to grasp the modal structure of law?

The modal structure of a law-sphere is, as we saw, an architectonic unity in the diversity of its structural moments. How can the unity be maintained here in the theoretically analyzed diversity? It is only because none of the moments stand on the same level, but are incorporated into a truly architectonic structure in which the cosmic temporal order of the aspects, and thus the place of each aspect in the mutual coherence of the aspects, expresses itself in the unique modal meaning of the aspect in question.

In addition, according to our cosmonomic idea, it must be the case that the original and irreducible character of the aspect is preserved, whilst, at the same time, the internal structural interconnections with all the rest of the aspects come to expression. This is only possible because in the modal structure there is a nuclear[1] moment that has an original meaning for this aspect alone. This nuclear moment impresses on all the rest of the structural moments its irreducible meaning, whilst, at the same time, some of the remaining moments point back in sequential order to the original nuclear moments that have an earlier place in the cosmic order and others sequentially point forward to the original nuclear moments or aspects that have a later place in the cosmic order of time.

Here there are two directions in the cosmic order of time, namely, a retrocipatory and an anticipatory direction. Both of them find their expression within the modal structure of the law-spheres.

Henceforth we shall call the nuclear moment that qualifies the modal structure of a law-sphere the "modal meaning-nucleus." The modal meaning-nuclei that point backwards we shall call "modal analogies" or "retrocipations." Those that point forward to later modal meaning-nuclei we shall call "modal anticipations."[2] And so we can describe the previously indicated directions in the cosmic order of time, respectively, as the retrocipatory (or founding) and the anticipatory directions.

It will then be clear that in the temporal order of the law-spheres there must be two limiting spheres, one of which can have no modal retrocipations in its modal structure, and the other can have no modal anticipations. One of the limiting spheres is that of quantity (number) because no aspects precede the aspect of number in the order of time. The other limiting sphere is that of faith (pistis) because no aspects succeed this law-sphere.

The analogies, as well as the anticipations, within the modal structures of the law-spheres remain qualified by the modal meaning-nucleus of the sphere in question. Therefore they do not assume the original meaning of the law-sphere to which they point back or of the law-spheres to which they point forward.

Furthermore, the fewer the number of analogies within the modal structure of a law-sphere the greater the number of anticipations there are. In this fashion the cosmic temporal structure of the aspects is pregnantly revealed and the place of each law-sphere in the order of the aspects can thus be analyzed.[3]

---

1 *Editor's note:* The term *kern* can also be translated in its literal sense as "kernel" or "core."

2 *Editor's note:* In his later works Dooyeweerd gave more precision to this categorization by acknowledging that both retrocipations and anticipations are sub-categories of the general category, analogies.

3 *Editor's note:* In the version of Dooyeweerd's *dictaat* used for this volume there followed a paragraph that appears to be misplaced. This is because it inexplicably interrupts the discussion of analogies with a general unrelated observation on the

As long as the modal anticipations in the structure of a law-sphere have not been realized we say that the law-sphere is still in a closed state. The anticipations disclose and deepen the meaning of the aspect because they approach the meaning of a later aspect. So it is clear that if the law begins to disclose its moral anticipations this must mean a very significant deepening of the meaning of law. One need only compare the above mentioned principle of *Erfolgshaftung* or primitive criminal law with the modern principle of punishment according to guilt.

Subsequently, we shall see that by this means the connection with the structures of the earlier aspects will also be deepened. The law-spheres that precede a particular law-sphere in the order of time will be called the substratum spheres of that particular law-sphere. The law-sphere in question is founded in these substratum spheres.

It will be clear then that a law-sphere has as many substratum spheres as it has analogies (retrocipations) present in its modal structure. To be precise, the analogical moments of meaning point back to the modal meaning-nuclei of earlier law-spheres. Every modal analogy is itself founded in the original meaning-nucleus of that law-sphere to which it ultimately points back.

Thus the first major undertaking of a true encyclopedia of the science of law, namely, to indicate the place that the jural aspect of reality assumes within the temporal coherence of the aspects, can now be actually commenced in a scientific fashion. And at the same time we have an indication of the only possible method whereby jural concept-formation can be put on a basis that is truly fruitful and free from arbitrariness. The basic concept of law must theoretically embrace the modal meaning of the jural law-sphere. And this modal meaning can only be found within the context of the entire temporal coherence of the modalities. At the same time, however, we encounter the internal limits of any theoretical definition.

In theoretical analysis of the modal structure of law, we can never go further than to theoretically differentiate the various structural moments that are qualified by the modal meaning-nucleus of the jural aspect. As we unify these moments synthetically into the fundamental concept of law, we shall inevitably encounter this irreducible modal meaning-nucleus that governs the meaning of the analogical and anticipatory moments. It is impossible to provide a more precise logical-analytical account of this meaning-nucleus because, within it, the modal sphere sovereignty of the jural

---

effect of the ground-motive of immanence philosophy on its account of the structure of reality! It could perhaps have been located at the beginning of the analysis of the analogical structure of the jural aspect of reality. The omitted paragraph reads: "Lacking a distinction between theoretical and pretheoretical presuppositions, the religious ground-motive within immanence philosophy constantly set itself in the place of true scientific investigation of the structure of reality. (Compare what was said above regarding the Historical School's concept of law.)"

aspect asserts itself over against the logical aspect. Every attempt to reduce this unique nuclear moment to something else produces completely indeterminate and therefore theoretically useless concept-formation. The modal meaning-nucleus of the aspect to be defined is thus the limit of all theoretical determination.

But this meaning-nucleus is only able to reveal its meaning in its unbreakable interconnection with the analogical and anticipatory moments, which bring to expression the connection of the jural aspect with all other aspects in the structure of law itself. The task of scientific concept-formation therefore is to analyze these moments theoretically in order to grasp them synthetically in connection with the modal meaning-nucleus.

We want now to demonstrate our method of analysis of the modal structure in relation to certain nonjuridical law-spheres, not only to show the reader that it is indeed of universal, encyclopedic significance, but also because it is necessary to obtain a proper insight into the structure of the remaining aspects if one wants to attain genuine insight into the structure of the jural aspect.

The first example to be chosen is the modal structure of the aspect of number. As already observed, this law-sphere (in the retrocipatory direction of time) is the first limiting sphere of our temporal cosmos, because there are no law-spheres that precede it. Therefore it has no analogical (retrocipatory) moments of meaning in its modal structure. The core meaning of number is only to be found in quantity. The temporal coherence of this meaning-nucleus with those of the other law-spheres can reveal itself therefore only in the anticipatory direction of time. The first anticipatory function of number is the anticipation to the meaning-nucleus of space.

In its structure, yet to be opened in an anticipating direction, number manifests itself in the natural or rational numerical values (the finite numbers). In its own modal meaning, however, number can approximate the modal sense of space, and therein reveals its first anticipatory function. The modal meaning-nucleus of space is continuous extension. In order to make clear how number, in its own modal sense of discrete quantity, can approximate continuous extension, consider a straight line on which there are two nonidentical points A and B. If we designate point A with the whole number 1 and point B with the whole number 2, then we can ascribe to each point in between a numerical value greater than 1 and less than 2. In this fashion there comes into being an infinite series of fractions which only find in 2 their limit, but which form, in the fullest sense of these words, an infinite, approximating series. These numerical functions have been called irrational because the total numerical value of the series is not able to be expressed in a finite (rational) numerical value (so, for example, $\sqrt{2}$, $\sqrt{3}$, $\sqrt{5}$, etc.). Here it is clear how discrete number approaches, within its own modal meaning, that of continuous space, without the anticipatory, irrational number functions ever taking on spatial meaning.

By contrast, we find in the modal meaning-structure of spatiality, analogies of (retrocipations to) the meaning-nucleus of number, both as to its law-side and its subject-side.

The modal meaning-nucleus of space is, as we saw, continuous extension. But there can be no continuous extension apart from dimensions or magnitudes in which it reveals itself.[1] Space may be of two, three, or more dimensions, but in its meaning-moment of dimensionality it still presupposes number. It appears therefore that at the law-side dimension is an analogy of number within the meaning of space. For dimensions are not themselves subjective spatial patterns, but only ways of ordering them. They are regular[2] determinations of those patterns. On the subject-side of space, the analogy of number reveals itself in the spatial point which always presupposes two intersecting straight or curved lines. Furthermore the following holds true: every spatial figure, even a one-dimensional straight line, can only function as a limited spatial figure in its delimitation by two points.

Now the modal meaning of space also displays anticipations, in the first place, towards the meaning of movement. In the original sense of space no movement is possible.[3] Space has a static character. A spatial figure can only exist in the simultaneous extension of its parts. In space, in its original meaning, there can therefore never be succession in movement's original meaning. But it is indeed possible for the various spatial positions of the figures to come so close to each other that the difference becomes infi-

---

1 *General Editor's note*: Dimension is a numerical analogy at the law-side and magnitude is a numerical analogy at the factual side of the spatial aspect. Although modern topology handles spaces without points, it still has to assume many local pieces (compare the "locale model of spaces" as explained by Mac Lane) and thus analogously reflects the primitive numerical meaning in the acceptance of a multiplicity of "objects."

2 *General Editor's note*: Although the Dutch text employs the word *"wetmatige"* in the phrase, *"wetmatige bepalingen"* (lit. law-conformative determinations/determinations conforming to a law), it does not make sense to translate it as such in this context. The problem is not merely one of language choice. In general, Dooyeweerd identifies the *universal side* of factual reality–evinced in the *law-conformative* (*wetmatige*) functioning of entities, processes and societal relationships–with the *law-side* of reality (the *law for* entities which determines and delimits the orderliness/regularity [*wetmatigheid*] of whatever is subjected to law). The untenability of this identification is evident in this case, because whereas it is clear that he has the *law for* spatial figures (that is, spatial *subjects*) in mind, his said identification causes him to use the term *"wetmatige"* which actually refers to the subject-side of reality. Any direct translation of this passage will highlight the incorrect identification of *law for* with *law-conformity of*.

3 The contrary conception rests on a scientifically unjustifiable confusion of space

nitely small. Think only of the continual increase of the number of sides of a polygon through which the circumference of the polygon increasingly approximates that of a circle. In a broader sense, in projective geometry and especially in so-called set theory, one speaks of transformations. In such cases, however, one should not be thinking of movement in the original sense of the word, any more than in the "movement" of points, straight-lines, corners, planes, etc. Here it is only a case of approximating concepts which comprise the anticipation to movement within the modal meaning of space.

In the modal structure of number, we also find an anticipation to the modal meaning of movement, namely, in the differential functions of number, which serve to approach the relationship between two variables to infinitely small differences (the differential quotient), in connection with which the one quantity (the function) is considered to be dependent on the other.

In the modal structure of the aspect of movement, in which again the meaning-nucleus is irreducible, there is involved, again of necessity, a numerical as well as a spatial analogy, both as to the law-side and also as to the subject-side of the law-sphere. According to the law-side, the spatial analogy expresses itself here in the direction of movement (the analogy of the spatial dimension). As to the subject-side, the spatial analogy is given in the field of movement of energy-mass, which, in the subject-object relation, is related to the objective space of movement (physical world-space). In modern physics since Einstein, it has been established that the properties of physical space are determined by matter as moving mass. From this it is immediately clear that this physical space cannot be identical with space in its original meaning, as the field of investigation of abstract geometry. The numerical analogy in the modal sense of movement, on the law-side, already resides in the moment of the direction of movement (one or more directions of movement), while it reveals itself, on the subject-side of this law-sphere, in the degree of the velocity of movement (impetus).

In the modal meaning-structure of the biotic law-sphere which comprises the organic aspect of reality (life), we discover an analogy of movement in the development of life. This analogy of necessity presupposes the movement of growth and, in its turn, metabolic movement. It also presupposes a spatial analogy in the organic bio-milieu as the biotic response-field of the living organism, and a numerical analogy in the nuclear meaning of the organic aspect which always presupposes a multi-

and movement in their original sense with the sensory-psychical space-and-movement image, i.e., with the analogies of space and movement in the modal meaning of the psychical aspect, of which we shall speak later on.

plicity of life-functions. All these analogies reveal themselves on the law-side as well as on the subject-side.

In the modal structure of the psychical law-sphere, in which the sensory aspect of reality is contained, we discover a biotic analogy in feeling-life that always rests on a bio-organic foundation; a kinematic analogy in the moment of emotion (feeling-movement); a spatial analogy in the feeling of space and in objective perceptual space (visual, tactile, and auditory space); a numerical analogy in sensory multiplicity. These analogies also reveal themselves both on the law-side and the subject-side.

In the modal structure of the logical law-sphere, in which the analytical aspect of reality is determined and which is qualified by the meaning-nucleus of the analytical aspect (logical distinguishing), we discover a sensory analogy in logical representation that fixes the analytical qualities of a thing simply in an image, that is, the pre-theoretical concept which is still rigidly bound to sensory impressions. This is a biotic analogy in the logical life of thought that rests on a bio-organic basis (namely, the functions of the brain) but which is nonetheless bound to the logical laws of thought, a kinematic analogy expressed as the movement of thought (logical process) which on the law-side is subject to the normative principle of sufficient ground.[1] This is a spatial analogy expressed as logical thought-space in which we analytically place side by side the logical multiplicity of conceptual attributes (numerical analogy) and bind them to a logical unity (analytical synthesis). In contrast we discover in the modal structure of the psychical law-sphere, which delimits the sensory aspect of reality, a logical anticipation in logical feeling.

How can we now, in the analysis of the modal meaning-structure, determine whether a meaning-moment, which is thereby disclosed, has a retrocipatory or an anticipatory character? For this purpose we must proceed from the modal structure in its still closed form, from the primary configuration of this structure in which the anticipatory moments do not yet reveal themselves, or, as we shall say from this point on, in which the anticipatory spheres are still closed. In contrast, we speak of disclosed or deepened configurations of a modal structure, when anticipatory moments of meaning display themselves within that structure. Thus in its closed configuration the modal structure only reveals itself in the unbreakable coherence of its meaning-nucleus and its retrocipations (analogies), although in the case of the numerical law-sphere, of course, in its meaning-nucleus alone. If a law-sphere indeed has substratum-spheres, then its modal meaning can never express itself apart from them. There-

---

[1] The principle of sufficient ground demands that there be sufficient logical grounds for every logical inference. Logical movement of thought reveals itself in every inference in which there is a progression from grounds to a conclusion. Thus in the deductive syllogism: (i) All men are mortal; (ii) Socrates is a man; (iii) Socrates is mortal.

fore the simplest form of its meaning-structure is given in the interconnection of nucleus and retrocipations.

Number reveals itself in its still-closed structure through its rational functions.[1] By contrast, in its opened structure, it reveals itself through its irrational functions, its differential functions, its imaginary functions, etc.

Thus movement, in its yet-to-be-opened structure, reveals itself in the natural gravitation of inorganic matter. In its opened structure, contrastingly, it reveals itself in motions of the metabolism directed by the organic function of life. Thus feeling reveals itself in its closed structure as the purely sensory feeling-life of the animal, but in its disclosed structure, in human feeling-life in which the normative feelings, such as logical feeling, cultural feeling, lingual feeling, social feeling, economic feeling, aesthetic feeling, jural feeling, feelings of love and hate, the feeling of assurance (feeling of faith) have developed themselves.

By proceeding then from the closed configuration of the modal meaning-structures, we discover the criterion for discerning whether a modal moment of meaning manifests the character of an analogy (retrocipation) or an anticipation.

So in the analysis of the modal meaning-structure of the logical law-sphere, it immediately appears that in the temporal order this law-sphere must precede the historical law-sphere, the lingual law-sphere, the economic, the jural law-sphere, etc. In the closed structure of the logical function of thought there is as yet no trace of the meaning-moment of logical control over form. The latter initially displays itself in disclosed theoretical thought wherein the systematic concept, which conceives matter in a scientific fashion, makes its entrance. In the pretheoretical concept which is still rigidly bound to sensory impressions, this anticipatory meaning-moment is lacking. The nontheoretical concept is still bound to sensory perception and does not acquaint us with the systematic coherence of phenomena. With such a concept we do not achieve logical control over the material. We shall now become acquainted with a historical anticipation in the moment of logical formative control, for the modal meaning-nucleus of the historical aspect is the cultural in the sense of free, controlling form-giving.

It is for this reason that the pretheoretical, logical aspect of thought as such does not have a history, while scientific thought definitely does have a history. Science certainly has its historical development. So also in the closed structure of the logical aspect of thought there is no trace of logical symbolism, in which logical analysis points forward in an anticipating

---

1 *General Editor's note:* A closer analysis of the meaning of number indeed reveals that fractions (the so-called rational numbers) actually already anticipate the spatial whole-parts relation with its entailed infinite divisibility (echoed in the infinite divisibility of every positive rational interval).

way to the meaning of language (symbolic signification). In logical symbolization, thought frees itself from its rigid dependence on sensory representation, and it can thereby conceive its *Gegenstand* abstractly. So, for instance, the abstraction of numbers or spatial figures from concrete things, of which they appear as aspects, is already an elevation above sensorily bound representations, as is symbolical thinking oriented to the symbolical signifying meaning of number and space.

Without difficulty we also discover, in economy of thought and logical harmony of the system, specific anticipations to the modal meaning of the economic and aesthetic law-spheres respectively; but these have a modal meaning of logical analysis. The principle of economy of thought does not play a role within logical analysis in its closed structure. It is a disclosure and deepening of the logical principle of sufficient reason insofar as it demands the exclusion of all superfluous logical grounds for a particular conclusion, and thus, in a logical sense, points ahead to the principle of economic saving. Only in systematic scientific thought, in which we seek to control the field of investigation theoretically, can this principle of the economy of thought disclose itself.

The jural anticipation in logical thought, searching for the logically *justified* ground, is also lacking in the closed structure of logical analysis. By means of this anticipation we confront the phenomena to be investigated as a scientific judge and not merely with the purely receptive attitude of naive thought.

Similarly lacking in the closed structure of the logical aspect is the anticipation to the modal meaning of morality. The meaning-nucleus of the latter is love in the normative sense of *agapē*. The modal structure of the logical aspect anticipates this as theoretical eros, the "Platonic" theoretical love of knowledge as a totality-idea.

Finally, also lacking in the closed structure of the logical aspect is the anticipation of the modal meaning of faith, the nucleus of which allows itself to be tentatively described as an ultimate temporal assurance concerning the absolute ground or origin of all things. In the disclosed structure of the logical aspect, we encounter the anticipation of this meaning-nucleus in the figure of logical certainty which expresses itself in the logical axiom.

The distinction between analogy and anticipation has been illustrated by means of various examples. By applying the criterion of this distinction to the jural law-sphere we are now able to establish the position of the jural aspect within the coherence of the normative law-spheres. It is intended to limit the investigation here to the relationship of the economic to the jural aspect.

Since Marxism (at least according to its current interpretation) characterizes law as a purely ideological superstructure upon the historical-economic structure of society and only allows law to be its ideological expression, there has been much debate about the question as to whether the economic order in fact determines the juridical order or whether, on the contrary, the legal order is foundational for all economic relationships.

The earlier-mentioned neo-Kantian legal scholar, Rudolf Stammler, was of the opinion in his *Wirtschaft und Recht nach der materialistischen Geschichtsauffassung* [Economics and Law according to the materialistic conception of History] (4th ed., 1921) that Marxism could be refuted by means of his doctrine that the historical-economic relationships only present an in-itself-unordered experiential material which is initially ordered and determined by law (or at least by means of a rule of social behavior) as a thought-form in experience. Law is thus an a priori category that makes possible the experience of economic relationships such as human cooperative social relationships. A historical-economic structure of society therefore, cannot exist apart from a legal order. By this it is supposed to be shown that the Marxist attempt to make economic relationships the basis of law is untenable in principle.

Now, leaving aside altogether our previous rejection of the critical method of neo-Kantianism, the assertion that economic relationships cannot exist in our experience apart from a legal order is by no means decisive in answering the question whether the economic aspect of reality lies at the foundation of the jural or whether the jural is foundational for the economic. This is because, in the temporal order of the world, all of the aspects are constantly and unbreakably intertwined with each other; it is indeed the case that no aspect can exist apart from the other aspects. The question now to be addressed is whether, in this order of the aspects, the economic precedes the jural or whether the jural precedes the economic.

From a serious analysis of the modal structure of law we learn how it is possible to point to necessary economic analogies within it. As to the law-side (norm-side) of the jural law-sphere the modal meaning-nucleus of law (that we shall later discover in the meaning-nucleus of retribution) only reveals itself, even within an as-yet-undisclosed legal order, through an economic analogy that demands proportionality in the satisfaction of certain legal rights and therefore rejects allowing excessive significance to certain legal interests. Where this meaning-moment is lacking we are outside the domain of law proper. The analogy in question is an analogy of the principle of frugality as the modal nucleus of the economic aspect.

In the primitive principle of *lex talionis*, "an eye for an eye, a tooth for a tooth," there is already an attempt to avoid excess, superfluity, in criminal legal retribution – as a particular manifestation of the principle of retribution – and to keep this sanction within the limits of proportionality. The economic analogy in the meaning of law[1] is already strongly expressed where murder, for instance, is punished with the death penalty. According to the strict principle of *talio*, the punishment is carried out as far as possible in the same manner as the crime, for example, where causing disfigurement is requited with the inflicting of a similar disfigurement. Also, the submitting of successive generations' blood-vengeance to the primitive principle of retribution leads immediately to prohibition of excesses and substitution of blood-vengeance by the demand for proportionate retribution.

Later, in the systematic analysis of the modal meaning of law, we shall come to recognize necessary economic analogies on the subject-side of this law-sphere in the jural subject-object relation as it appears in the configuration of subjective right and objective legal facts.

Thus it appears that the economic analogy, which has already come to expression in primitive designations for retribution, and which in turn are derived from economic activity, is essential in the closed modal structure of law. We shall, in due course, return to this point.

Therefore it is possible to assert with confidence that the economic aspect lies at the foundation of the jural and not the other way round. From his neo-Kantian standpoint it was not possible for Stammler to pose the problem regarding the relationship of law and economics in this sense because he did not recognize the modal structure as such. Because he regarded economic relationships in human society as unordered, experiential material, he also had to deny the the modal uniqueness of the economic aspect and was forced to deny a place for economics as a distinct special science. However, historical materialism certainly cannot be refuted in this way.

1.11 Antinomies and Illegitimate Fictions in Scientific Thinking: The Fictions of Legal Method[2]

The idea of the sphere sovereignty of the various aspects of reality is not an arbitrary hypothesis. That it must truly be founded in the divinely given temporal world-order is clear from the fact that every attempt to erase the modal boundaries of meaning between the law-spheres entangles itself in antinomies. These antinomies are not simply logical in character. Logical contradictions, which are forbidden by the principle of contradiction (*principium contradictionis*), concern the logical conflict of two contradictory judgments ($A=A$, $A \neq A$), both of which cannot be true at the same time. From a logical point of view, it remains un-

---

1 *Editor's note:* See note on p. 20.
2 *Editor's note*: Legal method (*rechtstechniek*) here refers to the method or "technique" of the practice of law, especially the judicial process of deciding cases, not the "scientific" method of legal analysis.

decided as to which of the two judgments has a claim to truth. If a logical argument is in conflict with the principle of contradiction, it is illogical but not a-logical. That is to say, in spite of its illogicality, it remains within the logical aspect. A logical contradiction remains logically qualified. By contrast, the theoretical contradiction in which thought becomes entangled, because it has abolished the modal boundary of meaning between two law-spheres, manifests itself in the fact that in our thought the unique laws pertaining to these law-spheres come into substantive conflict with each other.

Conflicts arising in this way we shall call true antinomies, in contradistinction to mere logical contradictions. The latter concern the logical aspect of these antinomies. In the true antinomy there is indeed a logical contradiction; but a logical contradiction is not of itself an antinomy. Where subjective behavior comes into conflict with the laws within particular normative law-spheres there is no question of an antinomy. Thus within the jural law-sphere there is no true antinomy between justice and injustice; within the economic law-sphere, between economical and uneconomical; in the analytical (logical) law-sphere, between logical and illogical; in the moral law-sphere, between love and hate; in the aesthetic law-sphere, between beautiful and ugly, etc.

In such cases it is only a question of contrarieties,[1] which come to expression within the normative law-spheres, and which are related to the normative character of these law-spheres. All such contrarieties are founded in the post-logical law-spheres.[2] That is to say, they presuppose the logical principle of contradiction, to which we referred above, and they are to be viewed therefore as logical retrocipations in these law-spheres.[3] They remain enclosed by the modal meaning-structure of the law-sphere in question. For example, an illegal act is still jurally quali-

---

1   Editor's note: Lit. "contrary opposites" (*contraire tegenstellingen*).
2   General Editor's note: From the next sentence it is clear that Dooyeweerd actually intends to say: All such contrarieties in the post-logical law-spheres are founded in the logical aspect.
3   With respect to the contrarieties founded in logical contradiction, one must further differentiate polar oppositions, such as sick-healthy, sensitive-insensitive, desire-aversion, joy-sorrow, etc., which we come across in the non-normative law-spheres. In his *Kritik der praktischen Vernunft* (pp. 347 ff.), Leonard Nelson accounts for the difference between the two kinds of opposition as follows: "The polar oppositions, on the one hand, are only supposed to appear in connection with physical interests (*Interesse*) and have to do with inner, factual (positive) differences of psychical activity. Contrarieties, on the other hand, refer only to *Gegen-stände* of logical judgments or decisions of will but just lack the polarity that is typical of the interested activity of feeling." The restriction of polar opposition to interestedness with the desire founded in it is, in my opinion, too narrow. In reality we already discover polarity in the biotic law-sphere (life-death, sickness-health) as well. But in such oppositions as movement-rest, round-square, we do not find any such polarity. These oppositions, to be precise, are only contrarieties in a logical sense, that is, insofar as they function in logical judgments.

fied and can only express itself within the modal structure of the jural law-sphere. By contrast, the true antinomy always reveals itself to theoretical thought in a mutual theoretical conflict between the law-spheres.

The term "antinomy" gives poignant expression to the type of theoretical contradiction we have in mind. The true theoretical antinomy arises by reason of the fact that thought sets itself in opposition to the cosmic order that regulates the mutual interrelation and coherence of the law-spheres.

This kind of antinomy is contradicted by the temporal cosmic world-order. Therefore the acceptance of the cosmic order of time as a temporal order of law, from a Christian standpoint, necessarily leads to recognition of the principle of the excluded antinomy as a cosmological principle of thought.

In the light of our preceding investigations, we must make it clear that the immanence standpoint inexorably leads theoretical thought into antinomies. Kant attempted to explain the theoretical antinomies as the result of transgressing the limits of possible human experience by theoretical thought. This attempted explanation, however, is inadequate because Kant makes the unwarranted identification of empirical reality with what is perceptible by the sense, as it is supposed to be ordered in a priori forms of consciousness, that is, forms of consciousness which found the very possibility of experience. It is impossible, however, for any of the law-spheres to fall outside the range of possible human experience. This is the case because temporal reality presents itself to human experiencing only in an unbreakable meaning-coherence of all the modal aspects. Every limitation of the totality of empirical reality to particular aspects of it rests on a theoretical abstraction that can never be squared with naive experience. If theoretical thought denies the modal aspects' sphere sovereignty, it always runs the danger of dissociating the modal analogies and anticipations that reside in the structure of a law-sphere from their appropriate meaning-nucleus. Instead, they are conceived in terms of the central meaning of the modal aspects to which they either point back or forward.

So, for instance, the Logicist School of mathematics attempts to reduce the mathematical to the logical aspect of reality with the aim of proclaiming logical multiplicity, which is included in each concept as a summation of logical characteristics, to be the origin of number. But, as we saw earlier, logical multiplicity is only a numerical analogy and presupposes the original meaning of number. The latter therefore can never be deduced from it.[1]

---

[1] *General Editor's note:* It is remarkable to note that the foremost mathematician of the twentieth century, David Hilbert, clearly pointed to this "catch 22" entailed in the logicist attempt to deduce the meaning of number from that of the logical-analytical mode. In his *Gesammelte Abhandlungen* Hilbert writes: "Only when we analyze attentively do we realize that in presenting the laws of logic we

Thus the Logicist School also attempted to construe space, in a purely logical manner, out of the continuous logical progression of one point of thought to another. As a consequence, logical thought-space, that is, the logical analogy of space, was elevated to the origin of geometrical space.¹ As a final consequence, the modal boundaries of number, space, movement, and logical analysis were completely obliterated with respect to one another. There arose, however, at the same time, theoretical antinomies which higher mathematics has tried without success to resolve. If an attempt is made to construct a continuum logically out of points, the points are thereby eliminated.

Such points were already known to the Greek philosophers. Zeno, the student of Parmenides, thought he could demonstrate that in reality movement and multiplicity cannot exist because the spatial distance that must be traversed in passing between two points is infinitely divisible, and it is impossible in reality to pass through an infinite number of points. In point of fact, he merely offered a strict proof of the mutual irreducibility of number, space, and movement.

So also in the science of law many antinomies have arisen because the boundaries between the jural and the other law-spheres have not been taken into account in the theoretical formation of concepts.

By way of a preliminary introduction we mention several examples:

Example 1
In the modal meaning of law there is an analogy of space, which manifests itself, as to its law-side, in the area of validity of legal norms and, as to its subject-side, in the location of a legal fact.

Within the framework of a naturalistic conception of reality, the attempt is made to interpret these spatial analogies as sensorily perceptible spatial relationships and thus to dissociate them from the meaning-nucleus of law. Now the spatial image of a thing or of an event is objectively given in sense perception in relation to possible subjective sense experience. Remember what we have said about the subject-object relation. I observe, for example, how a bullet fired from the barrel of a gun takes a certain trajec-

---

already had to employ certain arithmetical basic concepts, for example the concept of a set and partially also the concept of number, particularly as cardinal number [Anzahl]. Here we end up in a vicious circle and in order to avoid paradoxes it is necessary to come to a partially simultaneous development of the laws of logic and arithmetic" (*Analysis, Foundations of Mathematics, Physics, and Diverse Life History*, 2nd ed., vol. 3 [Berlin/New York, 1970], 199).

1 A beginning was made from the point as a supposed *Denksetzung* in logical space. Logical thought was supposed to construct a continuum by way of the continuous process of the movement of thought. It is evident here how spatial continuity is explained as a logical continuity of thought, movement as a logical movement of thought.

tory and finally strikes its target. By accurate subjective perception we experience the objective spatial image of this event.

Undoubtedly, the location of a thing or of an event can also be a datum in a jural sense, for instance, the place which a piece of land, as a legal object, occupies. This objectively given location, quite properly, has a jural meaning because it falls within a legal system's sphere of validity. The legal order, which subsumes legal relationships, depends on this fact. The relevant legal order will be that under which the piece of land functions as a legal object. But it is by no means always the case that the location of an act is objectively given in a jural sense.

Consider, for example, the legal fact to which we referred earlier, where an Amsterdam merchant places an order by telephone for a shipment of grain from a company located in Berlin. Now where did this agreement come into being? That aspect of the mutual action of the contracting parties which is susceptible to sense perception cannot give an objective clue to the solution because, as a subjective legal fact, the agreement is not able to be perceived by the senses. Yet, according to traditional doctrine, the answer to this question concerning the location of the agreement's formation depends on the issue: under whose civil law, the German or the Dutch, must the agreement be determined? The most diverse theories have been advanced to solve this question. According to some, the agreement is formed at the place where the shipment is arranged. According to others, it is where the shipment is received. According to yet a third point of view, both places are supposed to qualify as the place of formation.

The last theory, at least, approaches most closely to fixing the place of the transaction with respect to that side of it which is perceptible to the senses. But jurally viewed, it immediately leads to an antinomy. To be precise, it eliminates the jural unity of the agreement as a legal transaction and dissolves it – in conflict with its jural character – into two independent declarations of will. It may indeed be the case that the circumstances require that different parts of the agreement be judged according to different systems of law; but then the place of the agreement, of which there can only be one, cannot itself be made the exclusive criterion.

Example 2
Within the modal meaning of law, on its law-side, an analogy of movement[1] lies concealed that manifests itself in the legal consequences of a legal fact determined by the legal norm, and, on its subject-side, in the subjective (that is, the subjective-objective) causation of this fact.

According to the naturalistic conception of reality, subjective jural causality was conceived in a natural-scientific sense. In a consistent applica-

---

1   *Editor's note:* See note on p. 14.

tion of this natural-scientific concept of causality as factors in a causal chain, human acts were placed on the same level as natural phenomena, such as a flash of lightning or a falling stone. Human acts were simply incorporated into this causal chain as preconditions of the necessary occurrence of the effect in question, an effect that would not have occurred if these conditions had not been present. Thus the acts were interpreted according to the theory of *condicio sine qua non*.

However, this naturalistic concept of causality in the science of law necessarily leads to antinomies because it destroys any basis for jural accountability. If, for instance, the premeditated firing of a revolver by a murderer is only a link in a causal chain leading to the death of the victim, it functions at the same level as the mechanical motion of the projectile. Given the fact that the victim happened by chance to be within shooting range, then it is no longer possible to say that it was just the murderer's act which caused the death of the victim. That act is then only one of many preconditions for the occurrence of the effect.

One might just as well point to the acts of conception by grandparents and parents which led to the birth of the murderer as a cause of the effect that took place, presupposing that these acts of conception in their entirety could be treated as natural causal factors. For apart from these acts of conception the culprit would not have been present at all! Why therefore is the event solely attributed to that person?

In a natural-scientific chain of cause and effect, it is possible to enumerate an entire series of "conditions" that are equivalent to each other. Jural accountability, by contrast, is only possible if a human act can be regarded as the free cause of the event that has taken place. This can never be so if this behavior is only a link in a natural causal chain. If causality in a jural sense were identical with causality in a physical sense, then the basis for jural accountability would have been destroyed. It is clear, however, from the legal pattern of *causa omissionis*, that jural causality can only exist in an unbreakable connection with jural accountability.

By the mere dereliction of duty, by sitting still and doing nothing when it was appropriate to act, it is possible to cause damage in a jural sense. Think, for example, of a railroad worker who falls asleep at the switchpoint and whose dereliction of duty causes a train accident. This is not simply a question of fault divorced from any causal connection.

We shall see at a later point how fault in a jural sense presupposes the jural causation of the blameworthy acts. But the concept of causality in physics is only able to take account of positive functions of movement.[1] Negative conditions can never be causal in a physical sense. It is indeed the case that jural causality cannot exist, that it has no meaning, apart from

---
1   See note on p. 14.

the substratum of causality in the original sense of physical movement. But the sense that is original to the physical aspect is only an analogy in the subjective legal sense and must as such be qualified by the meaning-nucleus of law. If there is an obliteration of the modal boundaries of meaning between jural causality and causality in the original sense of physical movement, antinomy is unavoidable.

Example 3
A psychical analogy within the jural aspect is inseparable from the modal meaning of law. It is manifested, for instance, on the law-side, in the will of the law-former and, on the subject-side, in the jural will of the accountable legal subject who is subject to the legal norm. There is no possibility, however, of reducing this jural meaning of will to the psychical function of will in the sense of an emotional desire accompanied by the feeling that you are freely able to reach the desired goal.

This is clear from the following example. In the Netherlands, a statute comes into existence through the cooperation of the States General[1] and the Crown. Then a Bill is presented in the Second Chamber by Royal Proclamation. This Bill, assuming it has not been introduced by a member of the Chamber, having been drafted within one of the ministerial departments, is dealt with in the Cabinet, and in the meantime the advice of the Council of State is sought. During the deliberations of the Lower (First) Chamber, different members invoke their right to amend the Bill. Possibly contrary to the intention of the minister concerned and of other dissenting members of the Chamber, the Bill is then altered and amended. Finally, the Bill obtains approval, not because every individual member of the Chamber desires it in this form, but on the basis of a majority vote. If the Bill is of a highly technical nature, one can be certain that a large number of members of the Chamber who are not at home in this area, or who do not show any interest in it, are not likely to be familiar with its contents, although they vote for it, nonetheless. The Bill then goes to the Upper (Second) Chamber where it is passed. The last step occurs when the Crown gives its sanction to the Bill, whereby it is elevated to the status of law. Subsequently, the enactment is promulgated by publication in the Statute Book. This statute, in the form according to which law is created, is truly a declaration of the will of the legislature directed towards the formation of law (compare the Supreme Court decision, November 12, 1900, W.7525 in which the statute is expressly mentioned: "the intention of the legislators expressed in the text"). Thus the preamble of each Dutch law states: "Whereas We have taken into consideration that ... be it known that We,

---

1   *Editor's note:* i.e., Parliament.

having heard the Council of State, and in consultation with the States General, have thought fit and decreed, as we think fit and decree hereby ..."[1]

However, anyone should be able to see that this proclamation expressing the will of the law-giver is not identical with the factual psychical wishes and desires of the Queen and the members of the States General. It is a will in a normative, juristic sense, the content of which in due course obtains a more precise determination in the application of the statutory enactment. Nevertheless, the statute as a declaration of will that is constitutive of law is always attributed to the will of the legislator. Yet any attempt to explain the will of the law-giver as a will in a psychical sense necessarily entangles itself in antinomies. It then becomes necessary to speak of a psychical willing that is independent of the psychical, perceptual image and of the factual psychical desires and wishes of the persons involved, thus of willing that is in conflict with a truly psychical willing. On the other hand, one senses that the will of the law-giver, as a constant jural ordering, would be impossible if indeed it were fundamentally dependent upon subjective individual sensations, subjective desires, and representations of the persons involved in the task of preparing the law.

Consider also the following example: An ordinary person wants to purchase a life insurance policy. An insurance agent visits the person and explains the practical advantages of this or that policy. Finally, the person chooses one and receives an extensive printed policy full of clauses of which the insured understands little or nothing, if the time is taken to read them. In a juridical sense an agreement of will extends to the contents of the entire contract. But it cannot be maintained that the content of the juridical will is identical with the actual psychical content of the intentions of the contracting parties.

When the psychologistic theory of will in legal science all too obviously comes into conflict with the normative demands of law, it makes use of fictions in order to disguise the antinomies in which it has become entangled by reason of its elimination of the modal boundaries between a jural and a psychological concept of will.

Ernst Zitelmann, for instance, who is one of the best known adherents of this theory, introduced in his *Irrtum und Rechtsgeschäft* the concept of an unconscious psychological will in order to make the psychological concept of will useful for juristic purposes. In point of fact, it is clear that an unconscious psychological will is a pure fiction to which nothing corresponds on the psychical side of reality. For though the unconscious plays an important role in modern psychology, the psychological concept of the unconscious does not in any way correspond to the jural states of af-

---

[1] *Editor's note:* Compare the English text of the old article 81 of the Dutch Constitution (1972).

fairs which Zitelmann intended to accommodate within his concept of unconscious will.

Furthermore, the fiction has been an escape mechanism of long-standing in the science of law for glossing over the antinomies that have arisen because of the theoretical elimination of the boundaries between jural and nonjural data. But a fiction used in this way is a scientific untruth and is therefore inadmissible in scientific thought.

There also exists a quite different use of fiction, namely, as an aid to the practical formation of law by means of which legal norms that originally had a more restricted area of application are applied to a different situation that is considered appropriate for similar regulation.

So Roman law has an entire category of *actiones ficticiae*, that is, legal actions allowed by the praetor, by means of which the legal protection of a particular legal provision, on the basis of the old *jus civile*, applying only to Roman citizens, was extended by way of analogy to other similar legal relationships which fell outside the *actio civilis*. Of course, there can be no objection to this practical employment of the fiction.

By contrast, it is impossible to maintain the theoretical fiction because it conflicts with the demands of scientific truth. In modern legal science an attempt has been made to defend it as a constructive aid to legal method. In contradistinction to legal science, legal method is not supposed to be bound to the states of affairs given in reality but may freely operate with artificial constructions which can be utilized as if they related to real states of affairs. Such constructions of legal method are supposed to introduce a greater simplification into juristic thought because they present a shorthand account of what is an extremely complicated state of affairs; that is to say, the theoretical fiction is defended by an appeal to the principle of the economy of thought which we have come across in an earlier context.

The concept of legal personality, for example, is viewed as being such a purely technical legal construction. It is understood as constituting an organized corporation or foundation as an independent legal subject. The reasoning behind it is this: legal personality is a pure fiction of legal method. In reality, the only persons who exist are natural ones, individual people with psychological wills. At the basis of this conception, as shall be demonstrated when we systematically consider the subject of legal personality, there lies a peculiarly positivistic and individualistic view of reality that leads to jural antinomies because it does not conceive the jural aspect of reality in its proper cosmic relationship to, and coherence with, the other aspects.

An example of this reasoning is as follows: Only individual human persons have a will that is truly psychical, and are accountable and responsible for their acts. A corporation or a foundation cannot will as such and cannot be made accountable and responsible. However, a nonjural concept of will, accountability, and responsibility is being employed here. Since this unjurally defined concept comes into conflict, of course, with the juridical states of affairs, an attempt is made to make it serviceable for jural use by means of a technical legal fiction. Here also fiction serves to camouflage antinomies that have their origin in a theoretical distortion of the boundaries of meaning between the law-spheres. Such a use of fiction can never be justified by an appeal to the principle of economy of thought.

Rather, the true significance of the principle of economy of thought can only be appreciated when theoretical thought coincides with the requirements of scientific truth. We have done this by recognizing it as a deepening of the principle of sufficient reason. If this is not done, truth is deprived of its character as a supra-arbitrary law of thought. It is thereby made into a purely subjective indicator that consciously leads theoretical thought from the path of truth, and it becomes impossible for the theoretically inclined jurist to gain insight into the true states of affairs within the juridical field of investigation. As long as attempts are made, using technical fictions, to paper over the antinomies that emerge from the employment of concepts in the science of law that are unjuristically defined, the critical, scientific conscience is stifled and it is impossible to arrive at a self-critical insight into this indefensible way of proceeding.

PART 2

The Opening Process in the Normative Aspects of Reality: Law and History

2.1 The Sphere Universality of All the Modal Aspects and the Opening Process in the Normative Anticipatory Law-Spheres. The Relationship of Causality, Attribution,[1] Unlawfulness, and Fault[2]

The introductory investigation into the modal structure of the law-spheres acquainted us with the temporal order in which the latter are embedded. Their modal sphere sovereignty appeared to be founded, their place appeared to be determined, and their unbreakable coherence of meaning appeared to be guaranteed, in the cosmic order of time itself. The possibility of a philosophical encyclopedia that would be delivered from speculative constructions, and indeed would be considered as an indispensable foundation for a truly scientific theory, also appeared to be established by the same means. Within the modal structure of the law-sphere there was disclosed a temporal meaning-coherence with all other law-spheres guaranteed via the retrocipatory or analogical moments of meaning, on the one hand, and the anticipatory or forward-looking moments of meaning, on the other hand.

So it is possible to speak of the sphere universality of every law-sphere in accordance with its modal structure. The complete spectrum of meaning of the temporal cosmos is in principle mirrored in the modal meaning of every law-sphere.

The apparent ability of all the philosophical "isms" to be convincing is also explained in this way. For example, it is apparently possible in the abstract to carry through a psychologistic approach to all reality because the modal meaning of the sensory aspect indeed possesses sphere universal-

---

1 *Editor's note:* i.e., attribution or imputation (*toerekening*) of legal responsibility in the context of the treatment of legal "accountability" (*toerekeningsvatbaarheid*).
2 *Editor's note:* Dutch, as with German, has just the one term, *schuld*, to refer to both criminal and noncriminal blameable conduct. English-speaking (common law) jurisdictions for the most part, however, speak of "guilt" only in relation to criminal offences and of "fault" in connection with noncriminal (tortious) conduct. For the sake of economy "fault" here is used to cover, as Dooyeweerd intends, both criminal and noncriminal or civil wrongful conduct. Elsewhere, *schuld* is variously translated as "fault" or "guilt," depending on the context.

ity, that is to say, it exhibits the analogies and anticipations of the modal meaning of all the other aspects. Nevertheless, although psychologism apparently ascribes such high honor to the sensory law-sphere by exalting it as the "be all and end all" – compare the statement of Goethe's Faust, "*Gefühl ist alles*" (feeling is everything) – this absolutization not only means an immense impoverishment of the meaning of temporal reality taken in its entirety but at the same time an impoverishment of the sensory law-sphere itself. A modal aspect, such as feeling, can only retain its meaning character in its coherence with the rest of the modal aspects. This is consistently misunderstood on the immanence standpoint.

Now we saw earlier how the modal meaning of a law-sphere is able to manifest itself within concrete things, events, etc. in two forms: (i) a primary form, in which the anticipatory moments of the law-sphere are still closed and the modal meaning in its analogical moments remains rigidly bound to its founding aspects; (ii) a deepened or opened form, in which the law-sphere develops its anticipatory connections with the aspects of reality that come later in the order of time.

Thus we could say that in a primitive legal system retributive punishment still manifests itself in a closed form. Consistently, the gravity of the offense is only weighed in respect of the causal moments relating to its factual consequences that take place in the external world (the principle of *Erfolgshaftung*). We discovered within the meaning of law an analogy of physical causality (founded in the aspect of movement). In contrast, as the meaning of retributive punishment is deepened, the principle of punishment based on guilt arises.

Guilt, in a criminal legal sense, reveals an anticipation of guilt in the moral sense of the lack of a loving attitude, an attitude that can reveal itself in various relationships such as the love of country, love of parents and children, love of truth, love in general of one's neighbor, etc. As one weighs criminal legal guilt on the scales of retribution, penal retribution in its proper sense approximates the moral attitude of the agent. The meaning of retribution is therefore opened up and deepened.

An anticipation deepens modal meaning with respect to both its nucleus and its analogies[1]; thus it can never be conceived apart from them. Therefore, in the theory of criminal law, it is a mistake to treat the elements of jural causality, unlawfulness, and guilt, as is sometimes done, apart from, or even in opposition to, each other. The three basic concepts of criminal law: unlawfulness, guilt, and causality, belong together within the meaning of law. Guilt deepens the meaning of the offense with respect to its unlawfulness as well as its causality.

---

1 *Editor's note:* See note 2 on p. 103.

The principle of guilt, the principle of punishment according to guilt, does not invalidate the significance of the actual consequences of the offense; but it has become generally recognized that the jural damage which is caused by an unlawful act, in a legal community, is more weighty if, for example, it is done intentionally and with immoral motives than if guilt is lacking on the part of the agent. It is further acknowledged, at least in general, that the act is punishable only if guilt is present.

Precisely because the anticipatory phenomenon of guilt can never be conceived apart from the analogical moments in its modal meaning-structure, it becomes apparent that it must be conceived in a double meaning-relationship: (i) in a connection with the meaning of the spheres on which law is founded, and (ii) in a connection with the meaning of the anticipated sphere.

The situation is such that this multi-faceted relationship of jural guilt with the nonjural aspects expresses itself in modal analogies within the meaning of law itself. Thus it is impossible to conceive the jural meaning of guilt apart from the analogical moments of meaning in the modal structure of law. Jural guilt successively delimits its meaning through its connections with these analogical moments.

First is the connection with jural causality. Jural causality is an analogy of causality in the original sense of the aspect of movement. But causality itself can only reveal its jural meaning in its meaning-coherence with all of the subsequent analogical moments according to the sequential order that is prescribed by cosmic time.

Something can only be causal in a jural sense, whether it be as subjective behavior or whether as an objective legal fact, if it intrudes into legal life. What, however, is legal life? It is a biotic analogy within the meaning of law that can only reveal its jural meaning in a sequence of connections with all of the subsequent analogical moments. We discover the first more precise specification of meaning in the sensory (psychical) analogy of the will which can be held accountable. The life of law is a jural life of will in which every causal intervention is attributed to a will that is able to be held accountable. There is therefore no jural causality, in a subjective sense,[1] attributable to a will that is not capable of being held accountable.

Accountability itself, however, points beyond the sensory sphere of analogies to the logical sphere. Jural accountability is impossible apart from a relation to the logical principle of sufficient ground. Accountability presupposes a logical judgment that is sufficiently grounded logically. It can only relate to subjects who themselves are able to make logical distinctions. It presupposes in the first place a distinction between what in

---

1 We shall later speak of objective causality in connection with the juristic principle of risk.

law is and is not permitted, between lawfulness and unlawfulness. These are also logical analogies in the meaning of law, which, as we have seen earlier, are founded in the logical principle of contradiction (*principium contradictionis*).

Here we see, as a matter of course, the connection between jural causality and the unlawfulness of human behavior. The former cannot be understood apart from the latter. This is immediately apparent in the case of *causa omissionis*. The reverse is also true. There is no unlawfulness without causality in a juridical sense. This will instantly become clear, if it is recalled that an action is only forbidden by law and therefore has the quality of unlawfulness attached to it because, according to the judgment of the law-maker, it intrudes, in a disturbing manner, into the balance of legal interests that must be maintained by the legal system.

However, it is in no way required that this causal intrusion into legal life should carry a factual effect with it, such as, for instance, the death or wounding of a person, the damaging or destruction of someone's property, etc. In every instance of the description of a crime, where no particular result is expressly indicated, it is sufficient for the act to be viewed as being productive of danger in a general sense. When we specifically consider the concept of jural causality, we shall deal with this matter in more detail.

According to the modern concept of legal responsibility, it makes no sense to hold an animal legally responsible for a causal process. If there is no jural causality possible in a subjective sense without the jural imputation of unlawfulness, then it makes no sense either to impute to an animal, as a subject, a causal process within legal life. Animal behavior, for example, the biting of someone by a dog, according to modern insights, can only be taken into consideration in legal life as an objective legal fact which can never be viewed apart from subjective legal facts (human acts). The question to be asked is, Who is the dog's owner?

But the qualification, "according to modern insights," already indicates that jural causality cannot be conceived apart from the historical aspect and thus must differentiate itself more specifically in a historical analogy.

Thus in the Middle Ages it was very common for animals to be brought to trial. It was thereby assumed that animals too could be held subjectively accountable for the consequences of their acts. There was also a widespread belief in the causal efficacy of witchcraft. This relationship with the level of historical development manifests itself within criminal law in the juridical description of a delict as the giving of jural form to unlawful causal behavior. For jural form-giving is an analogy of free formative control in the original historical sense of cultural development, a point to which we shall return more fully later on. Jural causality can never be understood apart from this historical analogy of jural form-giving (the definition of the crime). It specifies its juridical meaning only in unbreakable connection with that analogy.

This historical analogy is more sharply specified through the legal significance of the causal legal act. Legal significance is a lingual analogy within the meaning of law because the meaning-nucleus of the lingual aspect is that of symbolical signification. In modern legal practice there is no longer any ascription of legal significance to witchcraft, for example, necromancy and such activities involving magic. For that very reason the legal system does not ascribe any juridical causal significance to it.

By what means, however, is the jural causal significance of an act established? In the first place, via conceptions of legal intercourse, which are generally established in the definition of the crime and to which a more precise delineation is given by the sentence. Here jural causality is specified more closely in an analogy of the social aspect. With reference to the question of jural causality the point at issue is, in the last analysis, never a purely natural-scientific one. It involves the concept adopted in legal usage relating to the causal connection of an act and its consequence. This is the case, even though there is a clear indication of the influence of science when it introduces changes to the conception employed in law through the historical analogy.

These conceptions of legal intercourse obtain a more precise juristic definition by reason of the fact that in subjective jural causality there is always an invasion of legal interests which are then brought into balance by the legal system. Legal life, in the final analysis, consists of a dynamic balancing of legal interests in which every excessive pursuit of individual interest immediately involves a disruption of the jural balance, which must again be restored. We discover here an economic analogy within the meaning of law which, in turn, is further defined by the aesthetic analogy of the legal harmony of interests. Jural causality therefore must always manifest itself as an upsetting of the dynamic balance of the legal interests that have been harmonized by the legal system. On the law-side of legal life, the legal consequences of the act must counter-balance this disturbing intrusion according to the standard of the legal proportionality of retribution. In criminal law this is achieved by means of punishment, in civil law by means of compensation.

Thus far we have delineated the jural meaning of causality in terms of the successive analogies closest to it. The anticipations, however, accompany the appearance of the jural phenomenon of fault or guilt. We should adhere strictly to the following insights gained in relation to the interconnections of the relevant legal concepts: there is no fault or guilt without unlawfulness, even though unlawfulness can exist without fault or guilt; there is no unlawfulness without jural form-giving (the definition of crimes) and causality; there is no subjective causation without accountability (otherwise objective causation is involved for which the legal subject is nevertheless held accountable according to strict liability in some fashion or other); there is no subjective accountability without a will that is accountable, etc.

But, within the meaning of law, the jural configuration of fault or guilt deepens all of these elements by relating them to the moral attitude of the actor and to moral standards, and by bringing to light the subjective jural blameworthiness of the agent.

Particularly in criminal law, this requires an individual assessment of the unlawful causal behavior and thus a refinement and deepening of the standard of judgment.

It is usually the case that accountability is only thought to be a requirement of guilt (or fault) in a juristic sense, and not of unlawfulness. If one understands being accountable in a very specific sense, then this is, without doubt, correct. For if it is taken in a specific sense, subjective accountability contains within itself the possibility of the subjective blameworthiness of the will, which indeed only appears when guilt is present. Without guilt unlawfulness involves nothing more than an act in conflict with a general standard of the legal order, and this judgment of unlawfulness, in legal practice, involves ascribing a causal intervention to the agent.

Insofar as accountability comes into consideration as a requirement for establishing an unlawful causal action, it must be understood therefore in the very general sense of a requirement for imputing (attributing) an act to a jurally responsible legal subject. To be able to say that X caused a person's death by a criminal act it must be possible, in a formal juridical sense, to attribute the result to X as having been caused by X's behavior. Taken by itself this attribution does not involve even the slightest suggestion of a judgment regarding the subjective blameworthiness of the action. It is possible that the unlawful act might have been committed under circumstances excluding all guilt on the part of the actor. Therefore, as a purely modal element of the meaning of law, accountability involves nothing more than what is required in general for *this* formal jural imputation. For this reason we can say that the unlawful act is indeed the act of X which has intruded in a causal manner into legal life.

Jural attribution always presupposes accountability. But the concrete standard that is applied in this context differs in principle, on the one hand, from a purely causal judgment and a judgment that something is unlawful and, on the other hand, from the judgment of fault or guilt. And that standard is always historically determined. The determination of causation and unlawfulness proceeds on the basis of the general standard of the legal order oriented to the normal person. The judgment of guilt or fault either proceeds according to the particular standard that ought to be applied to this specific person or, where it is based on a general standard (as is often the case in civil law), in each case there is required to be exercised the degree of care that might be expected of this specific person. In the latter case, the true ascription of fault is to be found in the very application of the general norm of care to the particular case of the wrongdoer who must therefore be allowed to show absence of fault.

With reference to civil law, some writers consider responsibility to be possibly dependent upon the accountability of the actor because of the unlawfulness of an act and failure to perform agreements. In addition they also only mention accountability here solely in connection with the determination of fault. Departing from the prevailing view, they then suppose that no accountability is required for fault in these cases and that fault is determined solely according to the standard of the normal person (cf. L. C. Hofmann, *Het Nederlansche Verbintenisrecht* (1941), 318; cf. the authors cited there in note 2). This conception appears to be supported by paragraph 1, article 1483 of the Civil Code which excludes appeal to the nullity of contracts entered into by minors, or persons who are lacking mental capacity, with reference to contracts that result from the commission of a criminal offence or from an act that caused loss to another.

Nevertheless, it must be immediately clear that in these cases also we are actually talking about jural attribution and, by implication, accountability, which in a modal sense are necessarily implied in the concepts, offense and act. If a minor or a mental patient is regarded as being responsible for the injury caused to other parties by the criminal act, then there is an implicit recognition, at least with reference to civil legal accountability, that this act can be imputed to them, that in this respect therefore they are regarded as normal, responsible persons.

This would involve a fiction only if, from start to finish, accountability was only allowed to apply in a particular sense and a subjective standard was thus applied a priori.

The question of guilt or fault must be posed here in a completely different way than it is put by Hofmann and his followers who, in actual fact, allow fault or guilt to be absorbed by unlawfulness. As we have seen, where fault or guilt is established according to the general standard of care exercised by a normal person, it also presupposes accountability of the particular person who performs the act. Minors who are under parental authority or receive parental support, or the delinquent who is under a guardian, may no doubt be regarded as individually accountable with respect to unlawful or illegal acts that inflict damage, to the extent that they are able to appreciate the blameworthiness of their acts. Insofar as this is not the case, the lack of individual accountability is jurally supplemented by the actor's caregiver or guardian who, for this purpose, must be jurally one with the actor. We shall return to this point later on.

Where, however, the actor in this situation is not at fault, in the sense of negligently failing to take preventive measures, and yet the minor or the minor's guardian is still held civilly accountable, it is not possible to base this accountability on fault but only on the unlawfulness of the act and the causation of damage.

It is quite proper in the practice of civil law to require this accountability whenever an inquiry is made into the reason for considering a person other than the actor to be the one to bear responsibility for the damage. It cannot be denied that in legal decisions where articles 1401 and following of the Civil Code are applied, fault-based responsibility in practice is sometimes resolved in material unlawfulness. In such cases legal science must then conclude that the requirement of fault has indeed been set aside. Scientifically, however, it is not permissible to eliminate the boundaries between the concept of unlawfulness and that of fault.

Hence it is impossible, for example, to conceive the jural phenomenon of guilt in its criminal-legal sense in isolation from biotic, psychical, logical, historical, social, and other elements, but even less so from the blameworthy directing of the wrongdoer's will in contravention of socio-moral norms. Yet guilt retains its own normative jural sense, and is never able to be reduced to an emotional feeling impulse accompanied by a perception of the assurance or the probability (or possibility) of the causal consequences of the act (the so-called psychological concept of guilt). Nor is it able to be reduced to guilt in a moral sense (a blameworthy lack of love for one's neighbor).

According to the established jurisprudence of the Hoge Raad, the notion of the certainty or probability of the causal course of the act is found to be an inherently jural one. Hence it is never merely a psychical feeling of certainty or probability, but always a probability or certainty on the basis of an existing discernment between good and evil imputable to the wrongdoer. It finds expression in the delict as the element of a jurally blameworthy attitude of will, such as one is to conclude, according to the normative standards of legal intercourse, from the circumstances wherein the punishable fact has occurred.

Even though jural intent can never be understood apart from its connection with the sensory life of the wrongdoer, it remains, nevertheless, an intrinsically jural phenomenon.

Thus, where intent (*dolus*) is lacking and there is only culpable negligence (*culpa*), it is impossible to establish the presence of a positive emotional impulse or perception which could form the content of the concept of guilt or fault. Therefore those who attempt to apply the psychological concept of guilt to guilt of this jural type discover that they are compelled to take refuge in a theoretical fiction in order to conceal the antinomy in which they have become involved.

If, instead, *culpa*, for lack of a positive psychological point of contact, is conceived in a normative juristic sense, whereas intent involving a sense of certainty or probability, as it is said, is not so conceived, then the unity of the jural concept of guilt has been abandoned. The unacceptable conclusion would then be drawn that the more serious form of guilt (intent, *dolus*) does not, while the less serious form (*culpa*), on the contrary, does involve jural blameworthiness.

If certain psychologists are followed in seeking the sensory content of *culpa* in a lack of proper social sensitivity, it is immediately apparent that this lack of the proper social sensitivity already presupposes jural guilt or fault, because it contains an anticipation to it. To be precise, you begin to apply a normative standard which psychology can never obtain from the structure of feeling itself. Only by applying the jural concept of guilt can it truly be established that during the commission of a crime there is lacking the appropriate state in the emotional life of the offender.

It is undoubtedly true that jural guilt can only exist on the basis of a normal emotional life in the offender. The requirement that a person be held individually accountable, without which there can be no question of guilt, allows us to see this indissoluble connection between guilt or fault and feeling-life.

But in relation to criminal law, guilt retains its sphere sovereignty with its own distinctive criminal legal meaning.

From the above encyclopedic determination of the place of the jural causal relation and the juridical phenomenon of guilt or fault, we are able to draw an important methodological conclusion. This will be particularly useful later on when we embark upon a separate treatment of the problem of causality in law.

In the jural assessment of an unlawful act, whenever, and to the extent that, fault or guilt, as a requirement of civil liability or criminal responsibility, is assumed, the jural causal relation is governed by the phenomenon of fault or guilt.

The judgment of unlawfulness will be deepened by the adjudging of fault or guilt as being present and will be able to orient itself to a material criterion (in civil law, for example, to the demand for good morals or due care in legal intercourse.) This deepening and orientation to a material criterion will be accompanied by a recognition that the causal connection between the unlawful behavior and the consequence will be conceived in a relatively narrow manner.[1]

---

1 In its decision of February 3, 1927, NJ 1927, 636 *(Haagsche Post Case)* the Hoge Raad speaks of a "reasonably foreseeable consequence."

Where, on the other hand, responsibility is not measured according to the principle of fault but according to strict liability, the causal connection will be conceived in a much broader sense and will not be judged according to a subjective test but according to an objective-jural (and only a jural) standard.[1] For the risk principle, as will be observed during the treatment of the jural subject-object relation, enables an objective causal chain, which is not affected by human volition, to be ascribed to a legal subject so as to make the subject accountable for its causal consequences.

To suppose that the question of causal connection can be treated entirely apart from the principles of fault (or guilt) and risk, is to adopt an unjuristic way of thinking. Where there is, jurally speaking, a question as to whether a result has been brought about through guilt or fault, the issue of guilt or fault takes precedence over that of causality. For, in a juridical sense, guilt or fault is nothing but a deepening of causality and unlawfulness.

Yet this does not imply that causality, unlawfulness, and guilt or fault coincide into one another. Even if (governed by the guilt or fault principle) an assessment of jural causality simply attributes a consequence to the wrongdoer as "reasonably foreseeable," in settling the question of fault, it will nevertheless be the case that the wrongdoer must still be allowed to establish his or her own innocence in respect of the consequence that was reasonably foreseeable and of which he or she was the cause in a jural sense, or with respect to the kind of behavior that is in conflict with the "due care that is appropriate in social intercourse." Furthermore, it is always possible that the general norm of care may not be applied to the particular wrongdoer because of special circumstances. Consider the decision of the Hoge Raad in the so-called *Grain Silo Case* (Decision HR, June 7, 1918, NJ 1918, 709; W10294).

> In order to examine a shipment of grain, an office worker had himself let down by a chute into the bin where the grain was being stored. Although the workmen had warned him that it could be dangerous to descend without a safety belt because of the gases that sometimes can be emitted from grain, he refused to wear the belt. The office worker having died from asphyxiation,[2] his father accused the owners of the silo of having committed an unlawful act because the workmen had allowed his son to descend without a safety belt, even though this had been at his own request.

---

1 Cf. the decision of the Hoge Raad, October 30, 1953, NJ 1954, 261: *State* v. *the Shoe Manufacturers*.
2 From a juridical point of view this is the objective-causal connection that was involved in the subjective causal activity of the workers.

Unlawfulness and causal connection, from a juridical standpoint, were undoubtedly attributable to the actions of the workers, in the sense that the manner in which they had acted was formally in conflict with the regulations, as well as materially in conflict with the safety requirements, since there was a reasonable expectation that their conduct would have the result it produced. Yet the Hoge Raad affirmed the decision of the *Hof's-Gravenhage* that the workers could be accused of "weakness" but not "fault."

If we look more closely at jural fault (or guilt) as an anticipatory meaning-figure, then it appears that the moral anticipation which reveals itself therein, in the first place, points to a moral meaning-figure which itself displays an opened form. Considered from the Christian standpoint, in moral fault or guilt which betrays a blameworthy failing of a person's inner attitude with respect to the norm of love of one's neighbor, there is, undoubtedly, an anticipation of guilt in the sense of faith (refusing to listen to God's word) which, in turn, points above time to the revelation of the guilt of sin before God in the root of the creation.

In a closed, primitive stage of human activity there is no place for guilt either in a jural sense, or in a moral sense, or in a faith sense. A real sense of sin cannot display itself here. In the jural figure of guilt, in other words, we encounter an opening process which cannot have any conclusion in time but which appears to take its point of departure in the supra-temporal root of creation.

And what we have established here concerning jural guilt or fault also holds true for all normative anticipations of the various law-spheres without exception.

For example, even the opening up of logical thought into theoretical, scientific thought ultimately anticipates an opening up of faith, whether it be in an apostate or a good direction.

And faith points beyond itself to the revelation of the *firm ground* and origin of the truth in the religious center of existence.

There resides here a difference in principle when comparing the non-normative anticipations which operate in the prelogical law-spheres. If we take, as an example, the movements of a plant growing in the wild, then we discover in these movements a clear anticipation to the biotic development of this natural organism.[1] But the organic life-function of the plant itself in its natural state continues to display a closed form. This life-function itself does not anticipate the subjective function of feeling because in its natural state the plant has no subjective feeling-life. Here a further opening up can only take place through the instrumentality of humankind

---

1 *General Editor's note:* Biotic development actually refers back to the kinematic aspect (it is therefore a retrocipation from the biotic aspect to the aspect of movement and not an anticipation).

with respect to the object-functions of the plant. As we have already seen, however, matters are entirely different with respect to the normative anticipations.

In the cosmic order of time, we might say that the entire process within which the normative anticipatory spheres of the various law-spheres are opened up is ultimately governed by the leading of faith-disclosure.

We must, however, take note of a second peculiarity of the opening process within the normative anticipatory spheres. To put the question more precisely: In which law-sphere does the opening process of the normative anticipations arise? This is a question that bears upon the temporal order of the law-spheres.

We discovered earlier that in this temporal order there are two directions which have been called, respectively, the anticipatory and the retrocipatory (or founding) directions. It must now be observed that the opening process within the normative law-spheres is always founded, in the retrocipatory direction of time, in the historical law-sphere. Development of the historical level of culture is the condition without which the opening up of the later law-spheres cannot occur. Only the opening up of the faith function is excepted from this cosmic founding. It is impossible to successfully introduce deepened principles of law, morality, social intercourse, language, economy, or art into a primitive society if the historical level of that society has not first been opened up by means of formative education.

Also, the opening up of the logical law-sphere is unilaterally dependent upon that of the normative anticipatory spheres in historical development.[1] It is impossible for abstract thought to develop in a people without its historico-cultural level having been opened up and developed. But it is not impossible for a historical opening up of culture to begin without the foundation of science. One need only reflect upon the formation of the Frankish kingdom under Clovis. With respect to the founding direction of time, the historical law-sphere is indeed the hub of the entire process of disclosure, while viewed from the side of the anticipatory direction of time, this entire process is subject to the leading of faith.

---

1 *General Editor's note:* Dooyeweerd argues that although the logical aspect precedes the historical aspect within the temporal order of aspects, the historical aspect may be disclosed while the logical aspect is not deepened as yet. According to its logical aspect, nonscientific thinking does not have a history (it may have a history according to its concrete social content). The deepening of nonscientific thinking takes place when a logical manner of *formative control* of a given *epistemic material* (*kennismateriaal*) occurs. Dooyeweerd argues that this is indirectly confirmed by the fact that the historicistic mode of thought does count scholarly thinking, but not naive thought, as a "cultural factor" (*Recht en Historie: referaat voor de drie-en-twintigste wetenschappelijke samenkomst der Vrije Universiteit*, [Assen: G. F. Hummelens Boekhandel en Electr. Drukkerij, July 13, 1938], 33, cf. notes 49 and 50 on p. 61).

In order to give ourselves a clear insight into this state of affairs, we must devote a few paragraphs to the modal structure of the historical aspect, to the aspect of faith, and to the place that must be assigned to both in the process of development of the normative anticipatory spheres.

2.2 Law and History: The Relationship of the Science of Legal Dogmatics[1] to the Science of Legal History

In the foregoing we have consistently proceeded on the assumption that history represents only a modal aspect of temporal reality and as such is contained in its own law-sphere.

This assumption, however, is diametrically opposed to current opinion. According to the latter, history is thought to embrace at least all of the normative aspects of temporal reality, insofar as it is assumed that science and languages, forms of social intercourse and economy, art and positive law, as well as positive morality and conceptions of faith are in the grip of a historical process of change and development, and as such are intrinsically historical phenomena. For those who adopt this traditional standpoint it is not necessary to lapse into a positivistic historicism which does not have an eye for anything but the changing historical facts, and does not acknowledge in the course of history any connection with supra-temporal "values." It is possible, for example, to adopt an idealistic standpoint and to believe in an eternal, supra-temporal world of rational ideas, ideas of truth, justice, moral freedom, beauty, and holiness. The latter are supposed to express themselves, to a greater or lesser extent, in the temporal course of historical development, or at least to give history its meaning insofar as the historical facts and events ought to be viewed in relationship to such "values."

But, within the actual course of positive science's development, so deeply rooted is the conception that the positive forms of social intercourse, the various languages, the positive forms of economic and jural life, of art, morality, and faith are essentially historical in character, that it seems to be a completely hopeless undertaking to begin lodging an objection against it.

Nevertheless, the following consideration alone ought to give rise to doubt as to the correctness of this conception. It may be undeniable that science, social life, economic life, the life of art and law, the life of morality and faith have a historical development; but this hardly establishes that they are completely absorbed by historical development. If, for example, it were assumed that positive law, presently in force in the Netherlands, is a purely historical phenomenon, then the science of positive law would have to be absorbed within the scientific descriptions of legal history.

---

1 *Editor's note:* Jurists in English-speaking common law jurisdictions more often speak of legal "doctrine."

This conception has in fact been defended and even has representatives amongst outstanding contemporary legal historians. But to date it has never been able to gain credence outside this circle. It is already refuted by the fact that the science of legal dogmatics, which investigates the positive law of an established legal order, and on which scientific jural concept-formation proper (founded on the general theory of law and the philosophy of law) and the development of legal doctrines must depend, is required to adopt an entirely different method than that of the science of history. The current view of the task of the science of law, nevertheless, is still this; that for scientific, systematic knowledge of a positive legal order in its internal coherence, the investigation of the historical development of existing legal institutions is indeed necessary, but that this investigation for the scientific jurist is, nevertheless, only able to serve as a supplementary science. We do not have to stop, however, with establishing the actual existence of the science of legal dogmatics alongside the science of legal history. Instead, we can go further and combat the overemphasis of the latter, which led to a historicist conception of legal science's field of investigation, with the much more appropriate weapon of immanent critique.

The attempt has been made to reduce positive law, law actually in force, to a completely historical phenomenon. But in what respect then does the history of law differ from the history of art, or the history of language, or the history of economics? Is it not objectionable to attempt to derive the criterion for distinguishing these fields of investigation from the changing historical phenomena? Rather, legal historians have in advance delimited their field of investigation, at least in a modal sense. Legal historians set out to investigate the historical development of the positive legal institutions of a particular society in successive periods of time. But in order to do this they must already understand how the jural aspect of society is differentiated from the nonjural aspects. In other words, they must have already placed, at least intuitively, a concept of law at the foundation of their investigations before they can delimit their field of investigation. For is it not true that legal historians cannot carry out their task in a satisfactory manner if they do not see the historical development of positive law in the most intimate connection with that of the economic institutions, the forms of language, the forms of social intercourse, the conceptions of faith and morality of the period to be investigated? Nevertheless, it cannot be contested that these fields of historical investigation are only able to perform a supporting role for the science of legal history.

Therefore, however it is viewed, the field of legal history cannot be delimited from other fields of historical investigation according to purely historical criteria. Instead, legal historians must already have a concept of the jural aspect of reality before they can initiate their investigations. Neither can they derive this concept from the various subjective conceptions concerning the essential character of positive law, which certainly differ from each other in the various periods of time. After all, the concept of law is an articulated concept of a theoretical kind and as such cannot be derived from ordinary experience. It would be necessary therefore to seek these subjective conceptions in the various phases of reflection in the philosophy of law. Naturally, these conceptions always have the closest connection with the historical course of development of society. In this respect, it is entirely true that the subjective concept of law has its own historical development, as does the science as a whole.

But this undeniable truth provides the most powerful argument against the historicizing of the modal structure of the jural law-sphere. Does not the subjective concept of theoretical truth also have its historical development? However, if theoretical truth, or even the concept of it, were itself no more than a historical phenomenon, then a truly theoretical science of history would become an impossibility. To the perennial question, What is truth? there would have to be the skeptical answer, What happens to be regarded as the truth by anyone in the course of historical development. But this statement is self-refuting because it makes an appeal to the validity of a permanent truth that does not change in the course of historical development.

And so a scientific delimitation of legal history would also become impossible, if the jural aspect of reality itself were not outside the historical aspect.

It must be remembered, furthermore, that there exists not only a science of legal history but also a sociology of law, a psychology of law, a science of legal logic, etc. Just as some legal historians have attempted to absorb the science of law into the science of history, so some legal sociologists have attempted to do the same with sociology, just as legal psychologists have thought to reduce it to psychology, legal logicians to the logic of law. No one of these is any more possible than any other.

Now, from the standpoint of the position we are attacking, it is indeed possible to say, "Your criticism pertains only to a historicizing of the constant modal structural-elements of law. There are, however, a good number of the representatives of the standpoint you are attacking who do not go this far, but only ascribe to law a historical character in its variable, positive manifestations of Dutch, German, English law, etc."

This objection is well taken. However, those who represent this moderate historical standpoint have, in so doing in any case, admitted that the very fundamental concepts of law, in which the modal structural-elements of law in question are conceived, cannot be derived from the science of history but must possess a supra-historical sense.

In the meantime, this admission is not found to be at all satisfactory. What is to be gained, after all, if only the abstract modal structure of the jural law-sphere is preserved from being invaded by the territory of changing historical phenomena, whilst, in the meantime, the variable content of positive law is completely abandoned to the historical viewpoint? On that account, the very nature of law would have become a theoretical abstraction, a mere category of thought. At the same time, it would always remain possible to dispute that temporal reality itself truly possessed a jural aspect contained in a unique law-sphere.

Therefore we must set our criticism of the standpoint in question upon a still deeper foundation. What is meant when we say that positive law has its own history? In order to answer this question it is first necessary to know what we truly ought to understand by history.

2.3 Law and History: The Modal Structure of the Historical Aspect[1]

To the question, What is history? there is an immediate response generally forthcoming in everyday life: That which has happened in the past. This answer is oriented exclusively to the naive attitude of experience, which, as we know, is directed not to the theoretical distinguishing of the modal aspects of reality but to concrete events. For this very reason, however, it does not adequately serve as a theoretical delimitation of the field of investigation for the science of history. First, it is not the case that history is limited to the past. This is appreciated even within the naive attitude of experience. It may indeed be true that in everyday life one may say of something that it is finished once and for all. "This now belongs to history." By this is meant, "This now belongs to the past." But it is just as true that in daily life, for example, on the occasion of some important event in national or international life, that no objection is raised against saying, "Today we are experiencing a historic event." Here there is a recognition that history also relates to the present. Indeed, it is even possible, without objection, to speak of the historical future of a people.

In the second place, the territory of history cannot be delimited according to the criterion, what has happened. We have already demonstrated in part 1.1 that actual events in principle function simultaneously within all aspects of reality. A block of stone falling, considered as a purely natural phenomenon, is not a historical event. But it can acquire an actual objective-historical significance if, for example, a piece of human culture is de-

---

1 See my *De Wijsbegeerte der Wetsidee*, vol. 2, 126 ff, and in particular my *Recht en Historie: referaat voor de drie-en-twintigste wetenschappelijke samenkomst der Vrije Universiteit*, (Assen: G. F. Hummelens Boekhandel en Electr. Drukkerij, July 13, 1938).

stroyed or a leading statesman is killed by the falling stone. In such cases, the natural phenomenon in question also displays its historical aspect.

So every human act displays a historical aspect alongside several which are themselves nonhistorical. One need only think of activities such as eating, smoking, writing, reading, etc. In the early Middle Ages, for example, the act of printing books was not yet known. The discovery and acceptance of printing in our society is undoubtedly a developmental process of tremendous historical significance which also gave reading a new historical form. But the concrete activity of reading manifests, in addition, many other modal aspects, such as the physical, the biotic, the sensory/psychical, the logical, etc., which are not themselves of a historical character, even though they stand in an unbreakable relationship with the historical aspect.

Precisely because actual people, acts, events, things, and societal relationships function in the course of historical development, it is of crucial importance to know what is the modal meaning of history. The question is not concerned with what is involved in historical development, but how it takes on a historical character. And for this purpose it is necessary, before starting with concrete reality itself, to direct attention to the diversity of the fundamental modal aspects in which this concrete reality functions.

For concrete reality also functions in the organic aspect of life, the aspect of movement, the aspect of feeling, the logical aspect, etc. It is as great a mistake to view a concrete human act as being exhausted in the aspect of movement, or in the aspect of life, as it is to think of it in its multi-faceted temporal reality as being entirely enclosed by historical development. The historicist standpoint primarily bases itself on the conception that true time is that of historical development or becoming. So it is then reasoned that everything is embraced by historical time in which the great stream of past, present, and future allows the entire course of life to unfold in a succession of moments. By contrast, the natural-scientific concept of time is not supposed to be an authentic concept of time but instead the construction of events in a fixed, spatial line.

In modern historicism it is assumed that historical becoming is the typical human mode of existence and that within it is revealed characteristic human freedom to project for itself the future, in contrast to the bare events of nature which lack this freedom and which take place according to a prescribed causal order. Such a position is held by Oswald Spengler, Martin Heidegger, and others. In any case, historical time is here identified with true, authentic time.

As we have demonstrated earlier, it is this very identification that is mistaken. The historical order of time is simply a modality of all-embracing cosmic time. Not even succession is characteristic of the historical mode of time. As a matter of fact, we discovered this in all of the modalities of time, beginning with kinematic time. It occurs in the organic time of development, in the duration of feeling, in the logical process of thought, in symbolic time, in the time of social intercourse, in economic, jural, aesthetic time, etc. The succession that is encountered in the historical order of time depends for its uniqueness exclusively on the modal meaning of the historical aspect.

It is undoubtedly correct that one cannot speak of history without reference to human freedom so as not to be restricted to the limits of what is given within nature but what is active in the making of projects for the future. However, that is no reason in itself to identify as history everything in time that transcends what is given in nature. Instead it is the modal meaning of the historical aspect that determines the "how" of all phenomena of historical becoming. The "what," that is, the concrete reality that functions in this modal aspect is always more than simply historical because it embraces all of the aspects of the temporal cosmos.

It is therefore advisable to make a distinction between history as the course of concrete events (what has happened) and the historical aspect in which it functions.

First it is necessary to give a more precise account of the modal meaning-nucleus of this aspect. This meaning-nucleus cannot be discovered, in any case, where current opinion seeks it, in "becoming" or "development," because without further qualification both of these concepts lack any modal precision and are thus susceptible to a variety of interpretations. The concept "development" is first encountered in the biological sense of the organic development of life, in which we discovered an analogy of the meaning-nucleus of movement. With respect to the concept of "becoming" (genesis), we primarily have in mind the developing within time of the structure which God has incorporated into the creation. On the basis of the divine act of creation, which does not itself fall within time, there follows the development of God's creatures in cosmic time, the development of the potentialities of creation into fully developed creatures. But even this becoming is not actually restricted to one aspect; it embraces all of transitory reality with regard to all of its aspects. Historical becoming is simply an aspect of this genesis and must therefore receive its modal profile from the meaning-core of the historical aspect.

Now every attempt to delimit the territory of the science of history over against that of the "natural sciences" has come up against the moment of culture. Indeed, within the framework of the humanistic ground-motive of nature and freedom, the distinction has been made entirely in these terms. Here "culture," however, was not conceived as a modal aspect of reality but rather as another kind of reality, a "spiritual" one, in contrast to the reality of nature.

Thus no distinction at all was made between the cultural aspect and reality. Reality certainly functions in the aspect of culture, but always possesses, in addition, individuality-structures that embrace all of the aspects without exception. This is a trap for all the "isms" in philosophy. Following this path, biologism arrived at an unlimited extension of the concept "life." The well-known German biologist Woltereck, for example, declared:

> Spiritual-psychical phenomena, accomplishments, products, belong to life just as much as, for instance, shell formation or the movement of protozoa. A temple or a book, a sonnet or a strategic plan are phenomena of life, the accomplishments of living beings; literally, the same holds true for the building activity of termites. Those who refuse to be instructed by this similarity will scarcely be in a position to arrive at a complete understanding of the extent and the content of the concept of life.[1]

Here again there is no distinction whatsoever between the biotic aspect of reality and the individuality-structures which function within this aspect.

The Historical School came to identify "culture" and "spiritual" reality mainly because, from the very beginning, it had tied culture to the national folk community and had identified that folk community, which itself is a concrete form of human society, with cultural community.

But a folk community also possesses a total individuality-structure that functions in all aspects without exception and thus can never be identified with its cultural aspect.

Even von Savigny was forced to acknowledge that the science of legal dogmatics cannot coincide with the science of legal history. He therefore sought a criterion that might serve to distinguish the two fields of investigation from each other. This criterion, however, could then no longer be derived from the modal structure of reality because there was a developing awareness that both of these sciences were directed to the investigation of the same historical, "cultural reality." There remained therefore only a subjective, methodological criterion, a distinction in the subjective, theoretical manner of viewing "historical reality." The historical manner of viewing law was supposed to conceive historical legal material as succession, the succession of its phases of development. By contrast, the science of legal dogmatics was supposed to view it in its simultaneity. In this way the science of legal history was supposed to follow the genetic while legal dogmatics was supposed to follow the systematic method of investigation.[2]

This criterion, which even today is quite generally followed, gets us absolutely nowhere. In the first place, the concepts "succession" and "simul-

---

1 Woltereck, *Ontologie des Lebendigen*, (Stuttgart: Ferdinand Enke Verlag, 1940), 52.
2 "This given manifold, however, is two-fold, to be specific, partly a simultaneous and partly a successive one, in terms of which there must necessarily arise a dual scientific treatment...The treatment of the successive manifold... is the very task of historical research..." von Savigny, *Zeitschrift für geschichtliche Rechtsissenschaft*, vol. I, (1815), 14.

taneity" are subject to all kinds of interpretation, apart from a definition of their modal meaning. For example, they are even used in physics, but the physical concepts of succession and simultaneity certainly cannot be used by the historian of law and for legal dogmatics. Furthermore, even when its modal meaning has been defined, the criterion in its generality is itself certainly not accurate. The historian also, in a real way, must take into consideration the simultaneity of historical events; and legal dogmatics just as surely must take account of the succession of legal facts and legal norms (think, for example, of the concepts "continuing delict" and "provisional law").

The opposition genetic-systematic also reveals all its defects once it is subjected to critical analysis. All scientific investigation possesses a systematic character. Not even the historian can work unsystematically. The Spanish author Ortega y Gasset, though strongly historically oriented, defined the science of history itself expressly as the systematic science of human life (a definition that is, by the way, truly historicist!). Those who do not conceive a historical phenomenon theoretically in its historical connections, but as a fact that stands in itself, do not provide a scientific description of history but only write a "potpourri" of news items. Indeed, but the very question at issue is, What is this modally defined difference?

The same holds for the genetic manner of viewing things. The science of law has its own formulation of the genetic problem in the doctrine of the sources of law. Here it is not a question of the historical but of the jural origin of positive law and the manner in which it comes into being.[1] By a systematic treatment of this doctrine we shall observe how the Historical School introduced a fundamental confusion, simply by losing sight of the jural character of the sources of law and by interpreting the jural process of origination in the formation of law as a historical process of development.

In modern times the attempt has again been made to divide the "cultural sciences" (that is to say, all those special sciences that are oriented to culture in contrast to nature), from a methodological point of view, into typifying and individualizing ones. The former then would supposedly adopt a typifying method in which the individual cultural phenomena are brought under a general type. The latter, on the contrary, would be oriented to an individualizing method in which it would be a question of describing what is strictly individual in this phenomena.

It was thought then that the science of legal dogmatics and also, for example, the science of economics could be put under the rubric of the typifying group, and that the strictly historical sciences, by contrast, would have to be associated with the individualizing group.

---

1 So, for instance, statutes, by-laws, treaties, regulations, etc., are juridical sources or originating forms of positive law.

But this criterion too is completely inappropriate to delimit legal dogmatics from legal history. Legal dogmatics can never be satisfied with an abstract schematism, with a typology of legal life; on the contrary, it must always conceive of legal norms and types of legal facts within the process of their ultimate concretization in the individual case. The scientific jurist must learn not only to conceive a legal relationship in its abstract type but also in its concrete individuality.

The earlier conception in legal science that legal rule, the legal facts of the case, and legal judgment relate to one another as a logical major premise, minor premise, and conclusion has now generally been abandoned. It may certainly not be exhumed from its grave as representative of the essential character of the jural-dogmatic method in contrast to the historical method.

On the other hand, the historian too must work with type-concepts. One need only think, for example, of concepts such as renaissance, feudalism, early capitalism, etc. So it appears that all of the difficulties in which historicism becomes entangled, when it attempts to delimit the true field of investigation of the science of history from that of the science of law and other sciences that have to do with the normative aspects of reality, issue from the overextension of the concept of culture, making it into a pseudo-concept of reality which embraces all of the normative aspects. Culture is not a kind of reality but only a modal aspect, a "way" of being.

What then are we to understand, by culture? It is simply this: a controlling manner of giving form to an existing material according to a free project.

When Aristotle construed the ancient polar ground-motive of Greek thought in terms of the form-matter schema there was already inherent within it an attempt to render harmless the ancient matter-motive of the nature-religion over against the form-motive of the culture religion by conceiving matter as purely complementary to form, as the "material" of form. This complementary relationship of form and material is indeed contained in the modal meaning of the aspect of culture.

There are indeed "forms" (forms of bodies) in the inorganic world and in the realm of plants and animals. But here, at least insofar as we consider the subjects and not the objective things that they construct, there is no trace of a relation of form and matter because the things of nature and the beings of nature are an integral product of creation and not simply the product of divine form-giving.

Only those things that are formed by plants and animals could be compared to culture. A bird, for, example, uses certain materials for building its nest. But animal form-giving is different in principle from cultural form-giving because animal forming through the ages has a rigid, uniform character; it is carried out purely by instinct, whilst culture formation possesses the character of free control according to a project. Only free control should, strictly speaking, be regarded as the modal meaning-nucleus of "culture," since the moment of "form-giving" already has an analogical character.[1] But free control can only reveal itself in giving form and therefore these two moments of meaning belong indissolubly together in the modal structure of the historical aspect.

When we speak of "free" control, it is certainly not the humanistic motive of freedom we have in mind. All that is meant is the ability to introduce variations according to one's own project in a free way.

That in "free control by means of giving of form" we have indeed hit upon the modal meaning-nucleus of the historical aspect appears from the fact that, on the one hand, all earlier law-spheres point forward in their historical anticipations to this central meaning of culture, whilst, on the other, all later ones point back to it in their historical analogies.[2]

The method of analysis adopted here, which could be described as the confrontation method, puts us in a position to discover in a precise manner the meaning-nuclei of the various law-spheres.

Thus we discovered, as a historical anticipation in the modal structure of the logical law-sphere, the moment of logical control, a moment which, as we saw, is able to develop itself initially in the systematic giving of form to the material to be investigated by scientific thought. This moment of logical control is lacking in prescientific thought.

In the modal structure of the psychical law-sphere, with its meaning-nucleus of feeling, it is also possible to discern the moment of formative control as a true anticipation to the historical aspect. That is to say, we discern it in the free feeling of form, on which rests the entire possibility of the higher formation of feeling-life in education, and which stands in an indissoluble interconnection with the disclosed historical stage of a society's development.

At a primitive level of culture it is as impossible to point out a differentiated feeling of form as it is to discern differentiated legal, moral, or aesthetic feeling. Instead, all of the feelings that are related to the normative aspects are only represented here in an undifferentiated feeling of solidarity of a tribe, a sib, or a clan. This has been pointed out emphatically by developmental psychology, that is, that area of psychology which studies the historical and genetic development of psychical life.

---

1 The moment of form only appears in its original sense in the structure of the spatial aspect. Physical, biotic, and sensory-psychical forms are already analogies of the spatial form or spatial figure.

2 *Editor's note:* See the glossary regarding use of the terms *anticipations*, *retrocipations*, and *analogies*.

On the other hand, in the modal structure of all law-spheres that are founded in the historical law-sphere, we necessarily encounter once again the moment of form (in the sense of free control) as historical analogies. Forms of language, forms of art, forms of law, forms of morality and forms of cultic faith are not only encountered when the level of a culture has been deepened but in primitive, yet-to-be-opened cultures also. Thus it is apparent that what we are dealing with here are historical analogies and not anticipations. From the unique character of the analogies in question it appears that here there is indeed no free formative control in an original historical sense but only analogies of culture-forming.

I want to demonstrate this with reference to the relationship of legal forming and historical culture-forming. It has been established that legal forming is grounded (founded) in historical culture-forming and thus can never be considered apart from it. But there remains, nevertheless, a clear modal distinction between them. Giving form to history requires power or historical influence. Formers of history are those who have power, in fact, as we shall see, power over persons. Legal forming, in its turn, demands legal power or jural competence. We shall see later on how this legal power therefore is also an essential characteristic of every legal source as a jural originating form of positive law.

Now legal power, considering its jural qualification, is a truly historical analogy of power in its original sense. It always rests on the foundation of historical power, but it cannot be reduced to it. Those who, in a historicist fashion, attempt to do this end up identifying power and law. Theoretically, it leads to the infamous antinomy because legal life never allows itself to be ruled by brute power.

Without doubt we have here established that the modal meaning-nucleus of the historical aspect is free control by means of the giving of form.

If, in this connection, attention is focused upon the subject-object relationship, on the subject-side of the historical law-sphere, it becomes immediately clear how the so-called natural things also possess a potential historical object-function, which is first disclosed by means of the subjective cultural activity of humankind as a historical subject.

To subjective, controlling form-giving corresponds the objective culturally formed object, or the objective cultural fact, that is to say, an occurrence in nature such as a flood, a volcanic eruption, etc., which acquires an object-function in human culture because it enters into a relationship with subjective cultural activity as a support or as a hindrance. It is therefore possible to understand the following proposition: wherever the tool is discovered as a cultural object we find ourselves within the territory of history.

We must now undertake a short investigation of the analogies that are observable in the modal structure of the historical aspect. Our method in uncovering the analogies has always been to demonstrate how a meaning-nucleus first delineates itself in the successive order of these analogies. Nevertheless, the analogies always remained qualified and determined by this meaning-nucleus.

Then we pointed to the difference in principle between cultural and animal form-giving. Cultural forming appeared to be qualified by formative control, in contrast to the instinctive and static character of animal form-giving. Here there already appears the indissoluble connection between the historical and the logical aspects, a coherence that must express itself in a logical analogy within the modal structure of the historical aspect.

There is no free, controlling giving of form apart from the ability to distinguish logically! Therefore nothing can be a subject in history that is at the same time not a subject in the logical law-sphere. The notion of "natural history," which is supposed to include not only the geological development of the layers of the earth but also the organic development of the realm of plants and animals, can only be attributed to the earlier mentioned historicist identification of the evolutionary process of development (genesis in the narrower sense) with historical development. In the same fashion, the Romanticist freedom-idealism aimed to conquer the old deterministic science-ideal in natural science by conceiving "nature" as a product of development from "free creative potentialities," a product of a "natural history," which is supposed to be merely the gateway to the history of culture.

The logical analogy in the modal structure of the historical aspect reveals itself first in the moment of historical attribution. In the historical process we do not reckon our way through an entire series of causal factors, but we attribute great cultural deeds to individuals as well as to collective historical subjects. After what was observed earlier concerning jural attribution as a logical analogy, we do not have to elucidate this point any further. Again it is to be expected therefore from the outset that we would also discover in the modal structure of history the analogy of the previously discussed logical contrarieties, which, as we have seen, can only be discovered in the normative aspects of reality.

This point is of the greatest importance because, by employing this modal structural analysis, we can expect clarification of the disputed point as to whether normative significance must be attributed to historical development, and if so, to what degree.

This controversial point has arisen especially since Friedrich Julius Stahl,[1] adopting the approach of the Historical School, set forth the proposition that historical development should only have secondary normative significance attached to it.

According to him, we are obliged to piously respect whatever has developed outside of human contrivance by means of the quietly working supra-personal powers of custom or tradition in the thread of historical continuity because the leading of God in history (Gottes Fügung) is supposed to be revealed here. At this point Stahl ties in with the thought already expressed by Fichte that history does not know any laws in the sense of universally valid rules, but that there is here asserted an irrational, hidden law-conformity in the sense of a divine providence. Expressed in a less Christian manner, this divine providence was also viewed as the *Schicksal* or the fate of a people.

Stahl himself observed the danger of such an appeal to God's guidance because even the revelation of evil in history does not fall outside of that guidance. Thus he took the Decalogue as the revealed will of God, as the primary norm of activity, and he placed historical development as a secondary norm under the judgment of moral law. If historical development does not come into conflict with an expressly revealed commandment of the moral law, then we must accept it as a norm.

Sharp criticism was brought to bear on this view of history by Leendertz in his thesis, *The Foundation of Governmental Authority in the Anti-revolutionary Doctrine of the State* (Leyden, 1911).[2] The neo-Kantian professor van der Vlugt was his promoter. Proceeding from the Kantian dualism of empirical reality (fact) and ideal norm, Leendertz argued that the anti-revolutionary view of history denied the boundary between fact and norm and ended up by accepting the *fait accompli*.

In spite of the unacceptable Kantian separation of "norm" and "fact of nature," conforming to the humanistic ground-motive of nature and freedom, there was nevertheless in this criticism the following element of truth: in conformity with the Historical School, Stahl conceived the norm of historical development in an irrationalistic fashion as a product of the subjective development of the national folk spirit in the historical process.

The irrationalistic conception always attempts to reduce the law-side of a law-sphere to the subject-side as it reveals itself in its individuality.

In the nature of the case, such an irrationalistic conception of the normative meaning of history is unacceptable from our standpoint. The subjec-

---

[1] A German anti-revolutionary, Stahl was a contemporary of von Savigny and the mentor of Groen Van Prinsterer during the second period of the intellectual development of the latter.

[2] *De grond van het overheidsgezag in de anti-revolutionnaire staatsleer.*

tive course of development in history can never be the norm of action. If history is embraced in a normative law-sphere, we shall have to search for the norms of historical development not on the subject-side but on the law-side of this law-sphere.

But the question whether the historical laws in this sense bear a normative character and thus whether the historical facts also bear a normative sense, that is to say, are only able to be understood in subjection to these norms, cannot be answered in a satisfactory way before we have learned to understand the place of the historical aspect in the temporal world-order.

We can now set forth the following thesis: *All law-spheres which are founded in the logical law-sphere necessarily bear a normative character because the logical analogy of contrariety, between what ought and what ought not to be, applies to their modal structure.*

This normativity would be impossible if the laws of these law-spheres did not manifest the character of norms or rules, of what ought to be. For this very reason therefore these laws cannot have the character of "natural laws" because the latter cannot allow for either accountability or responsible subjects nor the possibility of being responsible for breaking the law. Even on an initial glance, it is clear that this is indeed the case with the contrarieties: logical-illogical,[1] grammatically correct-grammatically incorrect, polite-impolite (e.g., proper-improper, gracious-ungracious, socially acceptable-socially unacceptable, tactful-tactless), economical-uneconomical, beautiful-ugly, just-unjust, moral-immoral, believing-unbelieving.

That this kind of opposition of normative contraries pertains to the modal structure of the historical aspect as a true logical analogy cannot be denied. It comes to expression here in the contrast between historical and unhistorical. The anti-normative character of the latter expresses itself in a pregnant fashion in the terms "reactionary" and "repristinating." This is because historical reaction or repristination involves a desire to seize upon dead elements from the past contrary to the norms of historical development.

A typical example of such a reactionary attitude contrary to the norms of historical development – the modal content of which, for the moment, is unknown – was presented by the counter-revolutionary spirit at the time

---

1 This logical contrariety is usually called "contradictory," because it can be only established under the aegis of the law of contradiction (*principium contradictionis*). *General Editor's note*: Traditional predicate logic distinguishes between four kinds of propositions: universal affirmative (A), universal negative (E), particular affirmative (I) and particular negative (O) propositions. Within the square of opposition A and E stand in a relation of *contrariety*, I and O stand in a relation of *subcontrariety*, while both A and O and I and E are related as *contradictories*.

of the Reformation. Both liberalism and the anti-revolutionary movements, each from its own standpoint, lodged objections against this counter-revolutionary movement. The latter did not limit itself to opposing the principles of the French Revolution; it also thought it could blot out everything that the revolutionary formers of history had brought into being "in the course of historical development." They wished to revert to the so-called feudal system of the old regime. In doing this they lost sight of the fact that this system was already a historical anachronism even at the time of the outbreak of the Revolution.

It is now clear that reaction as an anti-historical (not a-historical)[1] attitude can only have meaning if truly historical norms do indeed exist, whose modal meaning does not allow itself to be reduced to norms from other post-logical law-spheres.

Historical repristination as such is neither illogical, nor in conflict with the forms of social intercourse, nor uneconomical, nor unaesthetic. Neither is it unjust, because the reactionary movement can very well hold itself within the limits of the legal order and can seek its goal with juridically acceptable means. Nor is it immoral, because it can be motivated by a true love of the country. Its modal meaning can only be understood as a historical one.

Unless consistently refusing to speak of reactionary behavior, a person cannot deny the existence of truly historical norms without falling into self-contradiction. But it is possible to deny the anti-normative meaning pattern of historical repristination in theory. On the other hand, only the sinful practice of human society requires everyone to acknowledge its existence. It is always the case that every repristination brings its destructive influence to bear on the actual course of history. Reactionaries build on quicksand because they view a dead past as if it were still a powerful historical foundation. Indeed, they gain apparent success for a short period of time, if they are able to get power into their hands; nevertheless, their work will remain unfruitful for the future. After all, it is impossible to infuse life into a dead carcass. So the reviving of the old system of caste under King William I was not really a historically formative act. This system had lost its historical basis and under the new circumstances could only maintain a shadowy existence.

Therefore is historical development, nevertheless, a kind of natural process? Not at all. For it is impossible to adopt a reactionary, unhistorical attitude with reference to natural laws. The levelling of a reactionary cultural edifice and its replacement by a system that responds to the norms of historical development does not take place by itself, as it does in a natural

---

1 A-historical (privative "a") would mean that the act would not be of a historical character. An anti-historical act remains historical in character, even as an unjust act remains jural.

process; it demands once again the activity of free human forming in conformity with the normative principles of historical development.

Here we encounter a new characteristic of norms in contrast to natural laws. In all of the normative law-spheres, the laws are given only in the form of principles. They do not automatically bring about results in the subjective course of events, as is the case in a natural process. They appeal to the normative power of human judgment and require the giving of form, positivizing by human will.

This forming and positivizing of modal, normative principles is always founded in historical cultural development. It is for this reason that the forms of language and social intercourse, the forms of economics, art, and law, as well as the positive forms of morality continually vary with the development of history without themselves taking on a modal-historical meaning. As for the logical principles, the principle of identity *(principium identitatis)*, the principle of contradiction *(principium contradictionis)*, the principle of sufficient reason *(principium rationis sufficientis)*, they all demand human forming only in the context of deepened, theoretical thought.

In logical controlling by the systematic giving of form, we have in fact discovered a historical analogy.[1] Theoretical giving of form to normative logical principles occurs then for the first time in logic as a science, in which there is the attempt to render the logical laws of thought into exact formulas and to conceive them in their mutual systematic coherence.

Logic, also, has its historical development, beginning with the first attempts of the Greek thinkers to give the logical principles a theoretical form. Since then it has differentiated, in a synthetic sense, into a mathematical logic, a logic of the science of language, a logic of legal science, etc., and this process of differentiation has by no means come to an end.

In the pretheoretical attitude of thought there is, however, no question of a theoretico-logical giving of form to the principles of thought. Nevertheless, these principles of thought are applied in an intuitive, though often very imprecise fashion. In the ordinary everyday attitude of thought, illogical thought is indeed recognized, and there is an attempt to take logical principles into consideration. Even children ask for the sufficient ground of a judgment (Why do you say that?), and they are quite capable of noticing a logical contradiction in a story.

There is a fundamental confusion between logical principles of thought and the scientific forming of them, between the logical and the theoretico-logical, when the proposition is defended that primitive, and nonscientific thought, in general, does not yet recognize any logical principles.

---

[1] *Editor's note:* The use of "historical analogy" here is to be understood as an anticipation from the logical aspect to the historical aspect.

From the above mentioned state of affairs, it appears that, on the law-side of the historical aspect and of all aspects that are founded in the historical aspect, there is a peculiar interlacement of principles and subjective form-giving. This has been repeatedly misunderstood by the immanence standpoint. So an untenable opposition was posited between the "absolute" norms (logical, ethical, aesthetic), which are supposed to be eternal and in need of no human forming, and "empirical" norms (positive rules of law and social intercourse) which are supposed to have no absolute value and to rest completely on arbitrary human convention. We shall discuss this point in more detail later.

For present purposes it is sufficient to make the observation that the opposition in question rests upon the separation of two moments which in all modal norms belong unbreakably together, namely, the supra-arbitrary principle and human form-giving.

The logical analogy in the modal meaning of history has been sufficiently brought to light with the analysis of the normative character of historical development. If we now investigate more closely the nature of free formative control as the modal meaning-nucleus of the historical aspect, then it appears that there is a difference between this forming, in its original historical sense, on the law-side, and all-forming in the modal sense of later law-spheres. The nucleus of the former, in contrast to the latter, is in essence power-formation. But forming of language, social forming, legal forming, and aesthetic forming do not involve power forming as such. Power-forming is an original historical meaning configuration, which is qualified by the moment of control. Power is having free control.

Law-forming implies competence in a jural sense. Forming of social life implies the giving of an example and imitation. Historical forming, however, involves power, and more specifically, power over persons. That the competence of the (law-) former in the jural sphere, the example of leading groups in society, etc., are founded in the historical forms of power does not detract from the difference in meaning of these concepts.

Historical norms of development are not given form by just any individuals but by those who possess power. Power, insofar as it is power over persons, is a modal moment of meaning on the law-side of the historical aspect, just as legal power or competence for legal forming is a modal moment of meaning on the law-side of the jural aspect.

On the subject-side of the historical aspect, power manifests itself only in an objective direction as the mastery of the objective material to which form is given by way of a free project (so-called *Sachkultur*). Such a subjective power is more or less exerted by every cultural subject.[1] But in itself it is not power that qualifies someone to be a history-former. The lat-

---

1 In the jural aspect legal power expresses itself in a purely subjective sense as a sub-

ter is always power over persons which, however, often expresses itself by means of power over things.

The personal power of the former of history should not be confused with the simply psychical influence on the feeling-instincts of the mass, although it is undoubtedly bound up with a psychical analogy which is founded in this influence on feelings.[1] Power over persons has already impressed itself as a normative configuration by the logical analogy in the meaning of history. It is no private matter which can be imposed in solitude for one's own personal pleasure. Historical power comes to expression only in the process of forming history and imposes on its bearers the heaviest conceivable responsibility.

At the creation, the obtaining of power over the forces of nature was already imposed upon humanity as a normative historical task (Genesis 1: 26, 28). In this way God established an express ordinance for the process of culture-forming, which further expresses itself in connection with the culture of things (*Sachkultur*) in the advance of technology. Technology, however, can only have an influence in the process of the formation of history if the technical inventors obtain personal power in the area of culture in which they find themselves. For this purpose the mere mastery of the powers of nature is not sufficient. A discovery that remains buried with its inventor as a personal secret remains without influence in history. It must find entry into human society; to this end inventors require the power-formation in the circle of their contemporaries. They need power over persons.

Historical power is, however, a modal pattern of meaning that appears in all kinds of concrete forms, according to the particular nature of the cultural circle in which it is operative. So the state enters, in a formative way, into history by means of the power of the sword, the church by the way of the spiritual power of faith, science by the power of thought, the great artist by means of the power of aesthetic genius, the capitalist by means of the power of a pool of capital, etc. But history-formation, in its unique character, occurs in the course of a power struggle between historical tradition and the progressive will of the shaper of history, in which the latter experiences that history cannot be created in an arbitrary fashion but remains bound to a supra-arbitrary principle for all cultural development.

The will of the former of history, any more than that of the former of law, is not a willing in a psychical-sensory sense; it is a normative will-

---

jective power of will over a legal object (the ability to dispose of the object of a subjective right).

1   In the second volume of my *De Wijsbegeerte der Wetsidee*, I viewed power itself as a psychical analogy in the modal sense of the historical aspect. After further consideration I must acknowledge, however, that power is identical with the central moment of the historical aspect.

forming that only represents an analogy of psychical striving and makes its influence felt in the historical process of development to which the individual former of history is subjected. In its condensed form, tradition embodies the treasures of the ages which have been gathered in the course of centuries. New history-forming is possible only through exploring the vital moments of this tradition. Revolutionary arbitrariness is not able to form history. Naturally, it is possible, for example, for an invading people to destroy the culture of a people they subjugate; nevertheless, its new culture-forming remains bound to its own historical tradition.

In the power struggle between tradition and the will of the history-former, the latter must subject itself to the developmental norm of historical continuity. This was discovered by the history formers of the French Revolution, as well as the modern Bolshevik rulers in Russia. Many arbitrary revolutionary measures were cast aside by the historical stream of development without leaving a trace. By contrast, truly edifying work appears always to be subjected to the principle of historical continuity which penetrates the present and the future with the cultural development of the past. So the French Revolution could sweep away what remained of the feudal system because this system had already historically outlived itself. The establishment of the unified Netherlands in 1813 was undoubtedly part of a line of historical development. On the other hand, the elimination of the Christian-based calender in the French Revolution, for example, was a purely arbitrary act which purposely broke away from the Christian tradition.

The developmental moment of tradition's vital elements is a biotic analogy in the meaning of history, since the principle of development emerges for the first time in the meaning of organic life. Historical development occurs in cultural life. Yet behind the biotic analogy the analogy of movement which finds its expression in historical causality already manifests itself in the modal sense of cultural development.

We encounter the historical analogy of space in the modal configuration of cultural area and historical location.

Historical causality is not a physical causality of movement any more than is jural causality. The fact that there has been frequent confusion of the historical and the natural-scientific concepts of cause cannot be explained simply in terms of the naturalistic orientation of the science of history in the second half of the previous, and the beginning of this century. It is mainly to be explained, on the one hand, by a misconception of the significance of natural processes in the making of history and, on the other hand, by a mistaken reduction of historical power to psychical-sensory influence on human individuals.

The argument is as follows: The chain of causality in the historical process is formed, on the one side, by human activities, on the other side, by natural events such as famines, natural catastrophes or climatic influences. Human activities have a physico-psychical character and, in a view of the causal chain of the historical process, may only be viewed as links next to the natural causal factors. In other words, without warning, a natural-scientific view of causality was again introduced into the science of history, which, as we saw in a previous connection, has no place for real historical attribution. It was indeed conceded that, because history cannot obtain knowledge of all the causal factors, it must make a relatively arbitrary selection from them (Simmel, Huizinga). This entire way of viewing things, however, is mistaken.

Natural processes can only attain an objective function in the historical process through connection with human subjectivity in culture. The historical process is a normative one. Historical causality in a subjective sense implies attribution to a responsible subject. So, for example, a revolutionary attempt to destroy, or a reactionary effort, in history, does not evoke the opposition of tradition or revolution, respectively, in a natural way. Both are only a normatively sufficient basis for historical consequences which are brought into being by free, accountable, human activity.

The same applies, for example, to what is called in historical literature the major "causes" of the origin of the feudal system in the Frankish period. On the one hand, there was the external danger of the invasion of the Arabs and the inability of the Frankish army to oppose this with enough battle-ready troops. On the other hand, there existed the internal danger of the considerable private knightly power of the lords. These two factors demanded from the side of the Carolingian rulers a political act for saving the kingdom. They responded to this demand in a brilliant manner by incorporating the private knightly vassals into the military organization of the kingdom.

So, for example, a natural event, such as an earthquake or a flood, can only acquire an objective causality in the historical process if it again becomes a historical ground for free, subjective, human, formative activity in history. The reason for its objective historical causality, the natural event, in turn becomes a historical ground for free, subjective, human, formative activity in history.

Undoubtedly, a natural catastrophe can destroy a portion of human culture, even though such destruction only acquires historical significance in virtue of its connection with subjective human forming, whose products have been destroyed. But subjective forming in a historical sense is never a natural process. It cannot develop historical power as such, and therefore all attempts to draw parallels between human activity and natural factors in the causal process of historical development is an essentially unhistorical approach.

Finally, whenever psychical (emotional) factors are involved, these can never explain, or help to explain, the truly historical aspect of human activity because the historical aspect retains its own unique nature over against the psychical aspect.

In the historical course of the conflict between Anthony and Octavius, the relation between Anthony and Cleopatra certainly played an important role. It is, however, impossible to give a psychological explanation of the historical significance of Anthony's defeat in the naval battle of Actium based on his feelings of love for the beautiful Egyptian queen.

Psychological explanation based on factors of feeling only extends as far as the psychical aspect of the event.[1]

Historians who attempt to do this, in effect, move outside their own proper field of investigation and can give no more than an "impressionistic image" (Huizinga) of the psychical background. However, they should not treat the truly historical-causal factors in an "impressionistic way," or in an "arbitrary selection," if they have a proper understanding of their theoretical task. In this field, they will have to proceed in a genuinely systematic fashion.

2.4 The Modal Meaning of History in its Opened Structure: The Relation of Historical Ethnology and the Science of History

The modal moments of meaning that we have analyzed above are encountered in every cultural manifestation, even in the most primitive ones. That is the case because, as modal nucleus and analogies, in the earlier established sense of these terms, they are also part and parcel of the still-closed or primary configuration of history.

It is therefore also an expression of naturalistic-evolutionistic thought, when the older ethnology (the science of peoples) makes a distinction between peoples of culture who are supposed to possess civilization and primitive peoples who are supposed not to have any. This is the same kind of thinking that, for instance, attempted to derive the ordered arrange-

---

1 The situation becomes quite different if one takes into consideration the full act-structure of human existence. But that can only be expounded in a later context. An act, for example, a historico-politically qualified act of will, certainly cannot serve as a causal explanation of an action or behavior in the sense of the natural-scientific concept of causality because the action or behavior itself functions in all aspects of reality. An action can only be understood as the expression of such an act. In the current conception of physico-psychical causality, however, the purely psychically conceived will is allowed to present itself as the "cause" of the action in its physical (or preferably, physiological) aspect, muscle movement. This is indeed a very basic misconception of the true state of affairs.

ments of married and family life from a gradual evolution out of the animal stage of sexual promiscuity, or that construed animal herd life as the stage prior to the life of the state.

In the enthnological science of this century, these evolutionistic constructions have for a long period been recognized as speculative, having no basis in the factual material; instead, they are flatly contradicted by it. The truth of the matter is that the so-called primitive people are also actually people of culture[1] and thus have a history. But, in these primitive cultural circles, the meaning of history reveals itself in a closed, primitive form.

In this respect, it is striking that such primitive cultures are closed off within the narrow walls of undifferentiated primitive social forms, such as sibs (clans), folk communities and tribal relations. Strangers are enemies, hostages, outlaws (*ex lex*). They are without rights and without refuge, unless they find protection with a member of the tribe or the folk community. The historical tradition of such a primitive cultural sphere, thoroughly permeated as it is by mythology, is still rigidly bound to the natural conditions of life of the social grouping and is accepted by the members of the people as a supernatural, divine power. The protectors of this tradition very often even hold out against any influence of opened up cultural spheres, in particular, against the incursions of Western culture. Here tradition is all-powerful.

The communal order of the sib[2] or the tribe remains eternal and unchangeable. Every attempt to introduce change is regarded as atheistic. That this conception persisted even in Greek culture in its older, though already-opened, phases appears from the story of the Spartan, Chilon, who rejected the friendship of Solon when the latter dared to speak about the ability to alter the laws.

In order now to attain an opening, a deepening, of the modal meaning of history, the isolation of such a culture must be broken. It must enter into enriching interaction with other opened cultures. It must be taken up in the flow of the opened development of culture. At this point the conqueror's power of the sword is often an important factor. But peaceful factors, namely, missionary activity, colonization, and the establishment of commercial relationships also fulfill a most important role in the development of culture.

In the context of such a cultural development, all kinds of internally dead cultural forms can continue to be maintained by the tradition; but

---

1 I set aside here the distinction that is often made between culture in the sense of civilization or culture that is formed in the sphere of the state and culture in the broader sense of the word.
2 It can be established as a fact from modern ethnology that at the least developed level of culture the sib (i.e., in ancient Rome, the *gens*) is yet to be encountered. Cf H. Lowie, *Primitive Society* (1929), 105.

such forms of culture remain outside the real course of historical development. From that time on they belong to folklore, which, as we shall later see with greater precision, is not a legitimate theme for investigation by the genuine science of history.

Furthermore, having reached a relatively high level of development, a culture can become rigid and isolated. In that case, degeneration (decadence) sets in, unless once again there arise formers of history who succeed in breaking through the cultural isolation and lead the historical tradition along new paths.

But it is also a speculative, evolutionistic construction if one proclaims the primitive, closed cultural state to be the original state of culture and attempts to conceive historical development as a process of gradual progress. For such a construction the historical factual material does not offer any basis. Rather, in the story of the Tower of Babel, the Bible affirms that the isolation of cultures is in conflict with the divine ordinance for the process of historical development and therefore ought not be viewed as its normal beginning.

The opening process in history only occurs in accordance with the dictates of a modal norm of development. It may be called the norm of historical differentiation and integration which is observed in the entire coherence of the world order.

The historical norm of continuity, which we discovered in our preceding discussion, does not of itself give us a sufficient standard to establish the direction that God willed in his order of creation for the historical process of development. Moreover, when we established that the norm in question requires retaining the vital elements of the tradition to further the development of culture, this only brings out a biotic analogy in the modal structure of the historical aspect which, in its retrocipatory character (appealing to the nucleus of an earlier aspect), cannot of itself indicate a direction for the opening up of culture.

In itself, tradition can never function as the norm for historical development. It is only a subjective, historical-communal factor which embraces both good and bad elements. Those moments in the tradition, moreover, which are vital, and which are protected by sufficient historical power, do not provide any guarantee that they are amenable to further development in a truly disclosed historical process.

We require a criterion according to which the genuinely progressive course of historical development can be distinguished from the reactionary course. In our own time, the latter often initially masquerades as a development that strives in a forward-looking direction.

The norm of continuity demands further precision and is founded initially in the norm of historical differentiation. The content of this norm is the same as for the creation order in modally expressing itself through the historical process of development. For this norm requires the development of the various structures that are contained in the creation order, each according to its own nature in the process of cultural development. Historical development is only the historical aspect of the great process of becoming which, in all of its aspects, manifests a direction from the undifferentiated to the differentiated, and always has as its goal the unfolding of the structures of creation. For the unique traits of the different spheres of life cannot manifest themselves within the cultural aspect in an undifferentiated phase of society.

While the unfolding of culture, on the one hand, brings with it an increasing differentiation of human society within which various cultural spheres are formed, such as art, science, statecraft, the church, industry, etc., it leads, on the other hand, to the gradual shedding of the primitive undifferentiated forms of communal life which were dependent upon the isolation of the culture. Differentiation goes hand in hand with an integration of culture through which historical interaction takes on an international character, and ever-increasing parts of humanity become culturally intertwined with one another.

In the modal structure of history, the social anticipation in the sense of opened [social] intercourse now manifests itself. At the same time, however, the other anticipatory moments within the meaning of history also disclose themselves. The first to disclose itself is the anticipation to the meaning of language, symbolical signification.

Initially, what is historically significant is distinguished from what is historically insignificant. There is an urge to signify symbolically important historical events. This takes place in historical writing, monuments, inscriptions, memorials, honors, and in other ways. In the relatively uniform course of a closed culture, the muse of history does not yet discover any material for the chronicling of noteworthy events. Here mythology takes the place of historical description.

And here is also found the delimitation in principle of the investigative field of historical ethnology from that of the science of history proper.

The name "ethnology," or the science of peoples, does not itself indicate any modally defined field of investigation. A people is a concrete societal community, and functions as such in a similar way in all of the modal aspects of reality. Furthermore, a folk community exists as such, that is, without a differentiated state, only in primitive cultural relationships. This already establishes the principle that ethnology must limit its investigation to as-yet-undifferentiated cultures, or to the traces of primitive culture (folk lore) in already unfolded societies.

The question whether a science which investigates this primitive folk community in the coherence of all of its aspects is possible can only be considered later when we examine the problem of sociology. We limit ourselves now, however, to historical ethnology that studies the development of culture in primitive peoples in which the sociological problem is already presupposed, as will later become evident.

Since the aprioristic constructions of the older ethnology have been discredited – the older ethnology came under the influence of Darwin and economic-historical materialism – the insight that ethnology, as cultural ethnology, has a historical field of investigation, as does the science of history, and that within this field of investigation it must proceed not according to a natural-scientific, but a cultural-historical method, has increasingly been gaining ground.

Here, however, immediately lies the danger that the boundaries between these two sciences will be eliminated. To be specific, various proponents of the *Kulturkreislehre*, established in ethnology by Frobenius, who, on the basis of ethnological investigations, want to establish a cultural genealogy, do not observe any essential difference between historical ethnology and the science of history. In particular, they set themselves against the delimitation of its field of investigation which the science of history still maintains only investigates the development of culture transmitted in written sources, inscriptions, and monuments. They consider this criterion to be entirely subordinate to the fact that history is in essence an activity which is supposed to be indifferent to its symbolical signification.

In the light of our investigations above, this conception must be rejected as being incorrect in principle. To be precise, symbolical signifying of history appeared to be a trustworthy criterion for the disclosure of a culture which is always accompanied by an awakening into historical consciousness and a breaking out of rigidifying isolation.

The authentic science of history must only investigate the course of development of those cultures which have been absorbed into the developmental stream of disclosed cultures. Undoubtedly, under this rubric also fall the primitive phases of cultures. It can be documented that these have been incorporated into world history throughout the ages, as has been the case, for instance, with prehistorical Greek, Gallo-Celtic, and the Old German cultures.

On the other side, even the remains of primitive cultures that cling to developed cultures remain outside of the field of investigation for the science of history proper. Thus folklore in its entirety falls within the field of ethnology.

Finally, with respect to cultures which have arrived at a relatively high level of development but which have come to stand outside the stream of world history and have become static in their isolation (think of the old Maya and Inca cultures, the Hindu culture in Java, etc.), only in their static condition do these belong to ethnology's field of investigation. By contrast, their previous history of development is undoubtedly a theme for history proper.

What now is the importance of the strict distinction between the investigative fields of historical ethnology and the science of history proper? Its importance lies primarily in the fact that the method of both sciences, with all of their similarities, nevertheless, remains fundamentally different, a difference that is most intimately connected with the differences between isolated and developed cultures. Ethnologists who apply the culture-historical method will nonetheless have to follow an isolating, analytical method. According to this method, they begin with elementary or early cultures, and later primary cultures which have developed autochthonously, in complete isolation. Insofar as the later, secondary cultural spheres have developed out of a mixture of primary ones, it is nevertheless a requirement of ethnological method to analyze these secondary cultures and their elements. These elements therefore are again isolated with respect to one another. But for the science of history proper this is a completely useless method.

Furthermore, truly developed cultural spheres do not develop by the intermingling of isolated elementary and primary cultures, rather, they only unfold their historical individuality in relation to world history. This historical individuality, in other words, can only be understood in terms of international cultural intercourse. So, for example, the Dutch, English, French, or German cultures have not been built out of a superficial mixing of all sorts of primary cultural elements; their national historical traits were only formed in the modern disclosed development of culture. Naturally, this does not in any way exclude the borrowing of foreign cultural elements. The fruitful interaction of the civilized European peoples brought forth new historical individualities. In contrast, ethnology in its investigations, of Dutch culture for example, keeps searching for old tribal elements, such as those of the Frisian, Frankish, Saxon,[1] and the continuing existence of these old elements of culture in folk songs, folk costumes, mores, and customs. In short, it will investigate folklore in its entirety, which is of no interest to the science of history proper.

Ethnology and the science of history, in other words, have different conceptions of historical development, even though they are closely bound together in the modal structure of history.

Because this point, as will later emerge, is also of fundamental importance for legal history, we have to give some further attention to it in the discussion at hand. In part 2.3, the biotic analogy in historical develop-

---

[1] The encouraging renaissance of Frisian culture in most recent times, which allows the expectation of a historical future, has only been possible in opened up cultural development. It cannot be understood in terms of an isolated Frisian folklore.

ment was identified. It can now be observed in more detail that, in an isolated, closed culture, historical development does not actually rise above this analogy. It vegetates, confining itself to the possibilities of development which are present in its isolated existence. Influences from outside, for instance, the borrowing of new tools, are only passively received, without any internal impetus towards new cultural formations. Historical development manifests here a uniform course in rigid dependency on the organic conditions of life. If the bearers of the group's culture die out, the culture dies with them without leaving a trace behind in world history.

It is quite the reverse in the historical development of the disclosed spheres of culture. Essential tendencies for development of the old cultural centers of world history, Egypt, Babylon, Persia, Mycenae, Crete, Athens, Rome, Palestine, Arabia, etc., passed over into the culture of the Middle Ages and that of modern Western culture. By the fertilization of the German cultures, entirely new forms of civilization were brought forth in this way. This opened cultural development has been freed from strict dependence on the life-conditions of a tribe or a people. It does not vegetate within the narrow boundaries of isolated, undifferentiated cultural spheres, but like a flowing river constantly carves out for itself new channels.

This development exhibits a directed character. The meaning of history discloses itself in cultural development by directing itself to the meaning of the later law-spheres, in the last instance, to that of faith. It is not possible to grasp this historical evolution in a rigid concept. It is indeed possible, however, to grasp it in a theoretical limiting-concept,[1] an idea of development which in the final analysis relates the entire opening process to the religious root of the creation. This is essentially an idea of the origin, the root, and the direction of world history.

The historical idea of development is of necessity grounded in a cosmonomic idea. It must be placed at the foundation of the science of history proper if the latter is to maintain its distinctiveness over against historical ethnology. Furthermore, it undoubtedly includes a criterion for judging the course of history. The conception of this criterion, on the immanence standpoint, will be very different from that based upon the Christian transcendence standpoint.

The historical idea of development was conceived by the Enlightenment philosophy of history (Voltaire and his followers) as a steady progress of humanity, which emanated from a belief in the homogeneity of hu-

---

1 *Editor's note:* "Limiting concept" is the generally accepted translation of *grensbegrip*. However, the more literal "boundary-concept," or "understanding transcending the limits of a concept," perhaps gives a better indication of what Dooyeweerd actually means by the term "idea." The term "idea" designates a mode of human understanding transcending the limits of concept-formation.

man nature concentrated in autonomous reason. It was thought that the direction of the opening process was completely determined by the progress of science. Again other ideas of development were developed from the immanence standpoint by Herder, Kant, Fichte, Schelling, and Hegel.

Naturally, we shall return to this point when we examine the problem of the idea of law.[1] At this point we are only interested in the fact that there is no longer a place for a truly historical idea of development in the positivistic-historical approach to the science of history which, since the death of the great Leopold von Ranke, has become increasingly dominant in historical description.

This is explicable in terms of the peculiar orientation of this positivistic approach which has an eye for the variable subjective side of historical facts. It no longer believes, as did the earlier idealistic approach in immanence philosophy, in eternal ideas of reason which were supposed to be realized in the course of history. Because the historical process, on its subjective side, is absolutized, the historical process, in this positivistic conception, does not display any anticipation to the opened meaning of later law-spheres, let alone an orientation to the religious fullness of the meaning of history.

In terms of this positivistic preconception, the boundaries between ethnology and the science of history must also become vague. Insofar as the boundaries are still maintained, that is, by holding fast to the old criterion, the science of history has to restrict its investigations to cultural development whose remains are written sources, inscriptions, or monuments. It does this in the name of scientific tradition but without any insight into the true grounds for this criterion.

For those who would still attempt to write a world history from this positivistic-historicist standpoint, cultures are treated as kinds of plant-like organisms which are enclosed within themselves, the development of which only displays the biotic analogies of birth, maturation, old age, and death. It was Oswald Spengler, in particular, who attempted in his famous book, *The Decline of the West*, to give a true morphology of world cultures.

With respect to the history of law, it is striking that the Historical School has not yet managed to avoid the danger of viewing the disclosed national cultures as self-enclosed organisms which, at least in the early stages of development, produce their own law, language, economics, art, and social forms of intercourse in a conscious process of growth. The school's view of legal history immediately found itself in an embarrassing situation when it had to establish a place in the development of culture for that great legal process, the Germanic reception of Roman law. This applied especially to Puchta, a student of von Savigny, who gave it a biased

---

1 *Editor's note:* "Law" is used here in the juridical not cosmic sense.

nationalistic character. The Historical School could only attempt to explain this reception in terms of the historical spirit of the German people, an attempt that naturally was doomed to failure from the outset and brought sharp criticism upon itself. We shall return to this point again at the appropriate juncture.

Historical differentiation and integration, which is carried out according to the norm of development in the disclosure of culture – where we discovered an anticipation of the opened meaning of social intercourse – finds its parallel in a remarkable individualizing of the culture. Now for the first time there emerges the historical individuality of the former of history, as well as of the cultural sphere in which that person operates. At the same time nationality[1] and individual cultural artifacts now also achieve their most pregnant meaning. The individual personality is no longer absorbed within the confines of a closed cultural sphere but gains the opportunity to freely unfold its talents and its genius. At this point, the individual formers of history, whose formative work has world-historical significance, first set foot on the historical stage.

In primitive, isolated cultural spheres there is no lack of individual traits. But in itself this cultural individuality is of little interest to the science of history because it repeats itself in relative uniformity within the successive phases of cultural development, maintained by the power of a rigid cultural tradition. It is true that even here it is possible for particularly gifted individuals to emerge – ethnological researchers have repeatedly established this – but their cultural activity cannot truly be called opened up so long as the isolation in which they function is maintained by the tradition.

---

1 National individuality stands in sharp opposition to the "folk" in the ideology of national socialism. German nazism consciously attempted to suppress the typically national in favor of a great Germanic empire. It attempted to awaken a "folk" ideal in every people that was "elected" to participate in this kingdom. In essence, it was nothing more than an endeavor to revive a primitive, heathen folk-conception of German antiquity. The elevation of folk-lore to the real center of culture was entirely suited to this program. The emergence of a truly national individuality is in every case necessarily linked with a suppression of these folk-elements. They are retained by the tradition, partly as local idiosyncrasies which are interesting in themselves but gradually die out (local costumes, folk dances, etc.), partly as the ossified forms of a primitive, heathen phase of culture (such as Easter bonfires, Santa Claus, etc.) the origins of which are no longer understood. However, they have not a single internal connection with true national life. A nation is a community qualified in a politically-historical manner which has arisen in history through a coincidence of political circumstances. Community of religion, language, art, mores, and usages is not necessary for the existence of a nation (cf. the Swiss nation), but neither is it sufficient (cf. the medieval Dutch cultural community). National individuality stands under the test of a normative-national type that should be realized in an increasingly pure form in a people.

On the contrary, opened culture is always assuming new individual forms of a world-historical character on which individual formers of culture have placed their personal stamp.

This is also the kernel of truth in the opposition between the natural-scientific and the historical method of concept-formation introduced by the neo-Kantian thinker Heinrich Rickert. According to Rickert, natural science proceeds in a generalizing and "value-blind" fashion. It attempts to track down general law-conformities and does not therefore orient itself to cultural values. The science of history, by contrast, according to him, is only able to work in an individualizing way and in relation to values. It actually wants to grasp the individual in its relatedness to cultural values.

It must be observed that historical individuality in the first place can only derive its modal meaning from the cultural aspect as free, formative control. Culture cannot therefore, as Rickert supposed, be defined as "individual relatedness to values of a physico-psychical reality," that is, in his line of thought, an unqualified individual relation between the sensory kingdom of natural phenomena and the supra-sensory kingdom of values.

We saw that opened cultural individuality initially develops in the cultural intercourse of peoples. However, this individualizing can only develop fruitfully and in conformity with the historical norm of development if, along with it, the principle of cultural economy is taken into consideration. Here we encounter the economic anticipation in the modal meaning of history.

Every excessive development of power on the part of one differentiated culture sphere at the cost of another, every suffocating of a particular cultural factor, according to the divine ordinance for the process of development in history, leads to disharmony (aesthetic anticipation) and is avenged by God's world judgment in history (the jural anticipation: *Weltgeschichte* as *Weltgericht*).

Thus, in the 18th century, natural science's overdeveloped cultural power led to a disturbance of the balanced harmony of the elements of Western culture, a drying up of the life of faith, the triumph of a superficial utilitarian, popular morality, a rationalistic rigidifying of art forms, and to an atomizing and technicizing of legal life and economics.[1] Although it also worked in a historically formative way, the French Revolution, at the same time, brought historical judgment upon the divinizing of the mathematical method of analytical thinking.

This is because such a demonic overdevelopment of the cultural power of science always develops itself in cultural worship and divinization of

---

[1] For extensive discussion of this see my *De Wijsbegeerte der Wetsidee*, vol. 2, pp. 216- 217.

the formative power of science; here we touch on the last two anticipations in the modal meaning of history, the moral and the faith anticipations. Ultimately, it is being guided by an apostate faith that seeks the firm ground of cultural development in human reason, that is, in its natural-scientific function of thought.

Here we encounter the role of faith in the opening process, and this forces us to present a summary analysis of the modal sense of this boundary function. Before exploring this theme, however, I would like to utilize our newly acquired insight into the modal structure of the historical aspect in order to come to a provisional conclusion with respect to the treatment of the problem concerning the relationship of law and history.

2.5 The Relationship between Law and History Revisited: Is the Opposition between Historical and Systematic Thinking Correct?

In part 2.2 we concluded with the remark that we cannot be satisfied with only freeing the modal structure of the positive forms of law from historicization, while still regarding the entire variable content of legal phenomena as essentially historical in character.

In that connection we advanced the following proposition: as to its law- and subject-sides, positive law as such is not a historical phenomenon at all; it simply rests on the substructure of historical development. Another way of putting this is to say that positive law has its history, but does not itself have a historical character. In this meaningful form our proposition gets to the heart of the historical conception of law. It must arouse the nearly uniform opposition of modern conceptions of law that are rooted in the immanence standpoint insofar as these have adopted the historical view of temporal reality.

At first sight, our proposition undeniably appears strange to those still enmeshed in the ill-defined conception that views history as a process of coming into being and development in which the past, the present, and the future intermingle with each other. But it is for this very reason that we have devoted so much care and attention to an analysis of the modal character of historical development. Now that we have arrived at a provisional conclusion in this modal analysis of the historical aspect, the arguments that depend for their weight on such an ill-defined conception of history are no longer able to retain their hold on us.

We want first of all to continue debating various commonly acknowledged special problems in legal history. This will have the advantage of giving the reader a more concrete insight into the significance of our investigations for special scientific questions in legal history.

(A) Among legal historians, a well-known matter of dispute is whether the land grants of the Merovingian kings reduced those who received them to the status of vassals, or whether these grants only took on the characteristics of feudal law in the Carolingian period.

According to the historicist conception, the content of feudal law must be viewed as an exclusively historical phenomenon. Thus the historicist assumes that the question is a purely historical one. If, however, one views the question as a historian only, then the jural meaning of feudal law is of necessity completely eliminated.

This jural meaning, to be precise, is only capable of being conceived as a typical jural causal relationship between a legal relationship of persons that originated in the form of a feudal contract, involving a vassal and his feudal lord (superior),[1] and the granting to the vassal of a feudal estate given to him in fee (not as property-owner) with an accompanying right of use, possessing a typical juridical character, to which he might appeal against any claimants.

The entirety of this concrete legal phenomenon, which we call feudal law, it is true, originates out of a typically historical foundation. This historical substratum itself, however, has no jural meaning, and therefore should not be identified with feudal law.

What then is this historical foundation? It is a historical process of development, the origin of which extends far back into the Merovingian era and which continues into the Middle Ages. In this process of development, which we may characterize as the history of the feudal systems, there occurs a typical power struggle. On the one hand, it is a struggle between the state and the church. On the other hand, it is one between both of these and the power of the aristocracy. Furthermore, the political contest between the Frankish kingdom and the Arabs played a formative part in this entire evolution.

The Merovingian kings had already attempted to strengthen their position by having the aristocracy, which had gradually surrounded themselves with a private army, more tightly bound to their service by means of land grants. Nor did they hesitate to secularize ecclesiastical property when royal property did not suffice, a practice in violation of canon law which brought forth increasing protests from the church.

A similar politico-historical picture, exacerbated by the invasion of the Arabs, presents itself in the 8th century, with the Carolingians resorting to the expedient of again secularizing ecclesiastical property in order to present benefices to their powerful vassals.

From an economic-historical point of view, these benefices had a role no different from that of the Merovingian land grants. Furthermore, these land grants often only conveyed an inalienable right of enjoyment for the life of the beneficiary. The politico-historical situation in which both

---

1 In the feudal contract, the vassal places himself in the personal service of his lord by a "commendation," with a handshake and the expression of a vassal's oath; the lord assumes the duty to give shelter to and protect the vassal.

kinds of grants were made did not differ essentially from each other. The historical power-motif that lay at the foundation of both, namely, the need to bind the spiritual and worldly aristocracy to particular services of fealty to the king, was the same. And, considered from a purely historical point of view, was the vassal relationship any more than a service relationship that was formed to strengthen the power of the lord? Furthermore, *beneficium* was no more exclusively juridical in its technical meaning than was the later term *feudum*.

What grounds therefore does the historian have for allowing the feudal system to originate at the time of the secularization of ecclesiastical property under the Carolingians?

The well-known historian Alphonz Dopsch in fact defended the conception that vassalage and the system of benefices *in historischer Zeit niemals und nirgends getrennt*.[1] Likewise the Merovingian land grants were therefore already supposed to have created vassal obligations. The economic-historical causes of this form of compensation of vassal services Dopsch seeks in the *naturwirtschaftlichen Zersetzungsprozess des römischen Imperiums*,[2] that is to say, in the phenomenon that money in circulation was being steadily diminished by the bartering of goods, a process of disintegration in which the Merovingian kingdom was involved, as were the other German kingdoms.

The source material has already disproved this hypothesis; as if it could be known that vassalage and the system of benefices had not been independently occurring phenomena. But even leaving aside this erroneous hypothesis, it is true in any case that Dopsch eliminated what is a truly legal-historical question, namely, in which historical era did the feudal system originate?

According to the insightful description of the famous German legal historian Heinrich Brunner,[3] the Merovingian land grants must be juridically viewed as grants of restricted property[4] given for the purpose of remuneration on condition of faithful service on the part of the grantees. By contrast, feudal benefices were originally exclusively grants of secularized ecclesiastical property in the particular form of *precaria sub verbo regis* (that is to say, the loan of its goods by the church at the command of the king), under which no property at all changed hands. This is a jural state of

---

1 "...at no historical point in time were ever separated..." Alphonz Dopsch, *Grundlagen der europäische Kulturentwicklung*, vol. 2, no. 2 (1924): 305 ff.
2 "The natural-scientific process of replacing the Roman Empire."
3 Heinrich Brunner, *Die Landschenkungen der Merovinger und Agilofinger*, in *Sitzungsberichte der preuszischen Akademie der Wissenschaften* (1885), 1173 ff.
4 That is to say, not yet differentiated within civil property law, but a pattern of property in which the public legal authority and private legal power are still intermingled in an undifferentiated way.

affairs that cannot be understood merely in terms of historical development.

The historical development of feudal law is unbreakably interrelated with economic, national, and ecclesiastical history, but the historian who truly wants to study the legal history of the feudal system cannot conceive the typical jural pattern of the feudal system in terms of historical evolution. The modal meaning of history is, after all, different from that of law.

Heinrich Mitteis may be cited in support of this point. In respect of the above mentioned controversy between Dopsch and his opponents, he makes the following assertion in his book *Lehnrecht und Staatsgewalt* (1933, p. 115), which, at least as a practical guide for legal-historical investigation, is consistent with our own conclusions, even though the author still adheres to the traditional prejudice that feudal law is a historical phenomenon:

> The currently well articulated controversy regarding the genesis of the *Benefiziums* is probably better delimited from a methodological point of view. ... The historian will, driven by the urge to unite the social complex into a unity[1] encompassing a larger number of phenomena, try to subsume these phenomena under a common denominator. The jurist, on the other hand, in case the aim is not to give up jural categories altogether, will always feel bound to economic and social phenomena understood in juridical terms. The historian will therefore develop a larger picture of the *Benefizialwesens* than the juridical *Benefizialwesens* seen as an element of Lehnrecht. In the treatment of the latter one would only be able to commit oneself in that moment, because also the concrete legal relation between *Herr* and *Vasall* found a legal form within given variable limits.[2]

In his *Vom Lebenswert der Rechtsgeschichte* (Weimar, 1947) also, Mitteis makes a distinction between the politico-historical and the legal-historical method. Legal historians take their point of departure in law. All historical events are investigated with the use of distinctly legal categories. "Der Stoff der Geschichte und der Rechtsgeschichte ist der gleiche; nur die Betrachtungsweise ist verschieden."[3]

Furthermore, when he speaks (p. 69) about the necessity of juridical concept-formation for the history of law, he does not mean that legal history requires a fundamental concept of law in order to distinguish the jural

---

1 No doubt what is meant is a historical connection.
2 Undoubtedly this point has not been made clearly. It is not a question of more or less, but of a different modal aspect of the feudal system. But I do not in any way admit that Mitteis evinces a conscious insight into the modal structure of history and law; on the contrary, on this point he stays with the view that positive law is a historical phenomenon *sui generis*.
3 Heinrich Mitteis, *Vom Lebenswert der Rechtsgeschichte* (Weimar, 1947), 59. The subject-matter of history and legal history is the same; only the mode of investigation differs.

from the other normative sides of reality. The distinction is, to be sure, only the result of a mode of observation. What he really means is that the legal historian will better understand particular historical contexts in this fashion, because juridical concepts can sometimes be maintained in an analogical way. Early Renaissance (proto-Renaissance) or pre-Reformation, for instance, are historical conceptions, the jural analogy of which resides in the juridical concept "preparatory act" (pp. 70–71).

Furthermore, Mitteis sees in history a *"Fortschritt im Bewußtsein der Freiheit,"* that is, progress, through "being in accord with one's self," within the consciousness of the freedom (*Beisichselbstsein*) of the spirit, in the realization of human worth, in the conscious bringing into being of what must be (p. 83). Culture in its entirety is therefore historical life.

This conception is borrowed from Hegel. The historical is not a particular aspect of reality but it is reality in its entirety. The legal historian has the task of showing the progress toward freedom in the past and of making transparent and clear the consciousness of freedom and its limits (pp. 83, 84, 100). In this task lies the value of legal history for the forming of personality. According to Mitteis, legal history is of great significance for the science of history. He maintains that, "No single branch of legal science can dispense with the legal point of view" (p. 60).

This is the case because law has always taken and still occupies a very special place in life. Law is a *sozialer Primärfaktor*.[1] The relevance of legal history for the science of law, amongst other things, is that it serves as a propaedeutic and avoids the ossification of legal doctrine.[2]

(B) Is it in fact true that the Middle Ages did not know the distinction between public and private law? This is another issue that has come to the fore recently in legal history. Attention has been focused, in this respect, on the significance of a sharp distinction between the historical and the jural aspects. From this it also appears that legal historians are unable to distinguish the real jural structure of their factual material from historical development.

Even though there is presently a vehement discussion about the intrinsic value of the distinction between public and private law and about the criterion to be used in making it, we can say provisionally in explanation of these terms that, in contrast to private law, public law is inextricably bound up with the internal organization of the internal life of the state,[3]

---

1 Mitteis, *Vom Lebenswert der Rechtsgeschichte*, 60: a "primary social factor."
2 Mitteis, *Vom Lebenswert der Rechtsgeschichte*, 78–79. A similar discussion is found in Mitteis' book, *Über das Natuurecht*. We shall return to this point in the historical volume (vol. 2) of *Encyclopedia of the Science of Law*.
3 According to the Roman Catholic conception with that of the church also.

while private law regulates the other social relationships with respect to their jural aspect.

It may very well be true that this legal differentiation has not come into being in a particular phase of cultural development because the structure of the state has not yet been realized. In my opinion, this was indeed the case in the Middle Ages. But it is a faulty conception of public law, bound up as it is with the internal structure of the state, to think it has to be viewed as a historical phenomenon and that the historian might therefore be able to investigate the question we have posed exclusively from the standpoint of historical science.

The historian von Below, in his book *Der Deutsche Staat des Mittelalters*, had already subjected the dominant viewpoint to the acute criticism that the distinction between public and private law was unknown in the Middle Ages. He pointed to the necessity of juridically educating historians who want to engage themselves with a historico-legal question such as this. In particular, he criticized writers who had interpreted what he considered to be, in essence, public legal relationships in medieval society from an economic-historical point of view as concerned with seignorial land relationships or with relationships of villeinage.[1]

What we have here involves a question of the juridical interpretation of the source materials, a problem that cannot be solved from purely historical points of view.[2] Our insight is that this is not the case. How are legal historians to determine whether, for instance, the "prayer" of the feudal lord must be viewed as a genuine public legal impost or rather as a private legal duty on land, if they do not have any insight into the inner meaning of the structure of public law? And this juridical structure cannot be read off directly, anymore than feudal law can be read off simply from an analysis of the modal meaning of law, even though it has a typically juridical content.

Again, it may be – in my opinion it is – the case that the entire debate as to whether the prayer has a public-legal or a private-legal character is inapt for the legal states of affairs that prevailed during the Middle Ages because, at this time, legal life still had an undifferentiated character. Yet legal historians still find themselves confronting the problem as to what is the juridical character that must then be attributed to the prayer. This is a

---

1 In the case of von Below, too, this is not at all to say that he has a conscious insight into the modal differentiation of history and positive law. As with Mitteis, he holds fast to the traditional viewpoint of positive law as a historical phenomenon *sui generis*.
2 Cf. Emilio Betti, "Methode und Wert des heutigen Studium des Römsichen Rechts," *Tijdschrift voor rechtsgeschiedenis* XV, no. 2 (1937): 137 ff. for the necessity of the insights of legal dogmatics for the historical study of Roman law. The primary legal-historical question naturally is whether the medieval "prayer" can already be viewed as a differentiated (either public or private) legal phenomenon.

normative-juridical question, which cannot be answered solely in terms of the historical aspect.

(C) We have to make an additional observation concerning the distinction between the historical and legal-scientific forming of concepts.

The claim is often heard that legal dogmatics, in contradistinction to the science of history, works with abstract systematic concepts by means of which legal phenomena are theoretically systematized. The science of history, by contrast, is supposed to proceed not in a systematic way but only descriptively. Historical concepts are supposed to have a concrete, individual content and to simply identify the real events in a concrete way.

The proposition cannot be maintained in this form. We saw earlier that there is no scientific thought that is not systematic in the sense that it must grasp phenomena in a theoretical coherence. Furthermore, truly theoretical concepts can never have a purely descriptive content that would more or less represent reality in its entirety.

In fact, the science of history must proceed as systematically as the science of law. But historical systematics is quite different from that of legal science because the modal meaning of the historical field of investigation differs radically from the modal meaning of the jural.

The systematics of historical science comprises a theoretically abstracted examination of the historical developmental coherence in which every historically investigated phenomenon should be so conceived that its particular historical significance can be understood in terms of the entire context of a historical time-conception.

For example, it would be inconsistent with the practice of historical systematics if a collection of historical sources from the 8th and 9th centuries were interpreted in isolation from the entire cultural context of that time; this approach results in the historical data being torn out of their historical context.

Another instance of conflict with legal historical systematics occurs when the very sophisticated distinction between possession and the civil right of ownership, which already implies the ability to engage in a high degree of theoretical abstraction, is read back into the still quite primitive customary laws of the Frankish kingdom. Or if one wants to interpret a primitive delictual action procedure that is brought against a pirate, such as revindication, that is, an action seeking the return of property on account of loss of possession. Such an action for recovery, after all, presupposes the concept of an abstract property right, which remains in existence notwithstanding the loss of actual possession. But according to a truly historical way of thinking, such an abstract concept may not be presupposed during a cultural phase of German society where legal concepts are still rigidly bound to sensory representation and every legal transaction is performed with vivid symbolism in order to present its sensorily perceptible nature, as it were, before one's eyes.

The legal historian has the task of explaining the jural coherence of the positive forms of law that have developed out of the substratum of a defined historical period in a given context of historical development. In its investigations, however, juridical systematics must take the lead, in the sense that on each occasion the investigator must relate the historical developmental contexts, which lie at the foundation of the systematics, to the systematic-juridically conceived legal forms from their earliest stage of development. In this respect, the legal forms themselves ought to be viewed within the course of their own development; one should not begin with the already fully developed form.

This proposition may be elucidated by referring to our first illustration, the legal historical question regarding the historical period which must have given rise to the appearance of true feudal law. To answer this question it is first necessary to delineate, in a systematic juridical fashion, the feudal system itself as a positive legal configuration out of the concrete phenomena of life which are present in the source material. To do this one starts with the point of time at which the feudal system first began to develop.

Only after that can one fruitfully embark upon an investigation into the historical process of development of this feudal law and thus attempt to establish, in a legal historical way, what time period and under what historical conditions it is that vassalage and the system of benefices bind themselves to a new legal configuration, and how this legal configuration adapts itself in a modified form to the new historical situation. Those who attempt to reverse this relation between juridical and historical systematics are necessarily faced with a historical levelling of the jural aspect. Indeed, they are no longer writing legal history because true legal history is possible only if positive law is itself something other than its historical process of development. The historical aspect of a concrete societal configuration such as feudalism does not have its own history but is itself historical in character. Only that which in its inner meaning is more or other than a historical phenomenon is capable of having a history.

So the state, the church, family life, the industrial world, etc., have their historical development because they are concrete forms of society which function in all the aspects of reality, and thus also have their historical aspect.

So feudal law also has its history because, as the jural aspect of concrete feudalism, it is something other than the historical aspect of feudalism.

But the history of an abstract historico-developmental context is conceptually no more possible as a combination of words than is the expression, "the juridical side of feudal law." What is, modally-speaking, completely encompassed by the historical aspect cannot itself have a history.

From the above, it naturally follows that genuine legal dogmatics, which works with systematic juridical concepts, cannot in any way manifest a rigid character; instead, it remains bound to the historical development of legal life. The modal structure of legal life undoubtedly remains constant, retaining its validity for all times.[1] But the positive forms of law that realize themselves within this constant structure are of a variable character and change with the various phases of culture.

The civil legal figure of property in classical Roman law (*ius gentium*), for instance, remains strongly bound to Roman culture at its flowering and was not known, either in the primitive phase of Roman law, or in the old Germanic law. Only the civil legal structure of property law bears a constant character; but this structure demands positivizing, and the positive forms of law change with their historical phases.

That is not to say, however, that the positive legal forms themselves are historical phenomena, anymore than the science of legal dogmatics can be assimilated into the science of history.

The jural coherence of the positive forms of law carries a unique, irreducible character and yet remains unbreakably interwoven with the historical coherence of the evolution of culture.

2.6 The Modal Structure of Faith as the Temporal Boundary Function and its Place in the Opening Process

When we investigated the anticipatory moments in the modal structure of history, we finally encountered the anticipation in which the meaning of history points beyond itself to the meaning of belief as the second boundary function of our temporal cosmos. It appeared that, ultimately, the entire opening process in history stands under the leading of faith.

As the temporal modal boundary function of reality, believing should not, in any fashion whatsoever, be identified with religion, that is, with the central relationship of humankind to its Creator. As a subjective function, which is subjected to its own unique norms, faith is characteristic of all people, believers in Christ as well as those for whom faith reveals itself in an apostate direction.

There is apostate faith and faith that can become operative only through the Spirit of God. But both of them function within the modal structure of one and the same function which was already implanted in human nature

---

[1] This does not hold for a theoretical concept of law resulting from subjective theoretical investigation of this structure. The neo-Kantian conception of law as a universally valid subjective category of thought confuses this modal structure of law with the subjective concept of it and is refuted by the facts.

at the creation.[1] In both instances the following ought to be distinguished from one another: the subjective function, the norm, the content, the direction, the religious root, and the firm ground of faith. Faith truly reveals itself only in the unbreakable coherence of all of these moments; but in all this the modal function as such remains distinct from its supra-temporal root and its (true or supposed) firm ground, with which the difference in orientation and content between true and false faith has a direct connection.

The modal function of faith should not be identified therefore with the religious root of existence, with the heart, out of which are the issues of life. The faith-function, the logical function of thought, aesthetic valuation, etc., are distinct functions, which belong to various aspects of temporal reality, being contained in law-spheres with a unique, mutually irreducible character. The religious root of our entire existence, however, is not a modal function and is not incorporated into a temporal law-sphere.

The Bible (cf. II Cor. 5: 7; Rom. 8: 24; I Cor. 13: 12) also points us clearly to the temporal boundary character of true belief in Christ here on earth, which will be consummated in the full religious vision, in "seeing face to face." Even though the modal function of faith remains temporal in character, only within eternity does the consummation of faith, the full vision of faith, for the first time come within our purview. And the true firm ground of faith, naturally, is exalted above time in an absolute sense because it can only be found in God himself as the absolute source of truth.

I now want to initiate a brief investigation into the modal structure of the faith-function, insofar as this is necessary to gain insight into all kinds of questions that have a direct bearing upon the opening process in history.

This modal structure of *pistis* is completely misconstrued if the character of faith has not been conceived as the ultimate boundary function, that is to say, in its immediate relatedness to the transcendent root and origin of the creation.

Faith cannot exist as a temporal boundary function apart from the revelation of God, the Origin. In a nonspiritual and imprecise way of speaking, we indeed also talk of "believing," in the sense of having an opinion (Greek, *doxa*), a noncertain knowing. For example, one might say, "I be-

---

[1] The conception that faith is a completely unique function that was implanted in human nature at the creation was first retrieved for theology by Abraham Kuyper (cf. his *Encyclopaedie der heilige Godgeleerdheid*, vol. 2, par. 11). In scholastic theology it was completely lost because of the introduction of the false opposition between nature and grace. The center of human nature was then sought in reason. Faith was placed outside nature and considered as belonging to the sphere of grace, in Thomas Aquinas, as a supernatural gift of grace to the intellect (*donum superadditum intellectus*).

lieve I have seen you before." But the central modal sense of faith is the very opposite of that. It is, to be specific, a transcendental certainty in time concerning the firm ground of truth; it is being grasped in the heart of our existence by a revelation of the Origin of all things.[1]

This is the only meaning-nucleus that of itself points beyond time, and not merely via anticipatory moments of meaning, as is true of all the other meaning-nuclei.

Strictly speaking therefore it is impossible to form a concept of the modal sense of faith because its meaning-nucleus does not allow itself to be isolated from the One who transcends the possibility of all conceptualization. Every theoretical concept presupposes faith because it is dependent upon logical certainty with respect to the absolute Ground of Truth. And this assurance, as an anticipation to the modal meaning of faith, is in the final analysis unilaterally dependent upon original certainty with regard to the firm ground of truth, which can only be attained in faith.

The analysis of the modal structure of *pistis* is only able to present us with a theoretical idea, a boundary concept, of its nuclear meaning. Because this meaning-nucleus itself possesses a transcendental limiting character (that is to say, in its fundamental character it points itself beyond to the supra-temporal root and Origin of the entire temporal creation), all of the retrocipatory or analogical moments of meaning within the modal structure of the faith-aspect participate in this transcendental boundary character. There is the moral analogy of love connected with worship in faith (*cultus*), the jural analogy of justification by faith, the aesthetic analogy of the harmony of faith, the economic analogy of the sacrifices of faith in comparing the relative value of eternal and temporal things, the social analogy of the communion of faith with God and the communion of the saints, the symbolical analogy of the symbolism of faith (the belief signifying the meaning of God's revelation), the historical analogy of the forms of faith, the logical analogy of certain knowledge in faith, the psychical-sensory analogy of the confidence of faith, the biotic analogy of the life of faith (with its strengthening through preaching, proclamation, prayer, and the use of the sacraments), etc.

It is this very boundary character of the faith-function, its boundary position between eternity and time, that confronts Christian philosophy with the most difficult problems. If faith, as the transcendental boundary function of the temporal cosmos, is truly contained in a unique law-sphere, then, as a consequence, in this aspect as in all the other law-spheres, human subjectivity must be subjected to the unique laws that in this case, of course, are normative in character. Then it can only be divine revelation it-

---

1 Cf. the description of the meaning of faith in Hebrews 11.

self (which finds its religious fulfillment in Christ as the incarnate Word), in relation to its pistical aspect of meaning, that establishes the norm of faith and thus contains the principle (the law) for subjective believing.

But the Divine Self-revelation, which expresses itself in all of God's creation, "in all the works of his hands," shows in its temporal faith-dimension that it is connected with history. This is seen insofar as revelation (as special revelation of salvation) has a progressive character, just as the revelation of Jesus Christ itself has also entered history and has its historical meaning-side. From this we see that the meaning of faith is also capable of being opened up. In spite of the completely unique modal character of faith, this disclosure can never be grasped apart from historical development.

Is it also possible, in respect of faith, to speak of a closed, still-rigid structure and of an opened, deepened structure, such as appeared to be the case with respect to the other aspects of reality? Certainly not in the same sense. To be sure, in the case of the earlier law-spheres, the closed structure of the modal aspect only appeared to be given in the context of the meaning-nucleus and the retrocipations, while the deepened, or opened, structure first appeared to come to expression in the anticipatory moments of meaning.

But as we know, matters are completely different with respect to the modal structure of faith. Here, no doubt, the meaning-nucleus already points beyond time and all modal retrocipations also participate in this boundary character, while modal anticipations cannot be present in this structure because there are no other law-spheres subsequent to that of faith.

How then must the terms "closed" and "opened" structure in the modal sense of faith be understood?

From the beginning, Christian theology has made a distinction between the general revelation of God in nature (that is, in God's entire work of creation) and general and special Word-revelation. To locate the particular sense in which we may speak of a "closed structure" of the function of faith it is apparent that the point of connection will have to be sought in the revelation in nature.

In addition, however, attention must immediately be focused on the original, essential connection between "natural revelation" (*revelatio naturalis*) and general Word-revelation. At the creation of the cosmos God revealed himself within his creation, both in its religious root (the "heart" of the human being) and in its temporal coherence of meaning, through creating humankind in his image and bringing the divine fullness of being to a meaningful creaturely expression within the entire creation. But from the time of creation, this revelation of God within the nature of the cosmos was sustained and interpreted by the Word-revelation.

Encyclopedia of the Science of Law: Introduction - Part 2

Originally, and even after the Fall, this did not in any way have a particular but rather a thoroughly universal character, that is to say, it was directed to humankind as a whole. Commencing with Abraham, an independent line of development of a Word-revelation began that was no longer universal. Later, because of the threat of general apostasy, the people of Israel would provisionally become its selected bearer until the appearance of the Word itself in the flesh.[1]

Now in this Word-revelation God speaks to humanity, which is required to listen in faith. In this faithful listening to God's Word there is an initial disclosure to the insight of faith of the true sense of God's revelation in the nature of the creation, "in all the works of his hands." Apostasy begins therefore with an unwillingness to listen to God's Word, with the forsaking of that Word by the heart, which thereby leads to a closing-off of human *pistis* from God's speaking to us.

Apostasy from the Word-revelation, God's revelation in all his creation and primarily in the human heart, brought a judgement upon humankind. Where the heart closed itself off and abandoned God, the faith-function also became impervious to the light of God's Word. *Pistis*, however, retained its transcendental boundary character. It had to continue directing itself to a firm ground of truth which reveals itself in the creation. But it did this now by seeking that firm ground within the creation itself, in an idolatrous absolutizing of creaturely meaning. The direction of *pistis* became apostate; natural faith was transformed into unbelief in opposition to the Word-revelation. However, unbelief here must not be understood in a negative-logical sense; it must be understood negatively only within the meaning of the faith-function itself, in the sense of a fall regarding the subject, direction, and content of faith.

Now if it is true that apostate faith can only reveal itself in the modal sense of *pistis*, if, in other words, even the most apostate faith still retains its pistical character, then this modal function must be able to exist in a structurally closed condition. This structure, however, in contrast to the closed structure of the earlier modal functions, may be conceived as a closed structure of a transcendental sort. That is to say, it is directed towards a transcendent[2] being but is not itself transcendent.

"Closed structure," can be expressed thus: the boundary-point of the possibility of apostasy in faith life, whereby, under the leading of this apostate faith, all of the normative anticipatory moments of the earlier law-spheres remain closed. In other words, apostasy is that condition of

---

1 Cf. Herman Bavinck, *The Philosophy of Revelation: The Stone Lectures for 1908-1909, Princeton Theological Seminary* (London, Boston, and Calcutta: Longmans, Green and Co., 1909).
2 *General Editor's note*: The Dutch text here employs the mistaken word "transcendental" where it is clear that "transcendent" is meant.

faith, the leading boundary function, which renders the entire opening process in the normative law-spheres impossible.

It is of great importance to obtain an insight into this transcendental limiting point of the apostasy of faith because only from this point of departure can primitive cultures be understood. In this closed structure, faith can never be the point of contact for the positive development and meaning-disclosure of the faith-function which is part of human nature. It must, rather, be seen as a limiting point in the "degeneration," in the corruption and confusion of faith-life. *It can, however, function as a point of contact for a deepening of meaning, for an opening up of meaning in the process of the apostasy of faith.* We shall speak of this further in what follows.

For the positive development and deepening of the meaning of faith, in the full Christian sense, the point of contact will instead have to be sought in the structure of the pistical function as originally created in humankind, and in its initial receptivity to divine revelation. After the Fall, however, this initial opening up is only possible by the gracious operation of God's Spirit in the opening up of the heart. Certainly, this does not involve the creation of a new faith-function. But the initial opening up of apostate faith remains a radical reversal in the orientation of faith which is dependent upon the regeneration of the heart. By itself fallen human nature can never bring about this conversion.

Now that the function of faith, even at the transcendental boundary point of its apostasy from Word-revelation, appears unable to step outside the modal structure of its law-sphere and remains subjected to its modal structural law, a question arises as to the nature of the closed principle of revelation which, as a normative principle above all human contrivance and arbitrary volition, still controls even the most apostate faith. This closed (or restrictive) principle of revelation can only be understood in the light of the divine Word-revelation, in terms of the temporal cosmic law-order itself.

The closed structure of the logical and the postlogical aspects is always characterized by a rigid dependence on the prelogical aspects of reality, on the so-called natural dimensions of the cosmos (sensory feeling, organic life, movement, space, and number). The closed structure of *pistis* – the transcendental boundary point in the apostasy of faith, in connection with which all of the earlier normative meaning-functions (the moral, jural, aesthetic, economic, social, lingual, historical, and logical meaning functions) remain under the leading of the pistical aspect in a rigid, closed condition – can only be found therefore in the apostasy of faith towards a primitive divinization of the unknown (still-closed) natural powers, which control life and death, fertility and infertility, and in general the entire biotic-sensory substratum of primitive society.

With the divinization of the closed natural forces, human existence in its entirety becomes rigidly bound within its temporal normative functions to "irrational nature." The "night of nature" covers primitive society like a blanket. In other words, in this closed structure, subjective *pistis* has no other normative revelational principle than that of the transcendental certainty concerning the godhead which reveals itself immanently within closed natural forces that are required to be venerated in the cult of faith (that is, in the worship service).

This restrictive principle of revelation becomes a curse for humanity, resulting in the disorganization of its faith-life; but the principle itself is nevertheless firmly grounded in the divine world order and is thus elevated above all human arbitrariness. In the Word-revelation that finds its fulfillment in Jesus Christ, this principle is not set aside – God even reveals himself in the forces of nature – but rather it is disclosed in its true sense for the first time in relation to the fullness of meaning and the religious unity of divine law, through the whole-hearted service of God in the Christian freedom of being a child of God, which has initially been given to us by means of Christ's work of redemption.

In the closed structure of its apostasy, *pistis* lacks any orientation to religious self-reflection. The dispersion or disintegration of the awareness of personality, which we observe repeatedly in primitive peoples, comes to pistical expression in a remarkable way through the faith-representation of the divine as "mana." It was the ethnologist Codrington who first brought this mana-representation to attention in his well-known book *The Melanesians* (1891). Since then it has been discovered that it is spread among peoples over the entire earth, albeit, under different names (orenda, wakonda, manitu, dema, etc.).

After this discovery there developed a lively debate as to the true meaning of this mana-conception. As a provisional result of this debate we can truly say that this faith representation is characterized by a peculiar fluidity,[1] by a peculiar intermingling of the natural and the supernatural and of the personal and the impersonal. Mana, with its negative correlate, the taboo, is the divine and mysterious which, ubiquitously diffused in things, transcends the trusted everyday sphere of life, and in a kind of fragmentary and fluid way personifies itself in mythical figures. In this way, animals, humans, and spirits can function as inorganic things (for instance, stones), which make an impression because of their unusual form or size and which are seen as a kind of mask of the mysterious mana.

Totemism involves a faith-representation that is thoroughly imbued with belief in mana, whereby the clan venerates a particular animal or a

---

[1] Compare this with the principle of matter ($hul\bar{e}$) of the ancient Greek nature religions.

particular plant as the male or female ancestor of the tribe; the members of the clan identify themselves with the totem animal or the totem plant. They are eagles, kangaroos, date palms, etc. From all of this it is clear how diffuse and disorganized the conception of personality is in this primitive nature-faith.

In the meantime, we also discover in this closed structure of the faith-function that there is a retrocipatory meaning-coherence with the earlier law-spheres. The retrocipatory moments of meaning (analogies) are also included, as we have already observed, in the transcendental boundary character that is peculiar to the modal meaning-nucleus of the pistical aspect.

The law-sphere of faith is immediately founded in the moral law-sphere, which is qualified by the modal sense of love. This will be seen in more detail as we examine the distinction between law and morality. Naturally, love, in its full religious meaning, which in the New Testament is called "the fulfillment of the law," is not being referred to here but only its temporal modal meaning by which it is differentiated from all other modalities of meaning and is inextricably intertwined with these as typified in love between parent and child, conjugal love, love of country, etc.

The retrocipation of faith to this moral sense of love reveals itself in the cultic dimension that is characteristic of all true faith. This cultic element is also essential in the primitive, closed structure that faith manifests in the nature religions. In the veneration of the good and the exorcizing of the evil spirits that manifest themselves in the powers of nature, or so it is believed, is concealed a modal analogy that is immediately rooted in natural love for the power of life and in natural hate towards mysterious powers such as illness, death, barrenness, etc., which threaten the biotic existence of the primitive community.

Whenever this cultic element is lacking and there is only a primitive impulse to control the powers of nature by means of magic, it is not really possible to speak of a belief in God but only in magic. This does not in any way exclude the possibility that belief in God can be suffused with magical elements, which is indeed the case to a great degree with regard to the primitive belief in mana. Magic itself, however, is never to be identified simply with belief in God.

The central problem that now requires our special attention concerns the opening process of *pistis* in the apostate direction. What does this opening process involve and how is it possible? Answering these questions is also highly relevant for the conception of the historical idea of development in which the direction and the origin of the developmental process should be encompassed.

It cannot be denied that, after a period of primitive and undifferentiated faith in nature within the religions of the pagan peoples who have taken a leading position in world history, there has been the emergence of a process of faith-opening in an apostate direction. And this opening process has been directly connected with the emergence of these peoples from a more or less primitive stage of civilization.

So, in the development of the Greek representations of faith, we discover a clear transition from the originally primitive phase of nature, in which an impersonal religion of life predominates, to a phase of culture religion, in which the pantheon assumes idealized personal human forms and divine revelation in the normative personality-functions of science, culture, social life, economics, art, law, and morality is transformed into a polytheistic service of culture gods (historical analogy in the meaning of faith).

In his *Theogony*, the poet-philosopher Hesiod instructs the Greeks as to how the younger gods of measure, order, and harmony are to conquer the older nature gods of indeterminacy (Uranus) and limitlessness (Chronos, the god of limitless time, who devours his own children) and how they are to purify the earth from the grotesque monsters and the indeterminate ephemeral beings.

In Homer's epic, these younger gods, engaging in intercourse with each other and with humans, take on individual, personal form. In its developmental and opening-process, the service of idols transcends the primitive faith of nature, directs itself to the revelation of God in the normative aspects of the temporal cosmos, and begins to conceive of its gods in personal form.

Under the leading of this opening of faith, we also observe the historical norm of individualization and integration that we already saw taking hold in our analysis of the development of Greek civilization. The well-known neo-Kantian philosopher Ernst Cassirer, as has already been remarked in passing, also pointed this out from a completely different standpoint in his *Philosophie der symbolischen Formen* (II, 245–246). In the totemistic primitive life communities, he observes, the individuality of the members is still absorbed within the whole. However, as soon as the consciousness of faith elevates itself to the conception of personal gods, individuals begin to free themselves from being absorbed into the totality of the community. Now, for the first, time, individual persons acquire their independence and their "personal countenance" in contrast to the life of the clan and tribe. Correlatively, accompanying this orientation to the individual, there is at the same time a novel tendency towards the general, for the more inclusive social unities now elevate themselves above the narrow unity of the tribe or group. The personal gods of Homer are also the first, national gods of the Greeks. As such they become the creators of the Pan-Hellenic consciousness, for they are the Olympians, the universal gods of heaven whose worship is not restricted to a particular place. So there is carried out here liberation towards a personal consciousness and an elevation towards national consciousness in one and the same basic formative activity of faith.

Indeed, the opening of faith – which, in the last analysis, as the transcendental limiting function, takes the lead in the entire normative opening process within the earlier law-spheres – in apostasy from the divine Word-revelation is only understandable as a process of humankind's coming to self-awareness in its faith apostasy. In its modal structure of meaning, the function of faith does not have any modal sphere that it anticipates. Indeed, the only thing that apostate *pistis* can anticipate is the apostate root of existence which attempts to seek itself and its god in a personification of the normative aspects of the temporal cosmos. The function of faith in an apostate direction transcends the rigid enclosure of the primitive belief in nature as soon as apostate humanity becomes aware of the supremacy of the normative rational functions above the closed powers of nature, and, in a personifying divinization of these normative functions, it advances to religious self-reflection. Only in this process of coming to self-consciousness does apostate humanity also become aware of its freedom to form its historical future in a controlling way through a constant struggle with rigid tradition.

Manifesting itself here is the religious fundamental law of human existence, which retains its universal validity even in the state of apostasy, and which we have called the religious law of concentration. All self-knowledge is dependent upon knowledge of God. So even the apostate self only learns to know itself in relation to its idols, in which it absolutizes its temporal rational functions.

In the Egyptian pyramid texts, we find the oldest documentation of the gradual elevation of apostate self-consciousness to the normative-jural and moral functions of personality. We observe here how the ethical conception of selfhood accentuates itself in the belief in immortality and in the cult of the dead to the same degree in which the god of death, Osiris, is increasingly regarded as the judge of good and evil. In the older texts, he still functions only as a nature god who is coerced by means of magical formulas to receive favorably the soul of the deceased. Later on, magical incantation makes way for a plea of the soul before its judge, in which it defends its right to a favorable destination.

Under the guidance of the opening process in the apostasy of faith there also now occurs the opening up of the earlier normative law-spheres. It occurs initially in the law-sphere of historical development in which this entire opening process, as we saw, is founded, in the specific sense that a particular faith must first have attained historical power in order to be able to provide leadership to cultural development.

Where apostate faith has indeed acquired the power necessary for the forming of history and has thereby assumed leadership in the development of culture, this opening process cannot take place harmoniously. By reason of the divine world-order it must, in the nature of the case, come into conflict with the above-analyzed principle of cultural economy for opened cultural development. Furthermore, every divinization of an aspect of temporal reality signifies the absolutization of it at the expense of the sphere sovereignty of the remaining aspects. In historical development, this necessarily leads to the exaltation of the power of a particular cultural sphere at the expense of all the others.

As an illustration, we again refer to the divinization of natural-scientific thought at the time of the Enlightenment (18th century). In this period, the development of the entire culture comes under the tyranny of the belief in the all-sufficient power of natural science. By this absolutization of natural science, an individualistic, rationalistic and utilitarian stamp was impressed on this entire period of culture.

However, let us be clear as to what is involved here. It has already been pointed out that true historical formation remains bound to the principle of historical continuity. According to this principle, the power of tradition continues to offer a counterweight to any revolutionary subjectivism on the part of the shapers of history. So, for example, in our Western cultural development, the power of Christian principles has remained active in historical tradition, from which it has already become impossible to completely isolate the historical influence of Enlightenment faith. If apostasy could work itself out completely and purely in cultural development, then this would inevitably lead to a complete demonizing of culture.

We also recognize, however, God's common grace in the historical process, by means of which the spirit of apostasy is restrained and every exaltation of a particular cultural power elicits the reaction of others. The following illustrates that historical tradition remains operative as a beneficial conserving power in the process of cultural development: even reactionary movements – which over against the extreme arbitrariness of a revolutionary movement, attempt what is just as extreme, the repristination of a dead past – conspire to halt the exaltation of a particular cultural factor, though they, in turn, themselves evoke the opposition of progressive cultural powers.

Even in the face of all this, cultural development in a sinful world does not by any means manifest the image of a gradual linear progress. Instead, its course is that of a sinuous curve with high and low points, with action and reaction. It is never carried out harmoniously but always in a clashing disharmony. The Christian faith sees, in the entire historical process, the continuing conflict between the *civitas dei* and the *civitas terrena*, which, understood in the light of eschatology, ends in the definitive triumph of the kingdom of Christ.

Here we encounter a theme that will be developed in more detail within a later context. At this point, the aim has only been to determine the place of faith and history in the opening process.

PART 3

The Subject-Object Relation within the Modal Structure of the Law-Spheres and its Significance for the Science of Law

3.1 The General Significance of the Subject-Object Relation in the Modal Structure of the Law-Spheres with particular reference to the Jural Aspect

In our previous expositions, we repeatedly encountered a remarkable state of affairs within the modal structure of the law-spheres.

It became apparent, for instance, that a natural event, such as a flood, an earthquake, etc., has a subjective function only within certain aspects of reality (namely, in the number, space, and movement aspects), while, in all other aspects, it only appears in an objective function (merely as an object), which can only exist in a structural relationship to subjectivity within these aspects.

It is clear that in the aspect of feeling such a natural event cannot function as a subject. The event itself cannot experience in a sensory manner; instead, it is seen in its objective-sensory perceptual image. It is perceptible, in an objective-sensory way, exclusively for anyone who can see. Thus we also discerned how such a natural event is only able to occur in the historical law-sphere as an object, but can itself never be a subject in historical development.

The indicated object-functions that such a natural phenomenon has in the aspects of reality, in which it cannot appear as a subject, have meaning therefore only in relationship to the subject-functions within the same aspects. The objective-sensory perceptual image of a flash of lightning, for instance, only exists in relationship to possible subjective perception. It has no being "in itself," in abstraction.

Nevertheless, it is erroneous to suppose that such object-functions of reality are simply the product of subjective representation and that the true reality of a natural phenomenon is restricted to the aspects of reality which are investigated by physics and chemistry. However, this is a widely held opinion. With regard to a natural phenomenon, a distinction is then made between its mathematical and physico-chemical characteristics, which on the one hand, are believed to have an objective existence and belong to the reality of the phenomena itself, and, on the other hand, the sensory characteristics of color, smell, taste, etc., which are supposed to exist only for subjective perception, but do not possess any true objectivity, and which therefore cannot be ascribed to the reality of natural phenomena.

This conception, which arose under the influence of the over-extension of the limits of physics and chemistry, is erroneous in every respect. It completely misconstrues the relationship between subject and object as found in reality.

On the one hand, the functions which a natural phenomenon, such as an electrical discharge, has within the mathematical and physico-chemical aspects of reality are not at all objective but are subjective in character. The phenomenon, as a subject, truly possesses a spatial trajectory, and it functions as a subject within the physical aspect of movement and energy. On the other hand, its function within the psychico-sensory aspect of perception (as an object) is an objective and not a subjective one.

The view referred to above erroneously supposes that investigation by the special sciences is able to inform us with regard to the actual reality of a phenomenon. We have seen, instead, that the special sciences must in fact begin by abstracting from the concrete data in order to be able to theoretically study a particular aspect of reality which has been chosen as a field of investigation. The special sciences should never arrogate to themselves the theory of reality. This lies in principle outside the limits of their competency.

If it were true that the sensory dimension of a natural phenomenon only existed in the subjective representation, then one could no longer speak of a truly objective sensory-perceptual image. How would we then distinguish the perceptual image in a hallucination or a dream from the perceptual image of a real thing or a real natural phenomenon?

The true structure of the subject-object relation within temporal reality cannot be understood from the standpoint of immanence philosophy. It has already been pointed out that on this standpoint the subject is never regarded as *sujet*, as being subjected to the divine law-order.

Since Kant it has only been permissible to understand the subject-object relation in two senses: (i) in the epistemological sense, in which the entire empirical world is conceived as the object for the knowing subject; and (ii) in the practical-ethical sense, in which the entire empirical world becomes the object of the human will, that is, becomes the means for human purposes, in contrast to which the human person is viewed as "an end in itself" (*Selbstzweck*).

Taken in the first sense mentioned above, the object is erroneously identified with the theoretical *Gegenstand* of knowledge.[1] In turn, this *Gegenstand* is identified in equally erroneous fashion with what is gener-

---

[1] The confusion we refer to has also infiltrated the juridical terminology of our eastern neighbours. Thus G. Husserl, Professor at Kiel, begins his important book *Der*

ally valid, with law-conformity.[1] Thus, in the science of law, for example, the legal order, as the sum of universally valid legal norms, is called objective law (*recht*) in contradistinction to subjective law (*recht*) as the peculiar competence of a juridical subject.

First it should be observed that the identification of the object of human experience with the *Gegenstand* of theoretical knowledge must be mistaken *per se*. It has already been pointed out that the *Gegenstand* is the product of theoretical abstraction by means of which we set particular nonlogical aspects of reality over against the logical aspect of thought, making them into a theoretical problem for that attitude of thought. For this reason naive, pretheoretical experience cannot have a *Gegenstand*. In pretheoretical experience, however, we are indeed aware of subject-object relations. Thus everyone knows how to distinguish the objective-sensory perceptual image of a real tree from the subjective imagining of it.

In the second place, it is confusing to identify objectivity with universal validity or law-conformity. In its indissoluble relatedness to the subject, the object as well as the subject is subjected to the laws of its existence. So, for instance, the objective-sensory configuration of a tree is subject to the psychical laws which regulate sensory perception in its subject-object relationship. But the object is not identical with law-conformity. The objective sensory configuration of a tree, for instance, is just as individual as the subjective sensory experiencing of the individual person. Its individuality, however, is an objective individuality, that is to say, an individuality that is independent of the subjective individuality of the perception of the tree's configuration.

For the same reason it is confusing to use the expression "objective law," in the sense of the sum of universally valid juridical norms, in contrast to subjective law.

If we desire to obtain a proper insight into the place of the subject-object relation within reality, we are obliged to investigate it initially within the modal framework of the law-spheres. Only within this framework is the fundamental significance of this relation for the special sciences, and thus for the science of law, to be understood.

In the science of law the subject-object relationship is present in a twofold way:

Rechtsgegenstand (1933, p. 1) with the proposition: "The concept of the legal *Gegenstand* (legal object) stands in logical opposition to that of the legal subject."

[1] *General Editor's note:* Dooyeweerd does not acknowledge *universality* at the factual side of reality. As a consequence he uses the Dutch terms *wet* and *wetmatig* as synonyms, instead of realizing that having the *maat* of the *wet* (the "measure" of the "law") can only be a feature of something subjected to the law. In *being an atom* (the law-conformity of an atom) every *individual* atom in a *universal* way evinces that it conforms to the *law for* being an atom.

(i) In the figure of the jural object, that is, the object of a subjective jural relationship (a subjective right or a subjective jural obligation).

(ii) In the pattern of an objective jural fact, that is, a natural fact which itself never constitutes a subjective juridical relationship (that is, a relationship between jural subjects) but to which the legal order nevertheless attaches various jural consequences with reference to such a jural relationship. One need only think of the occurrence of a fire on premises that are covered by fire insurance.

The jural subject-object relationship is of the greatest importance; nevertheless, it has for the most part been ignored by the science of law. This has had a fateful influence on the development of a number of different basic legal concepts, such as subjective right, causality, legal facts, etc.[1]

Only in recent years has attention been given to the supra-arbitrary material structure of this relationship, in the previously mentioned book of Husserl, *Der Rechtsgegenstand*. He seeks this structure, however, only in juridico-logical states of affairs. In opposition to this, I maintain that a correct insight into the modal subject-object relation can only be gained by an investigation of the modal structure of reality itself. In order to approach this question we shall have to look more closely at two problems: (i) In which modal aspects does this relation appear? (ii) What can function as an object in a particular modal aspect?

Since this relation will be investigated later on, as it especially applies to the science of law, we shall restrict ourselves in this introduction to a more general, encyclopedic exposition.

3.2 The Limits of the Subject-Object Relation

We return for a moment to the modal subject-object relationship between sensory perception and the objective sensory perceptual image. As an example, we can take a rosebush in bloom. In the objective-sensory perceptual image to which subjective-sensory perception is directed, according to its modal structure, we find a multiplicity of objective sensory qualities in an objective-sensory spatial image. In this spatial image, a sensory image of the movements and of the life of the rosebush is also given. By careful observation it is certainly possible to discern whether the rosebush is living or is dead. True, we cannot see the subjective life processes, but we are able to perceive the objective-sensory expression of these life activities, their sensory image.

---

1 *Translator's note:* In the first edition the following paragraph followed at this point: "To be more specific, the true nature of this relationship is misinterpreted by the positivist conception of the jural subject and the jural object, according to which they are arbitrary fictions of juristic method (*rechtstechniek*) or are merely formal categories of legal science which can take on any content whatsoever."

From our previous investigations, we know what is involved here: analogies of number, space, movement, and organic life within the modal aspect of feeling. These analogies manifest themselves within subjective-sensory feeling, namely, in the sense of multiplicity, the sense of space, the feeling of movement, and feeling of life. But in the objective-sensory image these analogies are objectified; they have taken on an objective expression. The modal subject-functions, or the subject-object relations,[1] which the rosebush has in the pre-psychical aspects, are objectified in analogies within the sensory perceptual image.

Now it is undeniable that the life-function is the last subject-function that the rosebush has in reality.[2] In all later aspects it functions only as an object.

The question now arises whether it is only the analogies of its modal functions in the earlier law-spheres that are able to be expressed in the sensory object-function of the rosebush (thus in its objective-sensory perceptual image), or whether the anticipations of the later object-functions, which they have in the normative law-spheres, are also represented in this perceptual image.

In my work *De Wijsbegeerte der Wetsidee* (*The Philosophy of the Cosmonomic Idea*) I chose the former alternative. After carrying out my investigations further, however, I am of the opinion that I must revise this conception, in actual fact, already implicitly rejected in the third volume of the above work.

My earlier view certainly comes into conflict with the position we have earlier discussed, the "sphere universality" of every modal aspect of reality. Furthermore, the objective logical characteristics of the rosebush definitely express themselves by anticipation in the sensory perceptual image. If this were not the case, then in naive, nontheoretical thought, which still remains rigidly bound to sensory representation, we could not logically distinguish a plant from a stone. Here we discern the logical characteristics as they are embedded in the sensory configuration of the thing. In the objective-sensory diversity of form and shape the logical characteristics announce themselves by way of anticipation.

Likewise, the objective cultural function of a rosebush is observable in a sensory manner by way of anticipation. A rosebush that one comes across in the wild has an entirely different appearance from one that has been bred and cultivated. So the later object-functions of the plant also must be able to express themselves by way of anticipation in the sensory (objective-psychical) perceptual image.

---

1 For example, the biotic subject-object relation of the plant to the earth, water, or the light of the sun.
2 The view that attributes to plants an unconscious sensory life does not rest on an experimental foundation but on the philosophic prejudice that "nature does not tolerate any discontinuities." The so-called principle of continuity for this reason is a hindrance in obtaining a proper insight into the structure of plants and animals.

This does not appear to offer any difficulties with regard to the symbolic aspect of language, the social aspect, and the aesthetic aspect. In the sensory perceptual image of the rosebush one sees by way of anticipation its objective-symbolical meaning (which expresses itself in its name), its objective meaning in social life, and its objective aesthetic qualities.

Indeed, human sensory perception, in contrast to that of the animal, is in great measure characterized by symbolical anticipations. It is for this reason alone that it is possible for a person to recognize a thing at a glance because, in the sensorily perceived image of the thing, that person grasps its objective-symbolical meaning in social life. The animal, however, is completely bound to the emotional sensory impressions of its environment; it reacts immediately to these impressions in a motor-sensory fashion, and it can never come to a quiet reflection on things.

Within the sensory perceptual image of the rosebush, we also see by way of anticipation its objective aesthetic qualities, but always on a symbolic foundation. Those to whom the fine nuances of color and delicate form of a rosebush do not speak and mean nothing cannot see its objective natural beauty. The saying of Guido Gezelle, "To me flowers speak a language,"[1] is more than a simple poetic metaphor. As is the case with its cultural qualities, the aesthetic qualities of a plant are thus already revealed through anticipation in its objective sensory form. The aesthetic qualities and the social qualities rest upon a symbolic foundation, whilst the cultural do not.

It is much more difficult to obtain an insight into sensory objectifiability with respect to the jural object functions. After all, how would it be possible to perceive our flowering rosebush, in a sensory way, in respect of its function as a legal object? Is it only by way of anticipation?

Here we must refer back to what we have discovered in the meantime about the sequential order of the aspects in cosmic time. The jural law-sphere is based on the substratum of the law-sphere of language whose meaning-nucleus is that of symbolical signification. The jural significance of the rosebush therefore can only be expressed in its sensorily perceptible image by means of a sensorily perceptible sign or symbol.

The difference in principle between the jural aspect and the lingual, social, and aesthetic aspects, with reference to their sensory objectifiability, is that the jural functions of a thing can only be made perceptible to sense because someone provides them with a sensory sign. By contrast, the beauty of something and its symbolic significance in social life reveal themselves by way of anticipation in the sensorily perceptible image of the thing itself. In order to display the beauty of a rosebush, one does not

---

1 "Mij spreekt de blomme een tale."

have to attach any symbolic sign to it. This beauty manifests itself in the colors and in the sensory nuances of the living plant's form.

But if someone has not indicated the objective jural characteristics of a thing by means of an objective sensory sign, neither can these functions come to objective expression in the perceptual image. They become perceptible in a sensory fashion only by means of such attached signs. Whoever observes, for example, a hedge or a fence around the garden in which the rosebush is growing, can see that the garden belongs to someone. Whoever sees a book plate in a book, or the initials of the owner in an overcoat, observes, in the sensory perceptible image by way of anticipation, an expression of the article's ownership.

Indeed, the entire objective-sensory perceptibility of the jural functions of things in human society rests upon such sensory symbols which have been attached to them. Positive legal norms themselves are not recognizable either, apart from objective-sensory symbols. These symbols must continually be formed by human agency.

How is it then that the jural functions of things cannot express themselves in an objective-sensory manner within the things themselves but only by way of attached signs, while the symbolic and aesthetic qualities do indeed symbolize themselves in a sensory way within the things themselves? Could this be an indication that the jural functions are not attributable to the thing itself (although there is a structural relatedness to the jural subjectivity of a person) but that they play only a purely subjective role in human consciousness?

The latter is certainly not the case! Whether something is the property of the state or of a particular person, or whether it is temporarily a *res nullius*, makes a difference to its actual state of existence. If it is a *res nullius*, it will lack human cultivation and thus become neglected or revert to the wild. If it is an object of private ownership by a particular person in a civic community, then, within the limits set by law, they will be able to carry out their desires with respect to the thing, without having to make it serviceable to the common interest; whereas serving the common interest is just what is required with respect to objects of state ownership.

The object functions of a thing in the jural aspect are therefore not without significance for its real state of existence. They are not simply constructs of human thought, but they belong to the thing itself in a structural relationship to human subjectivity within these aspects. The fact that of themselves the jural object functions of a thing are not expressed in the objective-sensory perceptual image, whilst this is indeed the case with, for example, the objective lingual and aesthetic functions, requires a different explanation.

This explanation must be sought in the fact that the jural aspect of reality, as with the moral and faith aspects, is associated with the practical will-orientation of human life, whilst the lingual and the aesthetic aspects, in contrast, are, as such, related to the contemplative orientation of knowing and imagining.

Now the practical orientation of will requires that there be a realization of the inner acts of human life in the "external world," and this realization takes place in the act.[1] Only in the act can we actualize, that is, realize, the object functions of things within the jural aspect. The sensory objectification of these object functions also requires therefore a human act, such as the staking out of one's territory, or the affixing of a sensory sign.

Undoubtedly, the creation of a plastic work of art, such as a painting or a sculpture, also requires an act; but once the work of art has been brought into being, in its aesthetic object-functions it is again exclusively related to the contemplative orientation of knowing and imagining pertaining to human act-life. It no longer requires an actualizing of its aesthetic object functions by human activity. Its beauty, on the contrary, comes to direct expression in the sensory symbolism of its form, lines, and colors.

Finally, with regard to cultural activity, this is undoubtedly oriented in the direction of practical willing; but the cultural aspect does not rest on a symbolical foundation.[2] This explains why the modal cultural characteristics of a thing can objectify themselves within the sensory perceptual image without the affixing of a sensory symbol.[3]

The difficulty, which at first appeared to militate against the acceptance of the sensory objectifiability of the jural function of a thing, is solved. Without the possibility of such a sensory objectification legal life would be impossible.

There remains, however, a great difference indeed between the objective analogies and the objective anticipations in the sensory form of a thing. In this connection it is of little consequence whether these anticipations are already indicated in the sensory symbolism of the thing, or whether they require first the affixing of a sensory sign by human activity. The objective analogies are simply and directly given in the objective-sensory perceptual image. Within certain limits they are even accessible to the subjective sensory perception of the animal. A spatial form, move-

---

1 We shall return to this point in part 4.4.
2 This can also be shown genetically in terms of the development and the actualizing of the higher modal functions of the child. Before it starts to speak, a child in its first year has already began to use and to experiment with articulated sounds which do not yet have any symbolical meaning. Only after it has developed the free mastery of these sounds does it begin to form true words with lingual significance. See A. Gehlen, *Der Mensch*, 2nd ed. (1941), 137 ff.
3 This is not to say that we would also be able to sensorily perceive the practical destination of a cultural thing apart from a symbolic anticipation.

ment, or life process, in the macro-world, objectifies itself as a matter of course in the sensory perceptual image. Those with normal vision, and who use their eyes, cannot help but see it, at least, if there is enough light. That holds as a matter of course in nature.

In the case of the objective anticipations, however, the situation is altogether different. These relate to normative aspects of reality. They belong to the opened, or deepened objective perceptual image, and are only accessible to an opened, subjective feeling-function of consciousness. A creature that cannot think in a subjective logical manner will never be able to differentiate, within the sensory perceptual image, the objective traits that are characteristic from those that are not. An animal cannot discern within the sensory perceptual image any traces that it is the product of cultural activity because it is not itself a cultural subject but at best a cultural object. It cannot see any sensory symbols because it does not possess a subjective function of language, etc.

The normative anticipations in the objective-sensory form of a thing are dependent upon human disclosure; they are not present as a matter of course in the perceptual image itself (such as a spatial form or a moving image) but are, rather, presented to human beings as a hidden realm of meaning to be disclosed. Furthermore, this opening process, with reference to all objective anticipations of the post-symbolical normative aspects which are related to the practical orientation of will, must go hand in hand with an actualizing that can only take place by means of human activity.

Is the subject-object relation present in all of the law-spheres? The answer must be in the negative.

In a law-sphere whose modal structure does not manifest any analogies this relation cannot reveal itself. In the numerical aspect of reality therefore it must be absent because in this aspect there is nothing that can be objectified, for there are no aspects that precede this one in the order of cosmic time.

But in the aspect of space, the relation in question does indeed express itself, specifically, in the relation of a subjective spatial figure to its points. A point does not possess subjective extension in any spatial dimension. It is an objective analogy of number in the meaning-structure of space, which can exist only in an unbreakable relationship with subjective extension. For example, the three angular points of a triangle exist only in the intersection of the subjectively extended sides. The objective length of the sides depends upon these intersections. The points themselves are not subjective spatial figures but only have an objective function within this law-sphere.

The subject-object relation is also present in the biotic law-sphere. For example, a bird's nest itself does not live but is an object in the life of a bird. And so an inorganic means of sustenance, such as water, also has a biotic object-function without itself possessing a subject-function within this law-sphere.

Economic goods, as economic objects, exist only in a structural relation to subjective economic valuation.

A social object, such as a pleasant discussion room or an intimate living area in a home, only exists in relation to subjective human social intercourse. And so forth.

Within the object-realm of a law-sphere it is the retrocipations (analogies) of earlier aspects of reality that must be objectified, first of all. They are objectified in conformity with the constant order of succession prevailing amongst the different law-spheres. It is only upon the foundation of the objective analogies that objective anticipations can be based.

To cite an example, the life-function of a bird cannot objectify itself in a sensory manner within the objective-sensory image of a living bird apart from the function of movement, the spatial form, and the numerical relationships of the animal body. Life can express itself only in an objective-sensory fashion in a sensory spatial image of movement.

Now, is it possible for the subject itself to become an object within the modal aspects in which the subject-object relation has a place?

If we take again as an example the feeling aspect of reality, then it is undeniable that subjective feelings can be brought to objective-sensory expression. A feeling of joy expresses itself objectively in the facial expression, in the objective sound of the voice, etc. Subjective thought can also come to objective-logical expression in formulated concepts and judgments. The subjective aesthetic conception[1] of a painter allows itself to be objectified aesthetically in a painting. A subjective spatial configuration allows itself to be spatially objectified by way of spatial points, etc.

Yet this possibility of objectification has its internal limits in the modal structure of the subject-functions themselves. The subject itself never becomes an object within the same law-sphere. It cannot for the very reason that the modal object lacks subjectivity and possesses only a dependent function (as object) within the law-sphere, in unbreakable relation to subectivity.[2] The modal subject remains a subject in its modal structure. It

---

[1] What comes to objective imaginative expression in the work of art is actually the "intentional" aesthetic object, which is conceived by imagination, and, in this sense, is still only intended. But the intentional object itself is still a subjective conception.

[2] *General Editor's note:* Dooyeweerd did not realize that within the spatial aspect it is already possible for a subject to serve as an object too. A line, which is a subject in one dimension, can also function in a limiting (objective) sense in higher dimensions – e.g. limiting the surface of a square, or acting as the edge of a cube. In similar

resists any kind of objectification within the same law-sphere. In the objective facial expression the subjective feeling is never sensorily perceptible. The objective-sensory perceptible image of a laughing face does not itself feel any joy, but is simply an objective-sensory expression of the subjective feeling of joy.

In truth it is still analogies of earlier, or anticipations of later, aspects of reality which bring to expression individual subjectivity in the objective sphere of a modal aspect. But in such objective expressions of subjectivity within the same law-sphere, the former retain an unbreakable connection with the subject whose activity they bring to expression.

The objective-sensory configuration of a rosebush in bloom has an individuality that is completely indifferent to the individuality of the sensory subject that perceives it. But the objective facial expression in which a subjective sense of joy is mirrored remains, as an individual thing, inseparable from this subjective emotion of joy which is expressed in it. So also the aesthetic objectivity of a sculptural work of art retains the unique individuality of the subjective aesthetic conception which it brings to objective expression.

Insight into this state of affairs will later prove to be of great significance for the doctrine of subjective rights, particularly for insight into so-called personal rights (such as copyright, patent rights, trademark rights, the right to a company name), for the doctrine of the legal subject and the legal object, and for the doctrine of legal facts.\

---

fashion a surface can act as a limiting object in three dimensions, as when it delimits the volume of a cube.

PART 4

The Theory of the Individuality-Structures of Reality and their Forms of Interlacement as a Second Foundation for the Encyclopedia of the Science of Law

4.1 The Place of the Various Branches of Law in an Encyclopedia of the Science of Law

Up to this point we have only considered reality with regard to its abstract aspects. These appeared to be enclosed in law-spheres having a mutually irreducible modal structure.

The theory of the law-spheres in its relation to our cosmonomic idea provided the initial, necessary foundation for a true encyclopedia of the science of law. Only on this foundation did it appear at all possible to determine where the legal aspect is situated in the temporal coherence of the aspects and at the same time to establish the exact place of the science of law in the entire context of the special sciences. The place of the jural aspect in the order of the aspects seemed to reveal itself only by way of a precise analysis of the constant modal structure of law as to its law- and subject-sides. And only in this fashion did it appear to be possible to establish the meaning of the basic modal concepts of legal science, which are contained in the central concept of law itself, taking into account their internal connections with the basic concepts of the other special sciences.

Undoubtedly, this is the primary task of a formal encyclopedia of the science of law. This, however, is by no means its only task.

The basic concepts possess a very abstract character. In their mutual interrelatedness, they only provide a theoretical concept of the nature of the jural aspect of reality as it is simultaneously distinguished from, and internally connected with, all the other aspects.

The concepts: legal norm, legal subject and legal object, legal fact, subjective right and legal duty, area of validity and the locus of a legal fact, lawfulness and unlawfulness, jural attribution and accountability, jural will, jural causality (legal ground, legal consequence as to the law-side; the subjective or objective causality of, respectively, a legal transaction or objective legal fact, as to the subject-side), jural positivizing and the originating jural form (formal source of law), legal organ and jural competence (legal power), jural interpretation and legal significance, jural fault or guilt, good morals, good faith, etc. – none of these concepts belong to a particular division of the science of law as, for example, do the theory of civil law, commercial law, law of civil procedure, law of criminal procedure, and administrative law. Instead, they are basic concepts of the legal science as a whole, since they concern the foundational legal character of the jural law-sphere. In reality, the modal meaning of this law-sphere is not given in *abstracto* but only in a typical particularization within the individuality-structures of reality. Within these individuality-structures, legal norms, as well as subjective and objective legal facts and the legal objects that are subject to those norms, exhibit typical jural characteristics which are not simply modal.

We must attain clear insight into this state of affairs precisely because current notions concerning this subject in the science of law as well in the other empirical sciences, display considerable confusion.

The modal meaning of the jural norm is contained within the provision comprising article 119 of the Basic Law (*Grundgesetz*): The legislative power is exercised by the King and the States General together, as well as in the norm contained in article 1275 of the Civil Code: All contractual undertakings to do some positive act or to refrain from acting are satisfied by the payment of costs, damages, and interest where the party from whom performance is due fails to carry out his or her obligations. The modal sense of the legal norm is present also in a provision of the governing statute of the Dutch *Hervormde* church, or of the *Gereformeerde* churches, in the Netherlands, which regulates the manner of the convocation of a synod or the procedure for calling a minister.

The modal meaning of legal object applies to a house that is owned by me as private property, as much as it applies to a settlement or a public road of which the state is the owner, or to a particular performance (for example, the carrying out of a certain amount of work) to which one party by agreement has bound himself or herself in respect of another.

It is clear, however, that in reality there is no positive binding legal norm that is determined by the modal meaning of the jural law-sphere alone, any more than concrete legal subjects or objects exist which could be determined in such a modal-jural sense.

In modern legal usage, at least, the modal meaning of the legal norm always manifests itself in the typical differentiation of constitutional law, civil law, international law, ecclesiastical law, the internal law of associations, business law, and other legal norm systems.

The modal meaning of the legal subject in modern legal life is typified in the same manner. The subject in constitutional law has a different typical meaning from that of the subject in civil law, international law, ecclesiastical law, etc.

And so far as the modal meaning of the legal object is concerned, this is further concretely determined in a typical manner by the individuality-structures of things (for example, a house, a mine, a piece of ground, a factory), or by the specific nature of human performances (for example, painting a portrait, building a house, the carrying out of the duties of a porter), and, in general, by the specific nature of anything that can become a legal object. Here it also makes a great deal of difference in which typical spheres of society the legal objects function.

It should not be supposed that the particular nature of the legal norm, the legal subject or legal object in question would make no difference for rigorous juridical examination. On the contrary, juristically speaking, it makes a considerable difference, for instance, whether a person is the owner of an immovable thing (for example, a piece of land) or of a movable thing (for example, a horse, a bicycle). The content of the law of property is quite different with respect to each of these two instances. So also, in the various typical spheres of law, it will make a great deal of difference whether the one who is legally authorized is an individual person, a church, rather than a state, or a municipality. It is only in the sphere of civil law that this does not make any difference. We shall see in due course that this ties in precisely with the typical character of civil law.

If we now provisionally direct our attention towards the differentiation of legal norms in typical norm complexes, such as constitutional and administrative law, criminal law and criminal procedure, provincial and municipal law, civil law and civil procedure, civil commercial law and non-civil commercial law of free social intercourse, industrial law, ecclesiastical law, the internal law of associations, international law, etc., then we immediately encounter the question as to what it is that truly governs this typical differentiation.

We encounter here the problem of the material classifications of law and the criterion that is employed in connection with it. Its investigation comprises the second task of an encyclopedia of the science of law.

By material classifications we mean: classifications according to the typical internal character of the various norm complexes of a legal order.

Legal science acknowledges other classifications as well, such as a classification according to the originating forms (the formal sources) of positive law. Distinctions are then made between statutory law, customary law, jurisprudential law, treaty law, etc. As we examine the problem of the sources of law, we shall see, however, that this formal classification can only have scientific value when founded on an appropriate material classification. Indeed, material classification must have a position of prominence. Usually, however, formal classification is completely divorced from it and, as a consequence, it has no scientific value whatsoever.

Furthermore, we are acquainted with a means of classification according to the legal norm's area of validity: the classification into domestic and international law. In the way that it is usually made, this classification, as I view it, also lacks scientific value because it is divorced from a proper material classification and attempts, in an arbitrary way, to include all positive law in the typical sphere of law of the (national) state or in that of international relations between states. The sphere of validity of a jural norm-complex depends upon the material sphere of law within which it holds, not *vice versa*. So the canon law of the various church communities cannot be characterized, in a strict sense, as either national or international because a church community, as such, certainly does not have a national character; nor can its inner nature be understood as national in terms of the mutual relations between states. Ecclesiastical legal norms do not have a territorial but a personal sphere of application. That is to say, they only hold for members of the church. That does not alter the fact that a church community is formally constituted within the territory of a state and can be divided according to national boundaries (for example, the Dutch *Hervormde* church and the *Gereformeerde* church in the Netherlands). Therefore this only has jurisdictional significance for its internal law if it is constituted formally as a state church, or if its organization still clearly shows traces of its having occupied the position of being a state church. This, however, has nothing to do with the inner nature of the church.

Finally, there are other recognized schemes of classification which can in no way be viewed as fundamental classifications that embrace the entire range of positive law. If they are not to be rejected out of hand as being erroneous, they can only acquire scientific value based upon a proper material classification.

Into this category, for example, falls the distinction between coercive (or imperative) and supplementary (or regulatory) law. The criterion which is normally used in this regard is whether or not it is possible for a legislator to depart from a settled legal regulation without resulting in the nullification of the regulation from which there has been a departure. This classification only has scientific worth, as will be fully demonstrated when the problem of the sources of law is examined, if there has first been a proper delineation of the differentiated material spheres of law with their internal limits of competence, and an investigation into the mutual interconnections amongst these legal spheres. In any case, this classification is not all-inclusive because, in its original meaning, it only refers to law formed by the state, even though it must be admitted that it is also applied by practitioners of canon law to Roman Catholic ecclesiastical law. The latter is to be explained by the fact that ecclesiastical authority in the Roman Catholic church is organized formally, in many respects, after the example of the secular authority of government; but this can never accord with the true nature of the church institution.

Yet another classification of positive law is that into common and particular law (respectively, *jus commune* and *jus particulare*). The situation is represented as if there were a generally valid law. In this category is meant civil private law. Particular law, by contrast, is supposed to include only exceptions and supplementations to this *jus commune*. Insofar as such exceptions and supplementations are not explicitly or implicitly established, then common law must apply. This would hold especially within the sphere of public law, and more particularly within the sphere of administrative law which as *jus particulare* would contain only particular exceptions and supplementations to civil private law. This classification, at least according to the way in which it is made here, and, in particular, in its practical implications, is completely unscientific because it does not take into consideration at all the inner nature of the various legal spheres which must be placed at the foundation of the material classifications of positive law. We shall see later on that it is indeed meaningful to characterize civil private law, according to its inner nature, as *jus commune*. But there is no scientific justification for conceiving this *jus commune* in such a way that it would be applicable to all possible legal relationships, except where special regulations have not been established either explicitly or implicitly. Insofar as legal relationships do not have a civil character, civil law cannot be applied to them.

The classification of positive law into public and private law can only become meaningful for modern legal life, as will be later demonstrated, based upon a material classification of law according to the internal nature of the legal spheres. On the other hand, in societies which are still undifferentiated, it can only be regarded as a formal classification.

In contrast, classification of all positive law into material and formal law (in connection with which procedural law, in the widest sense of the term, is included under the latter), must simply be considered scientifically incorrect. This will be shown in more detail when we deal with legal procedure. There is no such thing as purely formal law. According to its nature, all positive law is material. The forms of law are inherent in every material law-sphere because the moment of form, as we have already observed whilst treating the problem of "law and history," belongs to the modal structure of the jural law-sphere. But in legal life they always manifest a typical inner nature related to the particular legal sphere in which they function.

Thus it is apparent throughout that the material classification of positive law is of fundamental importance for any other possible distinctions between the jural norm-complexes.

Do these material classifications now possess only a variable, historical significance, or do they have a fundamental value, and must they, as with the modal basic concepts of legal science, be oriented to constant structures of temporal reality which make possible the variable phenomena in the first place?

Without hesitation the prevailing conception answers this question in accord with the former of the two mentioned possibilities. This is so even when, as is the case in the neo-Kantian doctrine of law, it requires that there be a constant and a priori character for the concept of law itself, together with the modal basic concepts of legal science that are contained therein.[1]

At first glance there seems to be little that can be asserted to oppose this idea. It is self-evident that the material differentiation of the jural norm-complexes is governed, in the first place, by the character of human societal relationships. With regard to their jural aspect, the state, the church, the school, the family, free association, commerce, business organizations, mutual intercourse between states and that between private persons (including corporations or foundations), each have a typical material sphere of law with its own norm-complex. Now it cannot be denied that the above mentioned societal forms, in their differentiated character, only come into being in an opened up stage of cultural development. In part 2, when the opening process in the development of culture was investigated, it was seen that the primitive forms of society, such as the sib, the clan, folk, and tribal bond, still retain an undifferentiated character. In a primitive society therefore the sib, the folk, and tribal bond, fulfill all of the functions for which specifically differentiated forms of community develop at a higher level of culture. They simultaneously fulfill, to a certain degree, the role of the family, the state, the religious community, the school, trade, and industry, etc.

Is it not the case then that our modern forms of community are entirely historically determined? And are not the boundaries of their particular legal spheres therefore wholly variable? In the Middle Ages did not the sphere of ecclesiastical law also include a great part of what now falls within the sphere of state law? Has not the modern state, to a great extent, begun to participate in industry, the education of the people, social interrelationships, etc.? Does a modern Western European state still truly have something in common, for instance, with the ancient city state of the

---

1   But, as we have seen earlier, this cannot be correct. Only the modal structure of law, not the subjective concept of law, bears a truly constant character within the cosmic order of time. It is indeed possible to say that the concept of law bears a subjective, a priori and fundamental character for the special science of law, insofar as this creates only the possibility of juridical investigation as a special science. But, as a theoretical concept, it nevertheless remains historically founded. It cannot make any claim to constancy for the reason that theoretico-philosophical investigation should always penetrate deeper into the modal structure of law, and every result that is achieved is again susceptible to improvement and deepening.

Greeks, with the ancient Roman republic, or with the feudal state of the Middle Ages?

In the meantime, it will be clear, after what has been presented in parts 1 and 2 of this Introduction, that the conception of human society as a complex of completely variable historical phenomena proceeds from the typical positivistic-historicist prejudice; it considers the reality of human society only as to its historical aspect and identifies this aspect with reality in its fullness. This absolutization has become possible only because in this conception the basic modal structure of the historical law-sphere has been eliminated and there is only an eye for the variable phenomena which successively express themselves within this structure.

Now it must be immediately conceded that the organizational forms of human societal relationships are historically founded and possess a changing, variable character. They are the product of human formation which is dependent upon a whole series of factors. The forms of states, the forms of families, the forms of business, the forms of free social co-operation, or of social conflict, undoubtedly vary with different peoples in the different phases of their historical development.

But if, in the divine order of the world, there were not constant, basic structural principles for the state, the marriage community, the family unit, the wider community of family relations, business relations, the church community, etc., then the variable forms of the fundamental societal relationships in question would not be possible.[1] And by what internal criteria does one distinguish between state and church, state and industry, state and business corporation, state and family? It will become evident how positivism, which absolutizes the changing forms of human societal structures, is unable to provide any material criteria for the distinctions in question.

This is also the most fundamental reason why that approach, which still has a commanding position in the science of law, cannot produce a fitting account of the material classifications of law. In most of the introductions to the science of law there is not even an attempt to scientifically analyze the internal structural difference between state law, civil private law, the internal law of associations, law of trade and industry, church law, etc., and to give a respectable account of the mutual interrelationships of these particular spheres of law. One is supposed to be satisfied, for the most

---

1 It cannot be set forth as an objection to the constancy of the structures themselves that these structural principles in great measure are only first realized in society under particular historical conditions. To use this as an argument is also to necessarily deny the constancy of the structural difference between humankind and animals. For, in the genetic process, humankind only comes onto the scene in temporal reality after the animal world. The evolutionist hypothesis which, with its positivistic mentality, rejects the constancy of the creational structures, however, cannot agree with the Christian idea of creation.

part, with the presentation of a mere summary – on the whole far from complete – a loose juxtaposing of the material units of law. In addition to this, formal definitions are proposed which often give a very distorted image of actual legal life, and in any case do not provide insight into the intrinsic nature of the material legal spheres. So it is almost commonplace to identify civil law with private law which then, in turn, is set over against public law (state and administrative law, penal law, etc.). Private law, then, is supposed to regulate mutual relationships between citizens while public law, in contrast, is supposed to regulate relationships between citizens and government. This is a completely inaccurate representation of matters because in the first place there is a great deal of private law that does not have the character of civil law, and in the second place civil law is in principle independent of the citizenship of a particular state and instead regulates the civil-legal interactions between people, independently of their membership of a national community. Naturally, we shall return to this point in more detail at a later point.

The logical consequence of the positivist standpoint has been drawn by legal historians who deny any possibility of a material juridical classification in legal science. Logically, all law, according to them, is of a single kind because law is only supposed to be a form of human societal relationships and thus have a purely formal character. According to this conception, material distinctions between various norm-complexes can never have a juridical character. Thus the Kelsenian school is notable for having carried out, on that basis, a radical levelling of the material structural differences amongst the various jural norm-systems.

If it appears that it is not the modal structure of the jural law-sphere but rather the structural principles of human societal relationships that provide the basis for the foundation of the material differentiation of the jural norm-systems, then we would have to agree with the Kelsenian school when it avers that the material classifications of law are of a nonjural kind.

We are obliged therefore to initiate a more detailed investigation into the nature of the societal structures which are in view here and into the relation of these societal structures to the modal structure of the law-spheres.

First of all we must deal with the general problem concerning the individuality-structures of reality.

4.2 The Relationship of the Modal and the Individuality Structures of Reality. Law-Type and Law-Modality

Part 1 has already pointed out the difference in principle between the "theoretical attitude of knowing," which is required to analyze the various aspects of reality in a theoretical manner, and the "naive attitude of experiencing," which does not analyze reality with regard to its aspects but takes it as it presents itself, that is to say, in the structure of individual things, events, forms of social life, etc., and in their mutual interrelationships. As we saw, the modal aspects of reality are only implicitly experienced in this pretheoretical attitude of knowing in respect of concrete things, events, and forms of social life.

We also observed that concrete reality, as it presents itself in naive experience, functions in all the modal aspects without exception. There is no purely physical, or purely physico-psychical, reality. The physical and the psychical are only modal aspects of reality. And so there is also no purely jural reality, but only a jural aspect of reality.

Now what kind of phenomena are the structures of things, concrete events, and forms of social life in naive experience? They cannot be modal structures. An individual thing such as the chestnut tree in my garden, to be sure, functions simultaneously in all of the modal aspects. But I experience this thing as a concrete individual unity, as an individual totality, in spite of the unmistakable multiplicity of its modal aspects. This is possible only because the thing is given in a totality which groups the various aspects of its reality into a typical whole, and at the same time overarches these aspects. A concrete thing, as it were, is not just an agglomeration, the sum total of its modal functions; rather, it is the reverse. Its modal functions are functions of an individual whole, a concrete totality. The unity of the totality comes first; it is fundamental to the possibility of the existence of a thing.

The structural principle of a thing therefore does not stand on the same basis as the modal structure of a law-sphere. It overarches and penetrates the modal aspects and brings them into the coherence of a typical whole.

Now in part 1 we have seen that, in a general sense, the cosmic order of time – which maintains the unbroken coherence of the modal aspects, whilst preserving their modal sphere sovereignty, and which arranges them in an order of earlier and later – lies at the foundation of all of the law-spheres. The modal aspects already appeared to display their essentially temporal structure insofar as they showed themselves to be an expression of the cosmic order of time in their order of analogies and anticipations.

The same must also be established with respect to the individuality-structures of reality; these also are founded in the cosmic order of time. However, they are not purely modal but typical temporal structures, temporal structures of individual totalities which determine the subjective (or objective) temporal duration of these individual structures with respect to their nature.

So, for example, the individual duration of a plant's life (which, by the way, in its subjective existence can vary according to its different forms) is typically qualified by the individuality-structure of the living plant organism, which is a typical structure of time insofar as it binds the continued existence of the plant to the life-function.

In contrast, the duration of the existence of a work of art, for instance, is typically determined by the preservation of the aesthetically qualified form that the artist has given to the material. So also, the duration of the life of a house is typically determined by the preservation of its form, which is qualified by its objective destination in social life, and so forth. Following from our investigation, it will become apparent that it is the individuality-structure that gives to things their typical character.

There is, however, a second point of difference from the modal structure of reality. The modal structures maintain only a modal coherence amongst all of the phenomena that function within a law-sphere, irrespective of the individual character of these phenomena. No matter what may be the individual nature of a thing, viewed in a purely modal jural way, it only comes into consideration as a legal object.

By contrast, structural principles, which we are now proceeding to investigate, are just that, structures of individuality.

An apple tree differs from a stone not because it functions in different modal aspects but because, in whatever aspect of reality it may function, it displays therein a typical structure of individuality which is radically different from that of a stone.

An individuality-structure itself is not in nature a subjective (or objective) individuality.[1] Instead, it is a basic law-principle that lies at the foundation of the possibility of things, events, acts, forms of social life, etc., in their individual reality. It is a law-ordering[2] framework without which

---

[1] Naturally it has not been absolutely settled whether or not a differentiated structural principle has come to be realized in the great genetic process of the plant world. The theory of evolution, which denies the constancy of "kinds," comes into open conflict with the creation motive of divine Word-revelation only insofar as it misconstrues the constant structural principles that lie at the basis of the possibility of origination of the variable individual entities in the plant and animal realms, and of individual human beings within the developmental process. It is completely under the sway of the humanistic ideal of science in its over-emphasis on the natural-scientific method of thought and investigation.

It construes the facts in terms of the preconceived dogma that, in the development of natural kinds, nature manifests an unbroken continuity and thus does not recognize any essential difference between inorganic material and the living organism, between the realms of plants and animals, and between animals and human beings. A similar tendency is shown by the historicist and evolutionist conception of human society, which does not accept any constant structural difference between the family, the state, the church, etc., and which searches everywhere for transitional forms. As if the "transitional forms" themselves did not presuppose the existence of constant principles of structure! If everything were in a state of continual transition and flux, it would no longer be possible to speak meaningfully of a plant, an animal, a human being, a family, a state, a church, etc.

[2] *General Editor's note:* See note 2 on p. 106, on translation of "*wetmatige*."

those things cannot come into existence. An apple tree, in a general sense, is not an individual, real thing. Neither is it simply a name by which all possible individual apple trees are denoted. Even less is it only a concept that is supposed to have objective reality. On the contrary, it is a structural principle which, grounded in the temporal world order, is established by God's creative will.

But in contrast to the modal structural principles of reality, it is a law of individuality which guarantees the individual thing its typical nature and to which it is subjected as a subject (or object). These structural principles therefore will be called "type structures." Modal law-conformities are never type laws but only modal laws.

The type is always an individuality-type of a concrete, real whole. Thus the modal nature of the legal norm is not a specific jural type-norm. In contrast, constitutional, civil, or ecclesiastical legal norms, for example, are just that because they bring to typical jural expression, respectively, the character of the state, the character of civil relations between people that is made possible by the state, and the character of the church.

If we look more closely at the types of individuality that present themselves in various law-spheres, then it strikes us that some of them possess an original character in a particular modal aspect while others apparently point back to original individuality-types in an earlier aspect or point forward to original types in a later aspect.

There appears to be present in the individuality-structures of temporal reality therefore a state of affairs similar to that which we observed in the modal aspects. And here, once again, there is an accentuation of the intrinsic temporal character of the individuality-structures. Every attempt by metaphysics to elevate them to supra-temporal substances must be explained in terms that deny the cosmic order of time in which all of the structures of temporal reality are founded.

If this analogy with the modal structures is further elaborated, it is possible to speak of nuclear types and anticipatory types of individuality within the law-spheres.

As an example, we can take the love of parent and child. This is a characteristically moral type of individuality. It is the modal expression of the individuality-structure of the family community, in a narrower or broader sense, within its typical totality that embraces all aspects, a feature we shall later investigate. Love, as the modal meaning-nucleus of the moral aspect, thus obtains within this individuality-structure of human society a typical character which is distinguished from other types of moral love-relationships, such as the love of country, marital love, the love of one's neighbor in society, etc. To what then may the typical moral character of the love of parent and child be attributed? This can be referred back to the relationships of parent and child within the family in both the narrower and broader sense. It is evidently founded in the biotic relationship of descent, in the close bonds of blood relationship.

This community of those related by blood is an individuality-type that only possesses the original character of a nuclear-type in the organic aspect of life. The typical characteristic by which the love of parent and child is distinguished, for example, from the love of country is therefore never able to be conceived in a purely moral fashion but only in indissoluble connection with historical descent in which it is typically founded.[1] Therefore I maintain that this moral individuality-type does not have an original but an analogical character. Nevertheless, this kind of a love relationship is undoubtedly moral in nature. It gives a typical definition to the moral duties that pertain between parents and their children.

We come across anticipatory types of individuality, for example, in the spatial forms of seashells. In their typical geometrical form, these protective animal devices can only be conceived in terms of the typical object-functions that they fulfill in animal life. The same is true of the typical spatial forms of spider webs, bird and termite nests, etc.

In the arithmetical and spatial aspects of reality *per se*, we discover only anticipatory and not nuclear or analogical types[2] of individuality. Why this is the case we shall presently see. But in these aspects also the individuality and the type that determines it play an essential role. Hence there is a typical number of electrons (negatively charged particles) and protons (positively charged particles of the atom's nucleus) within the atomic structure of chemical elements, as well as in the molecules[3] of the various chemical compounds. It is also the case in the enormously complicated structure of the living cell. In the nucleus of the cells of its body, every kind of plant and animal has its own unique number of chromosomes (bearers of the inheritance characteristics). This is also true of the cells of the human body.

All of these types of individuality within the spatial or the arithmetical aspect can never be extracted from the modal aspects of number and space alone but only from the individuality-structures of reality. Within an individuality-structure, the ordering of the modal individuality-types, which

---

1 *Editor's note: Historische afstamming* (historical descent) appears to be a mistake. It should read *biotische afstamming* (biotic descent). Otherwise, which is more unlikely, *historische afstamming* could be taken as referring to the modal founding of the love of country.

2 *Editor's note:* By "analogical types" Dooyeweerd means "retrocipatory types." See note 2 on p. 103, on later refinement of "analogy" and "analogical" to encompass both retrocipations and anticipations.

3 A molecule is a grouping of atoms. The atom is the most primitive unity of a chemical element, such as hydrogen, oxygen, nitrogen, etc.

we have just described, into nuclear types, analogical types,[1] and anticipatory types plays an essential role.

But within the typical structural grouping of the aspects, this ordering is not the only one; it is not even the primary ordering. The primary ordering consists in this: a particular aspect is assigned the qualifying role of a typical destination (leading) function.

If the leading function itself does not manifest an original or nuclear type within this typical structural grouping, the second structural ordering acquires fundamental significance. In this case, it will be possible to point to a second modal aspect within the individuality-structure that in a typical fashion founds the individuality-type of the leading function because it comprises the nuclear type. In such a case the individuality-structure will then be characterized by two modal individuality-types which can then only be theoretically conceived in an indissoluble mutual coherence, namely, (i) the typical leading function; and (ii) the typical founding function.

For sound insight into this state of affairs we begin with a brief investigation of the individuality-structure of the living organism of a plant.

Before we begin, however, we must remark that in theoretical analysis the individuality-structure of things which are immediately accessible to naive experience do not appear to have a simple character, but instead are built up in a typical interlacing of simple structures which, nevertheless, are realized in a single individual whole. In order to discover things with a truly simple structure, it is necessary to penetrate into the micro-world of the elementary components of matter: electrons and protons (negatively and positively charged particles of matter).

The internal individuality-structure of a plant is already very intricate. It is a complex structural whole in which individuality-structures of very different kinds are united into a typical unity. The living organism of the plant, however, is only one of these structures, albeit, the characterizing one. It can only function, however, based upon the individuality-structures of its plasmatic "building blocks," which are of a completely different nature and which, in respect to their internal character, cannot be considered to be living. This state of affairs will only become clear when we have more thoroughly investigated the phenomenon of "enkapsis."

First, however, insight into the simple individuality-structure itself must be ensured in order that we may then successively embark upon an investigation into the very complicated mutual interlacements within the totality structures of things.

By way of example, let us take the structure of the living organism as a plant. For even if this structure in its simple character is not identical with the complex totality structure that we call a plant, it is – as will become ap-

---

1   *Editor's note*: See note 2 on p. 208.

parent – the component structure that gives to this structural totality its typical character and which qualifies it as a plant. It is not the structure of the lifeless building blocks themselves but the living organism (functioning in co-operation with innumerable cells), which binds these substances in its own service, that determines the internal nature of the plant's existence.

As an individuality-structure, the living organism of the plant ought not be confused with its modal function in the biotic aspect of reality. The living organism of the plant functions not only in this aspect but also functions in the physico-chemical aspect of movement,[1] in the aspect of space, and in that of quantity. In addition, it is represented in the post-biotic aspects of reality. It is therefore itself already a typical structure of totality which overarches all of its modal aspects, grouping them into a typical unity.

The attempt to analyze such a structure immediately confronts theoretical investigation with an apparently insoluble problem. Theoretical analysis involves a theoretical setting apart of what in reality is an indivisible whole.

Now we have seen that an individuality-structure is always a structure of totality that is rooted in the continuity of the cosmic order of time; the latter transcends the boundaries of the law-spheres which is why it is in itself inaccessible to theoretical analysis. Theoretical access to the individuality-structure therefore can never be given in the individual whole itself; instead, the latter is a presupposition of the structural analysis.

But an individual totality is, as we saw, always an individual unity in the diversity of its modal aspects. This diversity itself is accessible to theoretical analysis. If it is the case that the individual totality is already presupposed, lying at the foundation of the individual functions which the living plant organism has in the various law-spheres, then the typical structural principle of this whole must also come to typical expression in its modal aspects and thus, in this manner, becomes accessible to theoretical analysis. In other words, the individuality-structure expresses itself in every one of its modal aspects, just as the cosmic order of time was shown to express itself in the modal structure of the aspects, and via these appeared to be accessible to theoretical investigation.

The modal structure of an aspect appeared to be qualified by the modal meaning-nucleus, which impresses on all the other structural moments the irreducible meaning of the aspect in question. It might well be expected that in the individuality-structure, as the typical totality structure of the aspects, a qualifying aspect is also found which gives to the typical totality of the modal functions its irreducible character. That this is indeed the case we shall now seek to demonstrate.

---
1 *General Editor's note:* See note on p. 14.

In the first place, it is striking that not all of the modal functions within the individuality-structure of the living plant organism have the same role. The plant organism undoubtedly has modal functions within the law-spheres of number, space, and movement. The organism is built up from a number of cells, each of which has a spatial form and which are united with each other in a spatial form-whole, and there physico-chemical processes play a role within the movement aspect of the organism.

But so long as we only view the living organism within these first three modal aspects without taking account of the biotic aspect, there appears to be nothing to distinguish it as an individual whole from its environment. For mathematics, physics, and chemistry, the plant as a living organism does not have any role so long as scientists occupy themselves with the atomic or molecular structures of the building blocks. Modern chemistry has been successful in synthesizing a great number of the organic materials (excluding very complex compounds such as starch and proteins) without thereby requiring the interposition of anything like a hidden life-force.

This changes as soon as physics and chemistry, as bio-physics and bio-chemistry, respectively, begin to investigate the internal physico-chemical aspect of the living organism itself which clearly differs from the internal structures of the constituent elements. In this case, the individuality-structure of the living organic totality also impresses itself on theoretical investigation under the physico-chemical aspect of movement, even though there may still be many investigators who hold the opinion (naturally under the mechanistic influence of the deterministic-humanist ideal of science) that physics and chemistry will finally succeed in synthesizing even the organism of the living cell out of very complex protein compounds by purely physico-chemical means.

In bio-physics and in bio-chemistry, it is no longer a question of the internal molecular structures of material components but of the continuous building up and breaking down (assimilation and dissimilation) of substances under the influence of "bio-impulses," which always take hold just at the required time and place in service of the living whole, and thus constantly remain under the direction of the organic function of life. Only when we bring this function into consideration does it make any sense to speak of a plant organism. Why is this the case? It is because the biotic function, even though it is only itself a modal function of the living organism, has nevertheless a typical, central role within its individuality-structure.

First, the organic function of life appears to be the last subject-function that the plant organism possesses. In all of the later law-spheres, as we have seen, the plant functions no longer as a subject but only as an object.

Second, the organic function of life has the typical leading or directing role in the individuality-structure of the plant organism – and also of the plant as a complex structural totality – with respect to all of the modal functions which the organism has in the earlier aspects. In the internal structure of the living organism of the plant, every physico-chemical change occurs in a typical relationship with the organic life-functions. The internal movements of change in its matter, of assimilation and dissimilation, the movements of cell division, etc., are typically oriented to, and unlocked by, the life destination of the plant. The numerical and spatial relations in the internal sphere of the living plant organism are also unlocked by, and oriented to, the leading function of life. So, for example, there individually occurs within each cell organism a division into nucleus and protoplasm, and within each of these structural components a number of micro-components, each of which has its own function within the living whole. With respect to the spatial relationships, note should be taken of the typical way in which the spatial forms of the living whole are built up in the process of cell division, which takes place according to set, but typical, geometrical configurations.

None of this, however, alters the fact that the various modal functions of the living plant organism retain their own modal nature and remain subject to the laws of their own modal spheres. Physical movements and chemical changes, numerical and spatial relationships, also retain their own character within the organism of the cell; they do not themselves become living functions. But within the internal sphere of the living organism they are opened up in a typical fashion by the central biotic function; they possess typical anticipations toward the life-destination. The organic function of life is the typical destination function of the plant organism. At the same time it is the qualifying function of this organism because, in this individuality-structure, it plays the same role as the modal meaning-nucleus does in the modal structure of an aspect. Only if we pay attention to this qualifying or destination function of the plant organism, which is, at the same time, the destination function of the plant as a whole, does the individuality-structure of this living natural thing, as well as its earlier aspects of reality, allow itself to be identified over against its environment.

Of course, a plant also has external relationships to its environment. When it sways to and fro in a storm, in its modal function of movement, it obeys the modal laws of movement just as it does through its typical internal dynamics of growth and movements of change in its matter; but these external mechanical movements fall outside the sphere of the internal structural movements. They are not typically oriented to, and led by, the destination function of the plant.

It is therefore the organic life-function as destination function that qualifies the plant organism in its individuality-structure. And via the biotic destination function, this typical qualification also expresses itself in its object-functions in the post-biotic law-spheres.

Thus this will also hold for the function of a plant as a legal object. If I am the owner of a plant, then I am the owner of an individual whole that is determined by its own internal nature. The legal object is in this case a "nonfungible[1] object," in contradistinction to a merely "generically determined thing," such as a sum of money, a shipment of grain, which are indeed fungible. But the individuality of a plant as a nonsubstitutable thing, even jurally, remains bound to an individuality-structure that determines the type of thing it is. Its legal objectivity is typical and individualizing and not simply modal. The individuality-structure also comes to expression within the jural aspect itself.

If we pay attention provisionally to the modal character of the qualifying function only, without going on to investigate in more detail its particular type in a particular kind of plant, then we are already able to establish that the individuality-structure here has grouped the modal functions in a typical way. That is not to say that in this inner structure the general (time-) order of the aspects is changed. Indeed the latter lies at the foundation of all individuality-structures and is their presupposition. But the fact that it is the biotic function that plays the typical role of destination function for the plant cannot be deduced in any way from the general order of the law-spheres. This is only to be understood from the individuality-structures in which every conceivable plant is of necessity included.[2]

In the meantime the general basic framework of the individuality-structure is simply given, along with the modal determination of the qualifying function. Irrespective of their kind and their specific characteristics, all plants without exception are qualified by the biotic function as their destination function. This destination function determines the basic type of the entire realm of plants. The basic type, in which the qualifying function is thus determined modally only and not typically, will be called the "radical" type of the plant, while the qualifying function in this yet simple modal delineation may be called the "radical" function of the individuality-structure.

---

1 *Editor's note:* Fungible is a legal term applied to goods meaning "substitutable" or "replaceable."

2 The conception that is defended by some biologists, following the lead of the botanists Françé and Haberlandt, that even in the case of a plant it is possible to speak of a sensory (albeit unconscious) life of feeling, rests less upon sober factual material than upon the theoretical prejudice that there are no gaps in nature and that one cannot therefore acknowledge any essentially radical differences of structure between plants and animals. Whilst, in the case of the plant, it may be shown only that there are conduction channels for impressions of light and warmth, these are conceived by Françé and Haberlandt as sensory nerve pathways. This is an intrinsically philosophical interpretation that denies the structures of reality.

A radical type delimits an entire realm of temporal creatures. In this sense it is possible to distinguish three primary realms with various radical types: (i) the realm of physico-chemically qualified things, to which belong all chemical elements and compounds; (ii) the plant realm, with a biotic radical function; and (iii) the animal realm, in whose radical type the function of sensory feeling (the psychical function) fulfills the role of the qualifying function.

In this sense humanity does not constitute a realm because the human being is not qualified by a modal function. Its central position in the cosmos is located in the fact that it possesses a supra-temporal center of its temporal existence in which all of the modal functions of this existence find their integral root-unity.

The above mentioned three primary realms must be viewed, along with humanity in its bodily existence, as structures of reality of the first order because all other individuality-structures presuppose these structures of reality.

So, for example, plant and animal contrivances, which are always qualified respectively by a biotic and by a psychical object-function, presuppose the existence of a plant and animal realm to which they stand in a structural subject-object relationship. They are therefore second-order structures of reality, which exist only in relation to the plant and animal realms, and which in a broad sense can be included within these realms. The same holds for the very diversified human formations which can appear in all kinds of structural types, but which only have human meaning and existence in a subject-object relationship.

In addition, the forms of human society, such as the marriage bond, the family in both a narrower and broader sense, the state, the church, school, business organization, etc., which at a differentiated stage of culture manifest a great diversity of basic types, cannot be placed on the same level as humankind in the order of reality because they always presuppose temporal human existence. It is indeed true that these societal forms, at least insofar as they bear a differentiated character (which indeed would appear to be the case), are always qualified by a subject-function in one of the normative aspects. This does not give us the right to assert that they are a kind of *Überperson*, which has a status within reality equal to the individual human person. When examining the doctrine of legal personality, we shall become further acquainted with this conception, which has been defended by Otto Gierke and his school. This conception must be rejected in principle because the temporal societal forms are only realities of the second order which may never be placed on the same level as those of the first order.

The above mentioned radical types, which can be ascribed, in a secondary sense, to the individuality-structures of the second order, now, in their turn, embrace more inclusive and less inclusive groups of sub-types. These impose themselves immediately on theoretical investigation as soon as we consider the destination functions of the individuality-structures no longer only in their simple modal determination but in their typicalness.

The previously discussed ordering of the individuality-types into nuclear types, analogical types, and anticipatory types now becomes of decisive significance. Furthermore, insofar as the qualifying function does not manifest any original nuclear type, it is founded in an original individuality-type within an earlier modal aspect.

Therefore it is possible for the destination function to manifest an analogical individuality-type. It is not possible, however, for it to be of an anticipatory type. Anticipatory types can never qualify an individuality-structure with respect to its destination.

The sub-types we shall call "stem types," insofar as their structural peculiarities possess an altogether internal character and are thus unable to be explained in terms of the external relationship of the individuality-structure to other individuality-structures.

To the extent that the latter is indeed the case, we shall speak of "variability types." It must always be kept in mind, however, that the variable typicalness that an individuality-structure assumes by way of its interlacement with other individuality-structures never goes beyond its individual nature. So, adapting to their environments, animals and plants assume particular variability types. The polar fox, for example, assumes the white coat of its environment. A tree that is constantly exposed to the sea-wind takes on a typical form, for example, that resembling a column of smoke.

But these variability types are not impressed merely externally and mechanically upon animals and plants by their environment. The living organism itself assumes them in adapting to its environment. Nor is the internal nature of the plant and the animal denied in their variability types. The latter are therefore varieties of the stem types themselves and can never be conceived apart from them. Biology speaks of genotypes and phenotypes, by which the same thing is meant as by the terms stem types and variability types.

The particularizing of the stem type is carried through to the point where we at last strike an elementary type that itself does not include any narrower type but only individual beings or things.

The above mentioned ordering of the individuality-structures into radical types, into stem types in their gradual particularization to elementary types, and into variability types, is of universal applicability.

Thus it also holds for all objective human contrivances, such as works of art, utensils, dwellings, etc., and for the various structural types of human society. As we are yet to see, what is involved with the latter, for example, the family, the state, the church, and the business community is that they have different radical types. Stem types of the state, for example, are monarchies, aristocracies, democracies, and states with a mixed form of government. By contrast, variability types of the state, for example, are the church state, the industrial and the commercial state, etc. Thus the state church is a variability type of the church community.

As we continue our investigation, the fundamental significance of these structural-typical differentiations for the science of law will become increasingly apparent.

4.3 The Interlacement of the Individuality-Structures: Enkapsis and the Enkaptic Structural Whole

We must now direct our attention to the complicated manner in which the simple individuality-structures are interlaced with each other by the cosmic order of time and through which they are united, in part, within complex structural totalities.

To this end we proceed to investigate the individuality-structure of a work of art, and we choose as an illustration the famous sculpture of Praxiteles, *Hermes with the Son of Dionysius*. Here we discover peculiarities of structure, which recur in the case of the structures of human society to be investigated later.

If we attempt to establish what is the radical type of the art work in question, then it appears to be qualified by an aesthetic, hence, normative object-function. Considered modally, it is the aesthetic harmony of the conception which the artist has brought to objective expression in the marble image and which makes this entire image a work of art.

However, as soon as we consider the individuality type of the aesthetic destination function of the *Hermes* and thus investigate the stem type of the work of art in its gradual particularization, then it appears that (in the destination function) we are not concerned with an original nuclear type in the previously delineated sense.

The *Hermes* belongs to the stem type of plastic works of art, more particularly, to that of sculpture. The objective cultural form of the divine figures, which Praxiteles gave to the marble material, possesses, in the divine forms which have been represented (that is, the elementary type), the original nuclear type of individuality, which is the objective realization of the subjective aesthetic conception of the artist.

The aesthetic destination function of the *Hermes*, as to its individuality type, is founded in this cultural form (that is, an objective-historical function). The historical form-function is thus the typical founding function of the work of art. The (historical) aspect of form remains modally distinct from the aesthetic aspect in the Hermes. But in the individuality-structure both aspects are typically grouped in such a manner that the aesthetic object-function within it fulfills the role of the qualifying function and the objective historical function of form fulfills the role of the typical founding function. The founding function ought to be completely opened up by the leading aesthetic function. In a good work of art, the technical form should not assert itself at the expense of the aesthetic conception; it must give as complete an expression as possible to the aesthetic conception. In the Hermes, this is undoubtedly the case.

The inner structural principle expresses itself in all the modal functions of the work of art. These are truly subject-functions only in the first three aspects. In the later aspects, on the other hand, they are only object functions. Even in its jural aspect, as a juridical object, the Hermes remains this aesthetically qualified marble statue.

Both the destination and the founding functions have an objective, normative character. It is because of this that the work of art is the object of normative appreciation and as such is inaccessible to animal experience.

In the meantime, a new question raises its head. As a work of art, the Hermes is a marble statue. But what role does the marble play in it as a product of nature?

As a product of nature, this material has its own individuality-structure. As such it is physico-chemically qualified (within the modal aspect of movement) as a granular crystalline aggregate of limestone crystals, whose condition of being an aggregate is controlled under determinate geological conditions by the typical laws of calcium carbonate crystallization. Now the work of art itself is certainly no aggregate. An aggregate as such can be split up without difficulty into more or less homogeneous parts. It is a whole whose parts do not exist as uniform pieces of marble but are themselves determined by the inner structural law of the work of art and can only function as such within the individual totality of the work of art. The true parts of the work of art are the limbs of the divine figures which are formed of marble.

Within the structure of the work of art, therefore, the marble can only serve as formed material which gives expression to the art form.

Within this structure, the natural physico-chemical activity of the marble cannot fulfill the leading, qualifying role which it has in the product of nature. In that case, it would naturally present a constant threat (for example, because of cracks developing) to the cultural form which the artist has given to his material and in which, after all, the entire qualifying aesthetic conception is founded. Therefore Praxiteles took care by means of a technical process – he worked wax into the surface of the material – that the physico-chemical activity of the marble could not affect its surface, but remained subordinate to the expression of his aesthetic conception in the form of the divine figure.

Is the natural structure of the marble thus eliminated and taken up by the structure of the work of art? Not at all, for the marble remains marble. Artists cannot make it into flesh and blood. In their representational aesthetic activity, they remain bound to the structure of the material. But the structure of the material is, in a typical fashion, bound by, and interlaced with, that of the work of art. In the internal layers of the marble which are concealed under the external cultural form, it retains its own independent existence, its own individuality-structure.

It is only in the internal structure of the work of art that the marble no longer functions as a product of nature but acquires, in a formed image, the individuality type of the Hermes. It is only within this structure that its mathematical and physico-chemical functions are typically opened up and directed by the aesthetic composition. The work of art could not exist as an individual real thing if it did not also function in the prelogical aspects of reality. But the mathematical, physico-chemical, objective biotic, and objective sensory functions of the Hermes are nothing but the functions of the marble block that are bound up in the work of art.

In a marble statue therefore we discover an intertwinement of two individuality-structures that differ from each other, completely, in respect of their radical type. In this interlacement, each retains its own internal nature, its internal sphere sovereignty we may call it.

Such an interlacement of individuality-structures, which differ as to their radical type (or at least in their stem type), is called "enkapsis" in the Philosophy of the Cosmonomic Idea. The binding to which the structure of the marble is subjected within the structure of the work of art we call "enkaptic binding." And the functions which the marble thereby acquires within the structure of the work of art we call "enkaptic functions."

Enkapsis or enkaptic binding is to be found everywhere in temporal reality because the individuality-structures are not realized in isolation from one another but only in interlacements which are often of the most complex character.

Here we come across a situation which is entirely analogous to that encountered in the case of the modal structures. These also possess modal sphere sovereignty with respect to one another. No one of them is able to be reduced to any other but they are interrelated with one another in unbreakable coherence by the order of cosmic time.

The individuality-structures, too, are bound up with one another by the cosmic order of time that always occurs by means of a form, whether it be a physico-chemical, a biotic, an objective-sensory, or, as is the case with human beings, by means of a historico-cultural form. According to their individuality-structures, the forms of human society are always interwoven with each other, whether it be in their natural, original form or whether it be in a form of historical organization. We shall consider this later when we deal with the structures of society.

Thus the form, in whatever modal qualification it assumes, is always the nodal point of the enkaptic structural interlacements.

An individuality-structure that is enkaptically bound begins to manifest variability types in the form that interlaces it with another individuality-structure. Within the cultural form which is given by the artist, the marble, which has been technically worked on, becomes the means of expression for the artist's aesthetic conception. This typical character of the material, being a means of expression, cannot be understood in terms of the internal structure of the marble as a product of nature, even though this variability type still remains strictly bound to the internal nature of the marble as a product of nature.

The figure of enkapsis is entirely different from the relation of whole to part in every respect. Whatever is a part of a whole is exclusively determined by the individuality-structure of the whole. The part can never possess sphere sovereignty with respect to the whole. Indeed, the parts within the whole may possess autonomy, the boundaries of which, however, are dependent upon the demands of the whole, because the individuality-structure of the part does not differ in principle from that of the whole.

Enkapsis, by contrast, is only possible amongst individuality-structures which have a different radical type, or at least a different stem type. It is a form of interlacement which does not affect the internal sovereignty of the interwoven structures. Yet the enkaptic functions, which obtain an individuality-structure through the latter being bound into another individuality-structure, no longer fall within the internal orbit of the former but of the latter. In its enkaptic functions an individuality-structure thus does not possess sphere sovereignty.

Insight into this state of affairs appears to be of fundamental importance for the theory of human society because, in current conceptions, the difference in principle between sphere sovereignty and autonomy is consistently misunderstood.

Implicitly, this insight assumes fundamental importance for the theory of the sources of law because it is only by making a sharp distinction between the internal sphere sovereignty of radically different societal structures (such as, for example, state, church, and business organization) and the autonomy of the parts of one and the same societal whole (such as, for example, municipality and province within the state) can proper juridical insight be obtained into the mutual relationship of the original material spheres of competence with respect to the area of law formation.

Now the enkaptic structural interlacements, as they are encountered in reality, are themselves of various kinds. If we look more closely at the enkapsis of the structure of the marble in the individuality-structure of the

Hermes as a work of art, then it appears that the latter is founded in a one-sided dependence on the former, that is to say, the Hermes cannot exist as an objective work of art apart from the marble as a product of nature, but the reverse is quite possible. The marble is only bound into the form of the work of art; it originates in nature, however, in a free state. The type of enkaptic structural interlacement that we encounter here is that of unilateral founding.

A very different kind is that of correlative enkapsis in which the interlacement has a reciprocal character. We encounter correlative enkapsis, for example, in the intertwinement of the plant or the animal with its environment. Plants and animals are bound to their environment; but looking at the matter from the other side, a specific habitat is only a typical environment for particular types of plants and animals. In differentiated structures of society, we continually come across correlative enkapsis. Provisionally, however, we shall only focus on the type of unilateral founding which is encountered in all animal and human beings.

We encounter the same type in the structure of chemical compounds. Two hydrogen atoms and a single oxygen atom are bound in the physico-chemical form (configuration) of the molecule within the structure of a new element, water. Water can only exist in the physico-chemically qualified form H_2O into which the hydrogen and oxygen atoms are bound. But these atoms can appear in a free state as well.

We also encounter this type of enkapsis in the very complex structures within the plant and animal realms. The individuality-structure of the living plant organism, which we earlier analyzed, is unilaterally founded in the physico-chemically qualified structures of the components of the plant body. Here it is the biotic form of the body which interweaves these radically different structures into one another. Within this interlacement the components retain their internal sphere sovereignty. But they obtain an enkaptic function within the living organism. The mathematical and physico-chemical functions of this living organism are derived from the components, but follow, nevertheless, the internal structural law of the living organism.

Here also, as a result of enkaptic binding, the bound structures begin to manifest structural variability types which they do not have in their free state. Thus it is known, for example, that the components within the living organism manifest somewhat different physico-chemical characteristics than they do outside of it.[1] That is not to say, however, that they have changed their internal physico-chemical character. Protein and starch remain protein and starch, irrespective of whether they function in the living organism or are separated from it. We are only dealing here with variabil-

---

[1] This has been established, for example, in respect of proteins. Every living organism produces its own protein type that belongs to its stem type. A foreign type of protein that is introduced into a living organism has a toxic effect.

ity types of the materials, which they only assume in their enkaptic interlacement within the living organism.

Wherever we encounter this type of unilateral founding in the enkaptic structural interlacements, the individuality-structures, which are thus bound up, are (at least as a rule) united in a complex structural totality which we shall call an "enkaptic structural whole."

This enkaptic structural whole is not identical with any of the structures which are interwoven with one another within it, where the intertwined structures manifest a different radical type, but it is always qualified by its highest structure. According to its own complex individuality-structure, this enkaptic totality is a typical form-whole (that is, the typical founding function) which is qualified by the destination function of the highest structure that is interwoven within it (at least, insofar as it possesses such a radical function; this is naturally lacking, in a human being.) In the case of plants and animals this enkaptic structural whole is called the body. The body of a plant or an animal is not identical with its "living organism." It also includes within itself lifeless components which, nevertheless, belong to the body, such as, for example, the shells of molluscs, the armored back of a crocodile and, in general, calciferous (such as skeletons) or other parts (such as horns, hair, feathers, nails, etc.).

With regard to their inner structure, all material constituents of the living body, as has been seen, are in general already qualified in a physico-chemical and not in a typical biotic or physical way. They are not components of the living organism as such because they are not qualified in a subjective, biotic way with respect to their internal structure.

However, in their morphological binding within the form totality of the living body, they are indeed real existing components of it. In this connection, they do not follow the typical physico-chemical laws of the materials but the laws of form of the body as a morphological whole.

Thus, as a typically qualified morphological whole, the body of a plant and that of an animal intertwine diverse individuality-structures into an individual totality. In the animal body, superimposed on the individuality-structure of the living organism, there is a psychically (sensorily) qualified individuality-structure which is not present in the plant but which is the very feature which characterizes the animal as an enkaptic whole.

In the objective sensorily observable form (the typical founding function of the enkaptic whole), this psychical qualification of the animal body is expressed in its motor-sensory presence, which is lacking in the vegetatively qualified plant body. This motor-sensory figure of the animal body, which is already to be observed in one-celled micro-organisms (protozoa), is simply the morphological expression of the enkaptic structural whole comprising the animal. In its voluntary bodily movements, an animal responds out of a sensory-psychical response-center in which the impressions of the outside world are independently processed in a psychical way. It is only out of this sensory-psychical center that these responses express themselves as movements. By contrast, a plant only responds vegetatively. For example, it turns the top of its stem towards the light. But it lacks the capability of a psychical processing of the light and heat stimuli. The internal movements which are responses to the stimuli are only biotically directed.

4.4 The Enkaptic Structural Whole of the Human Body and Act-Life: The Relationship of Psychology and the Science of Law

The human body is the enkaptic structural whole that embraces the entire temporal individual existence of the human person. Within it, given in sequential order, the following individuality-structures are interlaced with one another in a unilateral founding relationship:

(i) the physico-chemically qualified structure of the components of the human body;

(ii) the biotically qualified structure of the living organism in which the vegetative or autonomous nervous system plays a typical role, insofar as this comprises the motor nerve pathways for the smooth, involuntary (not-subject-to-acts-of-the-will) muscles, which are in the service of the typical vegetative bodily processes;

(iii) the psychically qualified, motor-sensory structure, in which the animal nervous system plays a typical role, and which comprises the motor nerve pathways for the striated voluntary musculature;

(iv) the act-structure of the human body, within which the act-life of a person expresses itself according to the three fundamental directions: knowing, imagining, and willing, and within which the association-pathways of the cerebral cortex play an important role.

The four structures mentioned, as has become clear from our previous discussion, cannot be distinguished from each other morphologically, simply because they are unbreakably interlaced with each other within the form-whole of the body.

It is therefore just as impossible, for example, to place the autonomous nervous system, as a morphological whole, within the second body structure above (ii) as it is to locate the animal nervous system, in a morphological sense, under the third body structure (iii), and place the association pathways of the cerebrum within the act-structure (iv), though the associative nerve pathways are also present to a lesser extent in the cerebrum of the higher mammals. One can only say that they function in different typical ways and are only characterized in these typical functions in accordance with the bodily structures.

It is precisely these typical form-functions that provide an important experimental indication of the intrinsic structural diversity of the human body.

The Aristotelian scholastic doctrine that it is only the *anima rationalis* (as the only invisible "essential form" of the human body) that excites the vegetative and sensitive functions of the body – leaving out of consideration the conception we have rejected of the "rational soul" – cannot be squared with the empirical evidence. The body does not possess a simple structure.

By "acts," we understand the inner activities of human beings by means of which, under normative points of view (for instance, logical, aesthetic, cultural, jural, ethical, or pistical), they orient themselves intentionally (that is, intending or meaning) towards situations in reality or in their world of imagination, and make these their own by relating them to the "I" (as the individual religious center of the person's existence).

These acts always proceed from the supra-temporal (and thus integral) center of human nature, which the Bible in a pregnant religious sense calls the 'heart,' the 'soul,' or the 'spirit,' of the person. But it can only express itself within the human body as an enkaptic structural whole, more specifically, within its typical act-structure. The inner nature of acts resides in their intentional or meaning character. They only come to realization in the external world via a human action. The action brings to realization the intention of the act in which the three fundamental orientations of the act-life (knowing, imagining, and willing), within the motivated process of taking decisions, are intertwined and decision is translated into action.

There is no action without act; but not every act comes to realization in an action. So it is possible for a scientific act of knowing or an aesthetic act of imagining to remain entirely inwardly-directed. By contrast, an act of will, in its very nature, is oriented towards action. This has already appeared to be of importance in connection with legal life as a jural will-life.

What now do we understand by the "act-structure" of the human body? The act-structure is the highest individuality-structure of the human body. This means that it functions in all of the aspects of reality. Therefore, as a real act, the activity of thinking also has its internal physico-chemical, its biotic, and its psychical-emotional sides and should not be identified with its logical aspect.

In every act of thinking, the entire body and, in particular, the cerebral cortex is engaged in internal activity. This has been experimentally demonstrated since it is now possible to measure the electrical currents within the neurons (brain cells) produced by an act of thinking. It has also been ascertained that without the living cells of the cerebral cortex no experienceable thought-life is possible, even though this is not localized in special "fields" of the cerebrum, as are, for instance, sensory impressions and sensory images.

Taking account of this, the current view that acts are purely "spiritual" accomplishments which are independent of the bio-psychical "soma" are, at the same time, to be rejected in principle. This conception arises out of the well-known division (dichotomy) of temporal human existence into a material body and a spirit (or soul). We know, however, that according to divine Word-revelation, the human spirit or soul cannot be a temporal part of human existence but that it is the integral, religious center of temporal existence.

The conception of an act as a purely spiritual activity of the "soul," which is independent of the material body, has clearly arisen as a result of the theoretical *Gegenstand*-relation which we analyzed in part 1. The act has been described as "a spiritual experience of the I that in its content is intentionally related to a *Gegenstand*" (according to the whole of modern act-psychology, founded by Franz Brentano).

Now, we know that in the theoretical *Gegenstand*-relation the logical aspect of thought is set over against the nonlogical aspect of the field investigated by way of conscious abstraction. In this way it is possible to make all of the prelogical aspects of the body into a *Gegenstand* of the theoretical concept. But this abstract *Gegenstand*-relation was turned into a starting point, as though it corresponded to reality itself, and thus resulted in the acceptance of the idea that it is possible to effect an actual separation between the act of knowing and the material body as the *Gegenstand* of the act of knowing. We have become aware, in the meantime, that the *Gegenstand*-relation involves abstracting from the essentially temporal coherence and therefore it can never present reality itself but only a theoretical abstraction of it. Moreover, the theoretical *Gegenstand*-relation is in no way characteristic of all acts but only the theoretical acts of knowing.

The acts themselves, however, are indeed necessarily related to the I as the supra-temporal individual center. This already implies that the act-structure of the human body must differ in principle from the lower structures. In the act-structure, the body – as the total temporal form of existence – and the spirit (soul) – as the total and integral root-unity of human existence – are unbreakably related to each other *ex parte corporis*.

The act-structure itself retains its temporal bodily character. But it cannot exist apart from the spirit of the human person which transcends time and which itself comes to expression directly within the act-structure. For this very reason it lacks a qualifying function, unlike the lower individuality-structures.

One might for a moment suppose that all human acts are qualified by the function of faith, as the last limiting modal function. This view, however, is untenable.[1] If that were correct, all human acts would have to display a typical faith-qualification as, for example, is the case with prayer. But this, of course, is not so. Indeed, a theoretical act of knowing or an aesthetic act of imagining also function of necessity in the aspect of faith, but they are not typically qualified as acts of faith.

In reality human act-life is able to assume all of the possible normative qualifications because it happens to be within a bodily structure that does not itself possess any typical qualification but is directly oriented to the supra-temporal center of human existence. The scientific activity of knowing is of a typically theoretico-logical nature, the inward activity of prayer is typically pistical, the aesthetic activity of imagining is qualified in a typically aesthetic manner, etc. But the act-structure of the human body is itself unqualified, so that the soul or spirit – which transcends all temporal individuality-structures – would be capable of expressing itself in complete freedom within human act-life.

Individual acts therefore are able to assume a typical qualification which, as we shall see, is likewise determined by the individuality-structures of human society. But it takes place in a bodily act-structure which allows complete freedom for these typifications. It is only possible to say that act-life in the act-structure of the body is characterized by the three earlier-mentioned orientations of knowing, imagining, and willing. The latter, however, do not allow themselves to be divorced from each other as separate possibilities because they are in reality intertwined with each other. No act of will (volition) is possible apart from acts of knowing and imagining. It is indeed true, as we saw, that the distinct aspects of act-life are specifically related to the direction of willing, others to the direction of knowing, or to the direction of imagining.

Neither are these three orientations of the act-life, as such, any more typically qualified in the highest bodily structure. The direction of knowing, for example, is qualified theoretico-logically only in theoretical activity, but in the pretheoretical attitude of knowing it can take on any of the possible kinds of qualification. So, for example, when a congregation listens to an exposition of the Bible, the act of knowing is typically qualified

---

[1] I myself once defended this view in *Het tijdsprobleem in de Wijsbegeerte der Wetsidee* (The Problem of Time in the Philosophy of the Cosmonomic Idea) (1940), 222. By contrast, in *De Wijsbegeerte der Wetsidee*, vol. 3 (1936) I had already adopted the preferable approach.

as a faith-act. But in an industrial enterprise, where a foreman explains to the employee the operation of a new machine, the act of knowing is typically qualified by the technico-economic function of industrial life.

Furthermore, the three orientations of the act-life, knowing, imagining, and willing, do not possess an original character that is typical for the act-structure. Rather, they are founded in three orientations of intentional experiencing in the psychically qualified structure of the body, which we already encounter in the animal, namely, sensory knowing, sensory imagining, and sensory striving and desiring. These are not acts as such, because they are not related to a "self" and because the intentional experiencing here is not subject to the leading of normative points of view. Nevertheless, even the animal has a sensory knowledge of its environment; it possesses a sensory life of imagination (in which it has sensory representations of a purely intentional character, for example, of food, of impending danger; and compare animal dream life) and sensory desires and strivings (for the satisfaction of its needs). In human act-life these three orientations, however, are related to the self, and they are always directed by normative (logical, aesthetic, ethical, etc.) points of view.

It is for this reason that jural volition (willing) was earlier described as a sensory (psychical) analogy within the modal structure of law. The jural function of willing is only a modal aspect of an act of volition, which as such functions in all aspects of reality (in the logical aspect as well) but is nevertheless founded in the emotional feeling-desires. In the jural function of volition, too, the inner act-function retains its primacy even though (by reason of the founding of the jural aspect in the aspect of social intercourse and the lingual aspect)[1] it can never become operative in legal life without a declaration of will or an expression of the act in the external world. Those who want to allow jural volition to be exhausted in the declaration of will cannot provide the science of law with an account of the

---

[1] It is clear, moreover, that the inner act also has its lingual aspect. After all, we think in judgments which we express internally. The words, in which we think, are not yet expressed in the inner act via objective sensorily audible sounds but they are only intentional representations of sound with symbolic meaning. Imperceptibly, however, this interior speaking in thought can be transformed into "thinking aloud," whereby we give expression to the intentional verbal representations in objectively audible sounds, even though we may not direct this thinking aloud to anyone other than ourselves. The internal thought-act in this sense, however, does not have to take the form of a monologue in its lingual aspect. It can also occur intentionally in the form of dialogue through interior conversations with others, as when, for instance, we defend our opinions "in our thoughts" against the objections of others without these opponents actually being present. Because an act of volition never takes place without thought activity (I take the internal decision of will, "Tomorrow I shall do this or that" and internally utter this practical judgment, in which this decision is contained), the above also holds for the will-act (volition). Thus volition also has its inner lingual aspect.

juridical effect of mistake, coercion, and fraud on the validity of the declaration of will. Here there is a clear discrepancy between the will-act and its expression that can lead to the nullification of the declaration of will. It is not, however, a question of the psychical but of the jural function of the act, which is therefore assessed according to juridical standards.

From the explanation above it will have become clear that the traditional metaphysical conception of psychology as the science of the "human soul" is rejected. It is not possible to attain a scientific concept of the human soul as the supra-temporal integral root of human existence because all scientific conceptual knowledge is bound to the time-order.

Those who suppose that it is possible to make the human soul itself into a *Gegenstand* of conceptual knowledge conceive it – in the manner earlier indicated – as an abstract complex of modal functions, which are then made independent as "the spiritual soul" over against another abstract complex that is conceived as the "material body." We observed, however, that in temporal reality no dichotomy between body and soul exists, but that the human body is an enkaptic structural totality which intertwines four individuality-structures with one another within a single wholeness of form, and which is qualified by the highest of these individuality-structures, the act-structure. Human act-life, as we have seen, is not of a purely spiritual nature but plays itself out in the act-structure of the body, within which the logical and post-logical indissolubly cohere with the prelogical aspects. Act-life merely proceeds from the human soul which comes to expression in acts.

According to our conception, psychology is a special science whose field of investigation is delimited by the modal aspect of feeling. It has to scientifically investigate the human act-life within this aspect. That is to say, within its own, modally delimited, specialized field, it concerns itself with the typical individuality-structures of human act-life as these are found in human society. The same is true of the science of law within its own area of specialization. However, since acts, in their bodily structure, always proceed from the soul as the supra-temporal center, psychology has to place at the foundation of its special scientific investigations a transcendental idea of the human soul. The entire orientation of psychological investigation will depend upon the way in which this idea of the soul is conceived.

And so it is the case that psychology, in terms of such an idea of the soul, must investigate, for example, the activity of knowing and willing according to their emotional-psychical aspect. But in addition it must more specifically grasp these acts in their typical differentiation within the structures of society. Social psychology has already undertaken extensive investigations into these matters, and it is self-evident that it also has significance for legal science, namely, insofar as it analyzes the psychical individuality-structures. Social psychology, however, should never lose sight of the modal limitations of its own field of specialization and, adopting a psychological approach, declare itself to be a kind of foundational science for all normative special sciences.

The true totality science of human act-life is instead a philosophical theory of structure which, as crowning piece, takes the form of philosophical anthropology and which again, of course, ought to orient itself toward the data of experience. It stands in precisely the same relationship to empirical psychology as the philosophical theory of the structure of the living organism stands to empirical biology; and as philosophical sociology stands to the science of history, the science of language, the science of economics, the science of law, etc.

That the true structural theory of human act-life has been subsumed under psychology can be explained in terms of the traditional metaphysical conception of the soul as a grouping of functions independent of the material body. It really makes very little difference whether one is content with this dichotomizing of temporal human existence, or – as is very common in modern act-psychology – you introduce a trichotomy of body, psyche, and spirit, in which case only the spirit (as a complex of the higher functions of feeling, the logical function of thought, and the aesthetic and ethical functions) is conceived as being independent of the living body.

It is only possible for the encyclopedia of the sciences to be built upon a satisfactory foundation if there is a break in principle with all such false conceptions of totality.

We now return to the act-structure of the human body. The question arises then as to how is it possible here to speak of a true individuality-structure, if it is impossible to point to any qualifying destination function for it.

To be able to answer this question we must first of all take into consideration that an individuality-structure is nothing other than a typical unity in the diversity of its modal functions, which is founded in the cosmic order of time.

Because it appeared that with all of the previously investigated structures, such a unity could be brought into being only by the presence of a typical qualifying function, it cannot be concluded a priori that this is indeed the case. It should not be forgotten that, in the investigation of the structure of the human person's temporal bodily existence, the issue at stake, in the final analysis, concerns humankind itself which, as we know, occupies a central position in the temporal cosmos. With respect to the human person, the body, as the enkaptic structural whole, is a typical expression of the "spirit" as the religious root-unity, which has its individuality in the self.

This expresses itself morphologically in the objective sensory form-whole of the human body. The latter does not manifest a motor-sensory presence, as in the case of the animal body, but a spiritual presence – in the erect gait, the gleam in the eye, the powerful development of the cranium, the complete plasticity of the pattern of bodily movement, the free mobility of the hands for the purpose of labour (in contrast to the rigidly specialized functions of animal limbs) and, in general, in the lack of specialization of the body. While the animal is wholly specialized by reason of having claws, or gripping feet, a thick coat of fur, etc., for life within a limited habitat, the human body is not specialized for a particular environment. Humankind, in a spiritual sense, is created as the ruler of the temporal cosmos. Its bodily form is the temporal expression of this central position, and it is the act-structure, by reason of its essential relatedness to the spiritual center of the self, that impresses upon the human bodily form that typical stamp.

Human act-life has two levels, as modern depth psychology (the psychoanalysis of Freud and his school) has irrefutably demonstrated, namely, an unconscious substratum and a conscious superstratum. Consciousness is not restricted, as it was earlier thought, to the psychical aspect and the post-psychical aspects of human existence, whilst all of the prepsychical aspects have to be assigned to the unconscious. Instead, consciousness and unconsciousness are two forms of manifestation of one and the same reality, which function in all of the aspects without exception. Human consciousness, precisely because it is concentrated in a self-consciousness, includes all the aspects of reality; otherwise the question as to how these aspects could come into human consciousness would be insoluble. But the unconscious also functions in all aspects without exception. So it has been established that human act-life depends for its own continuity on the unconscious.

For instance, if, after months of fruitless searching for the solution of a scientific question, we turn our attention to other things for a while, sometimes it is possible the solution to the problem will spontaneously spring to mind. In that case, our thought-life has gone on unconsciously in the intervening time. If, after an interval of several years, we meet, for the second time, someone who made an unfavorable impression on us at first acquaintance, and we are reminded of this impression at the second meeting, then this impression has continued to work in the unconscious substratum of our feeling-life, even though it had receded below the threshold of our consciousness.

In post-hypnotic suggestion, a command that has been given during the suggestion state of "sleep" is carried out precisely at the instructed time. In what is otherwise a conscious condition, obedience is rendered unconsciously to a decision of will which has impressed itself in the subconscious. It is well-known, however, that ethical and faith factors can exert (just as unconsciously) a restraining influence upon the obedience of the one who has been given this suggestion.

In the normal structure of the act-life the unconscious is hierarchically subordinate to the conscious. Desires, ideas, etc., which are ruled out by a particular individual because of normative considerations are suppressed within the unconscious substratum of their act-life. In a serious psychopathic condition (namely, in the various forms of schizophrenia, hysteria, etc.), this act-structure is disturbed in a two-fold way:

(i) The hierarchical subordination of the unconscious to the conscious is broken. The former wrestles loose from consciousness and in many respects attains a position of dominance;

(ii) The central relation of the act-life to the self is broken in consciousness. Act-life, on account of this, disintegrates and there appears in the consciousness the well-known phenomena of "split personality." Patients speak about a part of their inner experiences in the third person, that is to say, they relate them to another, invented self. "He" thinks or wills this; "I" think or will something else. Also the harmonious working together of the various modal functions (for example, the function of feeling and the logical function) break down within the act-life.

In one way or other, it seems clear that in act-life there does indeed exist a typical structure which in its normal state guarantees the inner unity of this act-life. The central relatedness of the self, the harmonious concerted operation of the various modal functions, and the subordination of the unconscious to the conscious, protect the typically human unity in the act-structure of the human body. But the act-structure reveals at the same time its unique character over against all other individuality-structures in the following respect: its internal unity in the diversity of its modal functions is rooted transcendently in the central root-unity of human existence, in the soul or spirit, in which both the conscious and the unconscious act-life find their point of departure.

The lower individuality-structures that are bound up in the human body retain, over against the act-structure, their internal sphere sovereignty. They can only be controlled by the will in their enkaptic functions within the act-structure.

Insight into this state of affairs is of great importance, for example, for the juridical problem of responsibility.

It may be that the possibility of a conscious, normative directing of our actions by an act of will is temporarily precluded. In normal circumstances, the psychically qualified instincts (for example, self-preservation) do not come to free expression but are always bound up within the act-structure. If they temporarily break loose from their binding within the act-structure, they make a path for themselves with primitive force (think of a state of "panic"). In such a case the possibility of a free determination of will in a normative weighing of the motives and consequences of an action is lacking, and the foundation for jural accountability is eliminated.

Where there is permanently disabling development of the act-structure of the human body or its disruption due to illness (because of mental deficiency or complete insanity), lack of responsibility, naturally, is also permanent.

In the case of a delict that is committed under post-hypnotic suggestion, a foreign will has made itself the master of the act-life of the wrongdoer and thus the suggested action cannot be attributed to the one who carried it out.

We speak of "diminished responsibility" whenever the possibility of free determination of the will is only made difficult in more or less serious measure by a psychopathic tendency without it being thwarted altogether.

Glossary

[The following glossary of Dooyeweerd's technical terms and neologisms is reproduced and edited by Daniël F. M. Strauss, with the permission of its author, Albert M. Wolters, from C. T. McIntire, ed., *The Legacy of Herman Dooyeweerd: Reflections on Critical Philosophy in the Christian Tradition* (Lanham MD, 1985), 167–171.]

THIS GLOSSARY OF HERMAN DOOYEWEERD'S terms is an adapted version of the one published in L. Kalsbeek, *Contours of a Christian Philosophy* (Toronto: Wedge, 1975). It does not provide exhaustive technical definitions but gives hints and pointers for a better understanding. Entries marked with an asterisk are those terms which are used by Dooyeweerd in a way which is unusual in English-speaking philosophical contexts and are, therefore, a potential source of misunderstanding. Words or phrases in small caps and beginning with a capital letter refer to other entries in this glossary.

* **Analogy** (see LAW-SPHERE) – Collective name for a RETROCIPATION or an ANTICIPATION.

* **Anticipation** – An ANALOGY within one MODALITY referring to a later modality. An example is "efficiency," a meaning-moment which is found within the historical modality, but which points forward to the later economic modality. Contrast with RETROCIPATION.

* **Antinomy** – Literally "conflict of laws" (from Greek *anti*, "against," and *nomos*, "law"). A logical contradiction arising out of a failure to distinguish the different kinds of law valid in different MODALITIES. Since ontic laws do not conflict (*Principium Exclusae Antinomiae*), an antinomy is always a logical sign of ontological reductionism.

* **Antithesis** – Used by Dooyeweerd (following Abraham Kuyper) in a specifically religious sense to refer to the fundamental spiritual opposition between the kingdom of God and the kingdom of darkness. See Galatians 5:17. Since this is an opposition between regimes, not realms, it runs through every department of human life and culture, including philosophy and the academic enterprise as a whole, and through the heart of every believer as he or she struggles to live a life of undivided allegiance to God.

Aspect – A synonym for MODALITY.

Cosmonomic idea – Dooyeweerd's own English rendering of the Dutch term *wetsidee*. Occasionally equivalents are "transcendental ground idea" or "transcendental basic idea." The intention of this new term is to bring to expression that there exists an unbreakable coherence between God's *law* (nomos) and created reality (*cosmos*) factually subjected to God's law.

Dialectic – In Dooyeweerd's usage: an unresolvable tension, within a system or line of thought, between two logically irreconcilable polar positions. Such a dialectical tension is characteristic of each of the three non-Christian GROUND-MOTIVES which Dooyeweerd sees as having dominated Western thought.

*Enkapsis (enkaptic) – A neologism borrowed by Dooyeweerd from the Swiss biologist Heidenhain, and derived from the Greek *enkaptein*, "to swallow up." The term refers to the structural interlacements which can exist between things, plants, animals, and societal structures which have their own internal structural principle and independent qualifying function. As such, enkapsis is to be clearly distinguished from the part-whole relation, in which there is a common internal structure and qualifying function.

Factual Side – General designation of whatever is *subjected* to the LAW-SIDE of creation (see SUBJECT-SIDE).

Founding function – The earliest of the two modalities which characterize certain types of structural wholes. The other is called the GUIDING FUNCTION. For example, the founding function of the family is the biotic modality.

* Gegenstand – A German word for "object," used by Dooyeweerd as a technical term for a modality when abstracted from the coherence of time and opposed to the analytical function in the theoretical attitude of thought, thereby establishing the Gegenstand-relation. Gegenstand is therefore the technically precise word for the object of SCIENCE, while "object" itself is reserved for the objects of NAIVE EXPERIENCE.

Ground-motive – The Dutch term *grondmotief*, used by Dooyeweerd in the sense of fundamental motivation, driving force. He distinguished four basic ground-motives in the history of Western civilization:
(1) form and matter, which dominated pagan Greek philosophy; (2) nature and grace, which underlay medieval Christian synthesis thought (3) nature and freedom, which has shaped the philosophies of modern times; and (4) creation, fall, and redemption, which lies at the root of a radical and integrally scriptural philosophy.

Guiding function – The highest subject-function of a structural whole (e.g. stone, animal, business enterprise, or state). Except in the case of humans, this function is also said to QUALIFY the structural whole. It is called the guiding function because it "guides" or "leads" its earlier functions. For example, the guiding function of a plant is the biotic. The physical function of a plant (as studied, e.g. by biochemistry) is different from physical functioning elsewhere because of its being "guided" by the biotic. Also called "leading function."

Glossary

* **Heart** – The concentration point of human existence; the supratemporal focus of all human temporal functions; the religious root unity of humans. Dooyeweerd says that it was his rediscovery of the biblical idea of the heart as the central religious depth dimension of human multifaceted life which enabled him to wrestle free from neo-Kantianism and phenomenology. The Scriptures speak of this focal point also as "soul," "spirit," and "inner man." Philiosophical equivalents are Ego, I, I-ness, and Selfhood. It is the heart in this sense which survives death, and it is by the religious redirection of the heart in regeneration that all human temporal functions are renewed.

* **Immanence Philosophy** – A name for all non-Christian philosophy, which tries to find the ground and integration of reality *within* the created order. Unlike Christianity, which acknowledges a transcendent Creator above all things, immanence philosophy of necessity absolutizes some feature or aspect of creation itself.

* **Individuality-structure** – This term represents arguably one of the most difficult concepts in Dooyeweerd's philosophy. Coined in both Dutch and English by Dooyeweerd himself it has led sometimes to serious misunderstandings amongst scholars. Over the years there have been various attempts to come up with an alternate term, some of which are described below, but in the absence of a consensus it was decided to leave the term the way it is.

  It is the general name or the characteristic law (order) of concrete things, as given by virtue of creation. Individuality-structures belong to the law-side of reality. Dooyeweerd uses the term individuality-structure to indicate the applicability of a structural order *for* the existence of *individual* entities. Thus the *structural laws* for the state, for marriage, for works of art, for mosquitoes, for sodium chloride, and so forth are called individuality-structures. The idea of an individual whole is determined by an individuality-structure which precedes the theoretical analysis of its modal functions. The identity of an individual whole is a relative unity in a multiplicity of functions. (See MODALITY.) Van Riessen prefers to call this law for entities an *identity-structure*, since as such it guarantees the persistent **identity** of all **entities** (*Wijsbegeerte*, [Kampen, 1970], 158). In his work (*Alive, An Enquiry into the Origin and Meaning of Life* [Vallecito, California: Ross House Books, 1984]), M. Verbrugge introduces his own distinct systematic account concerning the nature of (what he calls) *functors*, a word first introduced by Hendrik Hart for the dimension of individuality-structures (cf. Hart: *Understanding Our World, Towards an Integral Ontology* [New York, 1984], 445–446). As a substitute for the notion of an individuality-structure, Verbrugge advances the term: *idionomy* (cf. *Alive*, 42, 81ff., 91ff.). Of course this term may also cause misunderstanding if it is taken to mean that each individual creature (subject) has its *own unique* law. What is intended is that every *type of law* (*nomos*) is meant to delimit and determine unique subjects. In other words, however *specified* the universality of the

235

law may be, it can never, in its bearing upon unique individual creatures, itself become something *uniquely individual*. Another way of grasping the meaning of Dooyeweerd's notion of an *individuality-structure* is, in following an oral suggestion by Roy Clouser (Zeist, August 1986), to call it a *type-law* (from Greek: *typonomy*). This simply means that all entities of a certain *type* conform to this law. The following perspective given by M.D. Stafleu elucidates this terminology in a *systematic way* (*Time and Again, A Systematic Analysis of the Foundations of Physics* [Toronto: Wedge Publishing Foundation, 1980], 6, 11): *typical laws* (type-laws/typonomies, such as the Coulomb law – applicable only to charged entities and the Pauli principle – applicable only to fermions) are special laws which apply to a limited class of entities only, whereas *modal laws* hold universally for all possible entities. D.F.M. Strauss ("Inleiding tot die Kosmologie." *SACUM*, [1980]) introduces the expression *entity structures*. The term **entity** comprises both the *individuality* and the *identity* of the thing concerned – therefore it accounts for the respective emphases found in Dooyeweerd's notion of *individuality-structures* and in Van Riessen's notion of *identity structures*. The following words of Dooyeweerd show that both the **individuality** and **identity** of an entity is determined by its individuality-structure: "In general we can establish that the factual temporal duration of a thing as an individual and identical whole is dependent on the preservation of its structure of individuality" (*A New Critique*, vol.3,79).

Irreducibility (irreducible) – Incapability of theoretical reduction. This is the negative way of referring to the unique distinctiveness of things and aspects which we find everywhere in creation and which theoretical thought must respect. Insofar as everything has its own peculiar created nature and character, it cannot be understood in terms of categories foreign to itself.

* **Law** – The notion of creational law is central to Dooyeweerd's philosophy. Everything in creation is subject to God's law for it, and accordingly law is the boundary between God and creation. Scriptural synonyms for law are "ordinance," "decree," "commandment," "word," and so on. Dooyeweerd stresses that law is not in opposition to, but the condition for true freedom. See also NORM and LAW-SIDE.

Law-Side – The created cosmos, for Dooyeweerd, has two correlative "sides": a law-side and a factual side (initially called: SUBJECT-SIDE). The former is simply the coherence of God's laws or ordinances for creation; the latter is the totality of created reality which is subject to those laws. It is important to note that the law-side always holds universally.

Law-Sphere (see MODAL STRUCTURE and MODALITY) – The circle of laws qualified by a unique, irreducible, and indefinable meaning-nucleus is known as a law-sphere. Within every law-sphere temporal reality has a modal function and in this function is subjected (French: *sujet*) to the laws of the modal spheres. Therefore every law-sphere has a law-side and a sub-

Glossary

ject-side that are given only in unbreakable correlation with each other. (See DIAGRAM on p. 241.)

* **Meaning** – Dooyeweerd uses the word "meaning" in an unusual sense. By it he means the referential, non-self-sufficient character of created reality in that it points beyond itself to God as Origin. Dooyeweerd stresses that reality *is* meaning in this sense and that, therefore, it does not *have* meaning. "Meaning" is the Christian alternative to the metaphysical substance of immanence philosophy. "Meaning" becomes almost a synonym for "reality." Note the many compounds formed from it: meaning-nucleus, meaning-side, meaning-moment, meaning-fullness.

* **Meaning-nucleus** – The indefinable core meaning of a MODALITY.

Modality (See MODAL STRUCTURE and LAW-SPHERE) – One of the fifteen fundamental ways of being distinguished by Dooyeweerd. As modes of being, they are sharply distinguished from the concrete things which function within them. Initially Dooyeweerd distinguished fourteen aspects only, but in 1950 he introduced the kinematical aspect of *uniform movement* between the spatial and the physical aspects. Modalities are also known as "modal functions," "modal aspects," or as "facets" of created reality. (See DIAGRAM on p. 241.)

Modal Structure (see MODALITY and LAW-SPHERE) – The peculiar constellation, in any given modality, of its meaning-moments (anticipatory, retrocipatory, nuclear). Contrast INDIVIDUALITY-STRUCTURE.

* **Naive experience** – Human experience insofar as it is not "theoretical" in Dooyeweerd's precise sense. "Naive" does not mean unsophisticated. Sometimes called "ordinary" or "everyday" experience. Dooyeweerd takes pains to emphasize that theory is embedded in this everyday experience and must not violate it.

Norm (normative) – Postpsychical laws, that is, modal laws for the analytical through pistical law-spheres (see LAW-SPHERE and DIAGRAM on p. 241). These laws are norms because they need to be positivized (see POSITIVIZE) and can be violated, in distinction from the "natural laws" of the pre-analytical spheres which are obeyed involuntarily (e.g., in a digestive process).

* **Nuclear-moment** – A synonym for MEANING-NUCLEUS and LAW-SPHERE, used to designate the indefinable core meaning of a MODALITY or aspect of created reality.

* **Object** – Something qualified by an object function and thus correlated to a subject-function. A work of art, for instance, is qualified by its correlation to the human subjective function of aesthetic appreciation. Similarly, the elements of a sacrament are pistical objects.

Opening process – The process by which latent modal anticipations are "opened" or actualized. The modal meaning is then said to be "deepened."

It is this process which makes possible the cultural development (differentiation) of society from a primitive ("closed," undifferentiated) stage. For example, by the opening or disclosure of the ethical anticipation in the juridical aspect, the modal meaning of the legal aspect is deepened and society can move from the principle of "an eye for an eye" to the consideration of extenuating circumstances in the administration of justice.

* **Philosophy** – In Dooyeweerd's precise systematic terminology, philosophy is the encyclopedic science, that is, its proper task is the theoretical investigation of the overall systematic integration of the various scientific disciplines and their fields of inquiry. Dooyeweerd also uses the term in a more inclusive sense, especially when he points out that all philosophy is rooted in a pretheoretical religious commitment and that some philosophical conception, in turn, lies at the root of all scientific scholarship.

Positivize – A word coined to translate the Dutch word *positiveren*, which means to make positive in the sense of being actually valid in a given time or place. For example, positive law is the legislation which is in force in a given country at a particular time; it is contrasted with the *legal principles* which lawmakers must positivize as legislation. In a general sense, it refers to the responsible implementation of all normative principles in human life as embodied, for example, in state legislation, economic policy, ethical guidelines, and so on.

Qualify – The GUIDING FUNCTION of a thing is said to qualify it in the sense of characterizing it. In this sense a plant is said to be qualified by the biotic and a state by the juridical [aspects].

* **Radical** – Dooyeweerd frequently uses this term with an implicit reference to the Greek meaning of *radix* = *root*. This usage must not be confused with the political connotation of the term *radical* in English. In other works Dooyeweerd sometimes paraphrases his use of the term radical with the phrase: *penetrating to the root of created reality*.

* **Religion (religious)** – For Dooyeweerd, religion is not an area or sphere of life but the all-encompassing and direction-giving root of it. It is service of God (or a substitute no-god) in every domain of human endeavor. As such, it is to be sharply distinguished from religious faith, which is but one of the many acts and attitudes of human existence. Religion is an affair of the HEART and so directs all human functions. Dooyeweerd says religion is "the innate impulse of the human selfhood to direct itself toward the *true* or toward a *pretended* absolute Origin of all temporal diversity of meaning" (*A New Critique*, vol.1, 57).

* **Retrocipation** – A feature in one MODALITY which refers to, is reminiscent of, an earlier one, yet retaining the modal qualification of the aspect in which it is found. The "extension" of a concept, for example, is a kind of logical space: it is a strictly logical affair, and yet it harks back to the spatial modality in its original sense. See ANTICIPATION.

Glossary

* **Science** – Two things are noted about Dooyeweerd's use of the term "science." In the first place, as a translation of the Dutch word *wetenschap* (analogous to the German word *Wissenschaft*), it embraces all scholarly study – not only the natural sciences but also the social sciences and the humanities, including theology and philosophy. In the second place, science is always, strictly speaking, a matter of modal abstraction, that is, of analytically lifting an aspect out of the temporal coherence in which it is found and examining it in the Gegenstand-relation. But in this investigation it does not focus its theoretical attention upon the modal structure of such an aspect itself; rather, it focuses on the coherence of the actual phenomena which function within that structure. Modal abstraction as such must be distinguished from NAIVE EXPERIENCE. In the first sense, therefore, "science" has a wider application in Dooyeweerd than is usual in English-speaking countries, but in the second sense it has a more restricted, technical meaning.

Sphere Sovereignty – A translation of Kuyper's phrase *souvereiniteit in eigen kring*, by which he meant that the various distinct spheres of human authority (such as family, church, school, and business enterprise) each have their own responsibility and decision-making power which may not be usurped by those in authority in another sphere, for example, the state. Dooyeweerd retains this usage but also extends it to mean the IRREDUCIBILITY of the modal aspects. This is the ontical principle on which the societal principle is based since each of the societal "spheres" mentioned is qualified by a different irreducible modality.

* **Subject** – Used in two senses by Dooyeweerd: (1) "subject" as distinguished from LAW, (2) "subject" as distinguished from OBJECT. The latter sense is roughly equivalent to common usage; the former is unusual and ambiguous. Since all things are "subject" to LAW, objects are also subjects in the first sense. Dooyeweerd's matured conception, however, does not show this ambiguity. By distinguishing between the *law-side* and the *factual side* of creation, both subject and object (sense (2)) are part of the factual side.

Subject-Side – The correlate of LAW-SIDE, preferably called the factual side. Another feature of the factual subject-side is that it is only here that individuality is found.

Substratum – The aggregate of modalities *preceding* a given aspect in the modal order. The arithmetic, spatial, kinematic, and physical, for example, together form the substratum for the biotic. They are also the necessary foundation upon which the biotic rests, and without which it cannot exist. See SUPERSTRATUM (and the DIAGRAM on p. 241).

Superstratum – The aggregate of modalities *following* a given aspect in the modal order. For example, the pistical, ethical, juridical and aesthetic together constitute the superstratum of the economic. See SUBSTRATUM.

* **Synthesis** – The combination, in a single philosophical conception, of characteristic themes from both pagan philosophy and biblical religion. It is this feature of the Christian intellectual tradition, present since patristic times, with which Dooyeweerd wants to make a radical break. Epistemologically seen, the term *synthesis* is used to designate the way in which a multiplicity of features is integrated within the unity of a concept. The re-union of the logical aspect of the theoretical act of thought with its non-logical "Gegenstand" is called an inter-modal meaning-synthesis.
* **Time** – In Dooyeweerd, a general ontological principle of intermodal continuity, with far wider application than our common notion of time, which is equated by him with the physical manifestation of this general cosmic time. It is, therefore, not coordinate with space. All created things, except the human HEART, are in time. At the law-side time expresses itself as time-order and at the factual side (including subject-subject and subject-object relations) as time duration.

Transcendental – A technical term from the philosophy of Kant denoting the a priori structural conditions which make human experience (specifically human knowledge and theoretical thought) possible. As such it is to be sharply distinguished from the term "transcendent." Furthermore, the basic (transcendental) Idea of a philosophy presupposes the transcendent and central sphere of consciousness (the human HEART). This constitutes the *second* meaning in which Dooyeweerd uses the term transcendental: through its transcendental ground-Idea philosophy points beyond itself to its ultimate religious foundation transcending the realm of thought.

Glossary

The different law-spheres of reality distinguished by Dooyeweerd*

CREATURES SUBJECTED TO GOD'S CREATIONAL LAW

	Law-Spheres (Aspects)	Meaning-nuclei
HUMAN	Certitudinal	certainty (to be sure)
	Ethical	love/troth
	Juridical	retribution
	Aesthetical	beautiful harmony
	Economical	frugality/avoid excesses
	Social	social intercourse
	Sign-mode	symbolical signification
	Cultural-historical	formative power/control
	Logical	analysis
BEINGS	Sensitive-psychical	sensitivity/feeling
	Biotical	organic life
	Physical	energy-operation
	Kinematic	unif. motion/constancy
	Spatial	continuous extension
	Numerical	discrete quantity

Left-side bracketing labels: HUMAN BEINGS / SOCIAL / LIFEFORMS & CULTURAL / CULTURAL / ANIMALS / PLANTS / THINGS

*Diagram and choice of terms by D.F.M. Strauss.

Index

A
actio civilis 120
actiones ficticiae 120
act-psychology 224, 228
act-structure 155, 222-231
administrative law 199, 204
Aeschylus 57
aesthetic aspect 13, 15, 31, 190, 192, 217
agapē 110
Albertus Magnus 61
an unlawful act 16, 125, 131-132
analogical concepts 83, 92-93
Anankē 51-54, 57-58
Anaxagoras 55-56
anima rationalis 62, 223
anticipations 103-104, 106, 110, 114, 127, 133-134, 145, 165, 176, 189-190, 192-195, 205, 212
anticipatory 103-106, 108-109, 123-125, 133-135, 158, 173, 175-177, 207-209, 215
antinomies 26, 112-115, 117, 119-121
antinomy 114
apeiron 64
Arabia 161
archē 53-54, 76
Archimedean point 34-37, 41, 44, 46-47, 76-78, 80-82, 90
Archimedes 34
Aristotelian scholasticism 92, 98
Aristotle 45, 50, 53, 56-58, 61, 63, 92, 143
astronomical theory 23
Athens 161
Augustine 60-61, 63

B
Babylon 161

basic concepts 20-22, 101, 124, 197, 201-202
battle of Waterloo 71
Benefiziums 168
Betti 170
bio-chemistry 211
biologism 36, 141
bio-milieu 107
bio-physics 211
Brentano 224
Bruno 64
brute power 145

C
capitalism 143
Cassirer 45, 181
causa omissionis 117, 126
central religious commandment 98
cerebral cortex 222, 224
cerebrum 223-224
Christian Gnosticism 59
Chronos 181
Civil
 – law 73, 87, 90, 93, 116, 127, 129-131, 198-199, 201, 204
 – liability 131
 – procedure 199
Civil Code 16-17, 19, 31, 86, 88, 129-130, 198
civitas dei 183
civitas terrena 183
Clement 60
Clovis 134
Codrington 179
Cohen 45
Commercial
 – law 199
 – agreement 15-18, 31
common law 24, 135, 201
Communal

- life 158
- norms 91, 93
conditio sine qua non 117
constant principles 206
Copernicus 64, 74
correlative enkapsis 220
Cosmic
- order of time 34, 76, 81-82, 98, 100, 103, 114, 123, 134, 202, 205, 207, 210, 216, 218, 228
- time 26, 29, 32, 79, 94, 100, 125, 139-140, 190, 193, 218
cosmonomic idea 11, 75, 85, 91, 95, 102, 189, 197, 218, 225
Crete 161
Criminal
- law 102, 104, 124, 126-128, 131, 199
- legal guilt 124
- legal retribution 111
- procedure 199
culpa 130-131
Cultural
- artifacts 163
- development 17, 30, 49, 80, 91, 126, 150, 152-153, 156, 158, 160-163, 165, 170, 182-183, 202
- intercourse 160, 164
culture religion 51-55, 143, 181
cultus 175
customary law 22, 171, 199

D

Darwin 73
deductive syllogism 108
Delphic oracle 37
demiurge 55, 57, 59
depth psychology 229
Descartes 65-66
differentia specifica 91-93
Differential
- functions 107, 109
- quotient 107
dikē 54
Dionysian movement 52
divine form 51, 55, 144, 216

dolus 130-131
donum superadditum 62
Dopsch 167-168
doxa 56, 174
Dutch jurisprudence 88

E

Ecclesiastical
- authorities 62
- law 198-200, 202
economic aspect 16, 31, 111-112
Egypt 161
Egyptian 155, 182
eidē 53
Einstein 107
Eleatic School 54
Empedocles 52
Encyclopedia of the Science of Law 11, 20-21, 81-82, 104, 169, 197, 199
enkapsis 209, 216, 218-220
Enlightenment 56, 64, 66, 71, 161, 183
Erfolgshaftung 102, 104, 124
ethnology 155-156, 158-162
everyday life 26, 32, 85, 138
evolutionistic constructions 156
ex lex 156
ex nihilo nihil fit 58
ex parte corporis 225

F

factual side 97, 187
fascism 75
fault 19, 117, 123, 127-133
feudal law 166, 168, 170, 172
feudalism 143, 172
Fichte 12, 20, 69, 71-72, 77, 147
folk community 141, 156, 158
folklore 157, 159
formative control 109, 144-146, 151, 164
form-matter motive 49-50, 53, 58, 60-61, 68
freedom-idealism 69-73, 146
French Revolution 149, 153, 164
Frobenius 159

Index

G

Galileo 14, 65
generic concept 92-93
genotypes 215
genus proximum 91-93
German
  – idealism 12, 74
  – law 17
Germanic law 173
Gnosticism 59-60
Goethe 124
Greek
  – religious consciousness 51
  – theoria 53
ground-motive 48-53, 56-63, 65-66, 68-69, 74, 76-78, 80-82, 97-98, 104, 140, 143, 147
Guido Gezelle 190
guilt 102, 104, 124-125, 127-133

H

Hägerström 24
heavenly bodies 23-24
Hegel 12, 20, 69, 77, 162, 169
Hegelian 74
Heidegger 139
Heraclitus 54-55
Herder 71, 162
Hesiod 51-52, 181
Historical
  – aspect 13, 17, 30, 51, 79-80, 109, 126, 135, 137-140, 144-146, 148, 151, 155, 157-158, 165, 170, 172, 203
  – development 13, 51, 71, 74-75, 80, 91, 109, 126, 134-137, 139, 146-151, 153, 155-158, 160-161, 165, 168-169, 171-173, 176, 182-183, 185, 203
  – differentiation 157, 163
  – materialism 112, 159
  – power 74, 145, 152-154, 157, 167, 182
  – School 71-72, 79-80, 91, 100, 104, 141-142, 147, 162-163
  – tradition 152-153, 156-157, 183
  – aspect 165
  – development 139, 165
  – tradition 183
historicism 36, 72-73, 75, 135, 139, 143
Hobbes 65-66, 77
Hofmann 129
Hoge Raad 86-88, 101, 130, 132-133
Homer 51-52, 181
hulē 50, 53, 55, 58, 179
human rights 73
Humanistic
  – freedom motive 50
  – ideal of personality 67-68, 70
  – philosophy 65-66, 68, 99
Hume 67-68
Husserl 188

I

idealistic conceptions 73
immanence philosophy 36-37, 45-46, 82, 84, 89, 98, 104, 162, 186
immanent critique 136
impetus 107, 161
individuality-structures 27, 46, 96, 141, 197-198, 204-205, 207-209, 213-216, 218-219, 221-222, 225, 227-228, 230
individuality-types 207-209, 215
industrial law 199
infinite universe 64
infinitesimal calculus 64
intellectus archetypus 45
internal law 198-200, 203
irrationalism 100

J

Jehovah 59
Jural
  – aspect 17-20, 23, 25, 31-32, 40, 43-44, 79, 85-86, 89, 91, 93, 95, 100-102, 104-105, 110, 118, 136-138, 151, 169,

172, 185, 190-192, 197, 202, 205, 226
- causality 18, 102, 117-118, 124-127, 132, 153, 197
- competence 145
- guilt 125, 131, 133
- harmonizing of interests 15
- volition 226
jurisprudence 22, 72, 86, 88, 130
Jus
- *civile* 120
- *commune* 201
- *gentium* 73, 173
- *particulare* 201
- *sumatur* 100

K

Kant 37-45, 47, 64, 66-70, 77-78, 82-84, 89, 95, 99, 114, 186
Kaufmann 54
Kelsen 43, 91, 99
kinematic aspect 14
Kuyper 174

L

late Scholasticism 62
Law
- of civil procedure 198
- of criminal procedure 198
- of religious concentration 45
law-conformity 71, 112, 147, 187, 206
law-giver 99, 119
law-side 32, 95-97, 99, 101, 106-108, 111, 115-116, 118, 127, 147-148, 151, 197
law-sphere 11, 94-97, 99-105, 107-115, 121, 123-124, 133-135, 137-138, 144-151, 161-162, 174-178, 180, 182, 185, 187, 189-190, 193-195, 197-198, 201, 203-207, 210-211, 213
Leendertz 147
Legal
- aspect 197
- consequences 18, 31, 99, 116, 127
- ground 18, 101, 197

- harmony 127
- historians 136-137, 165, 168-170, 204
- interpretation 17
- logic 137
- object 116, 190, 195, 197-199, 206, 213
- philosophy 21, 49, 89
- rule 22, 86, 99, 143
- science 20, 25, 89, 92, 119-120, 130, 136, 143, 150, 169, 171, 188, 197, 199, 201-202, 204, 228
- system 102, 116, 124, 126-127
- theory 22, 100
Leibniz 45, 64, 66, 68
Lex
- *naturalis* 97
- *talionis* 111
linguistic interpretation 17
Logical
- aspect 17, 29-30, 34-38, 40-42, 44, 75, 79, 82, 104, 109-110, 113-114, 139, 146, 187, 224, 226
- contradiction 112-113
- control 109, 144, 150
- discontinuity 32
- principle of identity 54
logical-analytical function 68
Logos 54-55, 60
Lundstedt 24-25

M

Marcion 59
Marxism 73, 110-111
materialism 66, 77, 112, 159
mathematicism 36
meaning-coherence 114, 123, 125, 180
meaning-nucleus 103-111, 114-115, 118, 127, 140, 144-146, 151, 175-176, 180, 190, 207, 210, 212
medieval synthesis 61
metabolism 109
metaphysical psychology 67, 83

metaphysics 53, 58, 66-67, 74-75, 82-83, 207
Middle Ages 61-62, 65, 126, 139, 161, 166, 169-170, 202-203
Mitteis 168-170
modal structures 94, 100, 103, 205-207, 218
Moira 52
molluscs 221
moral aspect 15, 19, 32, 42, 101-102, 207
moral law 45, 69, 97-98, 113, 147, 180
morphē 50
Mount Olympus 51
Mycenae 161
mystery worship 52
mythology 55, 156, 158

N

naive experience 23-24, 26-28, 32-33, 39-40, 65, 75, 114, 205, 209
National
 – community 73, 75, 204
 – socialism 75, 163
natura naturata 64
Natural
 – history 72, 146
 – law 27, 55, 68, 70-73, 97-98, 148-150
natural-scientific causality 68
nature and freedom 49, 63, 65, 67-69, 72, 76, 78, 97, 140, 147
neo-Kantian 43, 45, 74, 91, 99, 111-112, 147, 164, 173, 181, 202
Neoplatonic 61, 63
Neoplatonism 60-61
Newton 65, 98
Nietzsche 73-74
nonjural aspects of reality 86, 89
nonlogical aspects of reality 28, 34, 187
nontheoretical thought 189
normative principles 150
nous 55-59
numerical aspect 14, 19, 193

O

objectivity 39, 84, 186-187, 195
Olympic pantheon 50-51
Olympus 51-52
opening process 123, 133-134, 157, 161, 165, 173-174, 177, 180-184, 193, 202
opening-process 181
orenda 179
Orestea 57
Orestes 57
organic aspect 14, 51, 107, 139, 208
Origen 60
Orphism 52, 54, 57
Ortega y Gasset 142
ownership 31, 99, 171, 191

P

Palestine 161
Parmenides 54-55, 115
Pater Angelicus 62
Persia 161
personality-ideal 65, 69-70, 72-75, 77
Phaidrus 56
phenotypes 215
Philo 60
philosophical anthropology 228
philosophy of law 21, 43, 85, 90, 136-137
physical aspect 14, 18, 23, 29, 42, 118, 186
physical causality 18, 101, 124, 153
physicalism 36
physico-chemical 14, 27, 33, 37-38, 185-186, 210-212, 214, 217-218, 220-222, 224
physis 53, 61
pistical aspect 175, 178, 180
pistis 53, 56, 103, 174-175, 177-180, 182
Plato 52-54, 56-58, 64
Platonic 57, 61, 110
poet-theologians 51

positive law   13, 21-22, 26, 90, 99, 135-138, 142, 145, 165, 168, 170, 172, 191, 199-201
Positivistic
- approach   21, 162
- standpoint   84
post-hypnotic suggestion   230-231
prescientific attitude of experience   23
prima materia   63
Principium
- *contradictionis*   112, 148, 150
- *identitatis*   150
- *rationis sufficientis*   150
Principle
- of sufficient ground   30, 108, 125
- of sufficient reason   110, 121, 150
private law   169-170, 201, 203-204
process of differentiation   150
prooté hulē   58
Protagoras   55
protein compounds   211
psychical aspect   17-18, 25, 27, 43, 107, 155, 228-229
psychologism   124
psychologistic   68, 91, 100, 119, 123
psychology of law   137
psychopathic condition   230
public law   169-170, 201, 204
Puchta   162
Pythagorean school   52

R

radical type   214-216, 218-219, 221
rational soul   52, 58
reasonably forseeable   132
Reformation   61, 63-64, 74, 148, 169
Religious
- dualism   76
- synthesis   48, 61-62, 69
Res
- *cogitans*   66
- *extensiva*   66
- *nullius*   191

retrocipations   103-104, 106, 108, 113, 144, 176, 194
retrocipatory   103, 105, 108, 123, 134, 157, 175, 180
revelatio naturalis   176
rheuston   53
Rickert   164
risk principle   128, 132
Roman Catholicism   49-50, 62, 74, 76
romanticism   70
Rome   156, 161
root-community   47-48, 76, 81, 96
Rousseau   66-67

S

Santa Claus   163
Schelling   12, 20, 69, 72, 77
Schicksal   147
Schlegel   70
scholastic philosophy   56, 76
science of law   11-12, 20-22, 24, 43, 79, 81-82, 89, 92, 94, 101-102, 115, 120-121, 136-137, 142-143, 169, 171, 185, 187-188, 197-199, 203, 216, 222, 226-228
science-ideal   66, 68, 71, 83, 97, 146
Scientific
- honesty   26
- knowledge   11, 43, 67, 84
Sensory
- aspect   14, 43, 108, 123, 186
- experience   24, 41
- impressions   28, 42, 109, 190, 224
set theory   107
sexual libido   61
simpliciter   92
Social
- aspect   88, 127, 190
- intercourse   13, 16, 27, 30, 91, 98, 132, 134-136, 140, 149-151, 163, 194, 199, 226
- life   15, 27, 135, 151, 181, 190, 205-206
- rules   16, 93
sociology of law   137

Index

Socrates 37, 56, 108
spatial aspect 29, 144, 208
special science 11-12, 15, 20-21, 23-26, 28, 33, 36-37, 39, 84-85, 89-90, 101, 112, 142, 186-187, 197, 202, 227-228
Spengler 139, 162
sphere sovereignty 82, 91, 100, 104, 112, 114, 125, 131, 183, 205, 218-220, 230
sphere universality 123
split personality 230
Stahl 71, 147
Stammler 43, 111-112
States General 118-119, 198
stem types 215-216
structure of reality 22, 25-26, 78, 89, 104, 141, 188, 206
Subjective
 – legal facts 126
 – right 99, 112, 188, 195, 197
subject-object relation 40, 96-97, 107, 112, 115, 132, 145, 185-189, 193-194, 214
supra-sensory forms of being 53
supra-theoretical presuppositions 79, 82, 84-85
Supreme Court 86, 118
symbolical signification 127, 159, 190

T

theologia naturalis 83
Theoretical
 – abstraction 25-26, 38, 40-42, 47, 59, 114, 138, 171, 187, 224
 – antithesis 41, 49, 69
 – concept-formation 50, 85
 – idea 20, 32, 79-80, 175
 – synthesis 35-36, 39, 41, 43-44, 47, 49-50, 69, 75-76, 78, 81-82, 90
 – thought 14, 28-29, 32-37, 41-42, 44, 47-50, 56, 61, 66-69, 75-84, 90-91, 100, 109, 113-114, 121, 150
 – view of reality 24-26, 60
 – view of totality 33-35, 76-77
thinking ego 38, 47, 76
Thomas Aquinas 61, 68
Timaeus 57
time-duration 32
totemism 45, 179
transcendence standpoint 37, 161
Transcendental
 – criticism 35, 49, 82, 84
 – critique 29, 35, 39, 48, 50, 75, 77, 82-83
 – forms 41
 – ground-idea 75, 81, 91
 – presuppositions 42, 68
Transcendental-logical
 – subject 41, 47, 77, 82
 – unity of apperception 38
tuchē 51
types of individuality 207-208

U

unilateral founding 220-222
unlawfulness 123-124, 126-133, 197
Uranus 181

V

variability types 215-216, 219-221
Volkgeist 79
volonté générale 70
von Below 170
von Savigny 72, 91, 141-142, 147, 162

W

Woltereck 141
Word-revelation 44-46, 48, 58-60, 63, 81-82, 176-179, 182, 206, 224
world history 159-162, 180

Z

Zeno 115
Zeus 57
Zevenbergen 11
Zitelmann 119-120

www.ingramcontent.com/pod-product-compliance
Lightning Source LLC
Chambersburg PA
CBHW032032290426
44110CB00012B/764